STRATEGIES

FOR ACTIVE CITIZENSHIP

Kateri M. Drexler

Gwen Garcelon

PEARSON

Prentice
Hall

Upper Saddle River, New Jersey
Columbus, Ohio

Library of Congress Cataloging-in-Publication Data

Drexler, Kateri M.
   Strategies for active citizenship / Kateri M. Drexler, Gwen Garcelon
       p. cm.
   Includes bibliographical references and index.
   ISBN 0-13-117295-6
  1.   Citizenship--United States. 2.   Civics. I. Garcelon, Gwen.
II. Title.

JK1759.D75 2005
323.6'5'0973--dc22

2004009144

Vice President and Publisher: Jeffery W. Johnston
Senior Acquisitions Editor: Sande Johnson
Editorial Assistant: Erin Anderson
Production Editor: Holcomb Hathaway
Design Coordinator: Diane C. Lorenzo
Cover Designer: Ali Mohrman
Cover Image: Index Stock
Text Designer: Aerocraft Charter Art Service
Production Manager: Susan Hannahs
Director of Marketing: Ann Castel Davis
Marketing Manager: Eric Murray

This book was set in Janson Text by Carlisle Communications, Ltd. It was printed and bound by R.R. Donnelley
& Sons Company. The cover was printed by Phoenix Color Corp.

Pearson Education Ltd.
Pearson Education Australia Pty. Limited
Pearson Education Singapore Pte. Ltd.
Pearson Education North Asia Ltd.

Pearson Education Canada, Ltd.
Pearson Educación de Mexico, S. A. de C. V.
Pearson Education—Japan
Pearson Education Malaysia Pte. Ltd.

10 9 8 7 6 5 4 3 2 1
ISBN 0-13-117295-6

Contents

Preface   *ix*

1 SELF-AWARENESS AND ACTIVE CITIZENSHIP   1

DETERMINING VALUES   2
Identifying Life Areas   2
Identifying Values   4
Creating a Mission Statement   5
Acting with Integrity   6
Congruence   6
Understanding Motivation   8
Reflecting   9

TRANSLATING VALUES AND MOTIVATION INTO GOALS   10
Types of Goals   10
Prioritizing   11
Dealing with Conflicting Goals   12
Goal Setting   12

CHOOSING WHERE AND HOW TO ENGAGE AS CITIZENS   15
Effective Engagement   16
Understanding Our Problem-Solving Preferences   16
Myers-Briggs Type Indicator Instrument   22
Matching Styles and Values to Action   23

APPLICATIONS   23

2 CRITICAL THINKING AND PROBLEM SOLVING FOR SOCIAL ISSUES 27

CRITICAL THINKING 28

Evaluate Sources of Information 29

Maintain Objectivity 33

Identify Stakeholders and Perspectives 34

Separate Facts and Opinions 34

Evaluate the Context 35

Recognize False Logic and Bias 36

Use Your Values 36

Critical Thinking Exercise: Christopher Columbus 37

PROBLEM SOLVING 38

Step One: Define the Problem 39

Step Two: Gather Information 40

Step Three: Interpret the Information 41

Step Four: Develop Possible Solutions 41

Step Five: Evaluate Possible Solutions and Choose the Best One 42

Step Six: Evaluate Success 43

Obstacles to Problem Solving 43

Problem-Solving Exercise: Global Poverty 44

APPLICATIONS 47

3 RESOURCE MANAGEMENT FOR ACTIVE CITIZENSHIP 53

TIME MANAGEMENT 54

Steps in Time Management 55

Time Management for Active Citizenship 59

Tools of Time Management 60

Time Bandits 61

FINANCIAL MANAGEMENT 62

Managing Beliefs 63

Budgeting 63

PERSONAL RESOURCE MANAGEMENT 67

Other People 67

Health and Personal Well-Being 68

APPLICATIONS 71

4   ACTION STRATEGIES AND PROJECT MANAGEMENT   75

CREATING AN ACTION STRATEGY   76
    Review the Issue or Project   76
    Create a Vision   78
    Identify Desired Goals   79
    Choose Resources and Partners   79
    Create a Timeline and a Plan   81
    Consider Possible Obstacles and Resistance   82
    Allow for Change   82
    Evaluate the Outcome   82

STAYING ON TRACK   83
    Revisit Goals   83
    Face the Fear of Failure   84
    Face the Fear of Success   85
    Put Off Procrastination   85
    Reinvent the Standard   86
    Delay Gratification   87

SAMPLE ACTION PLAN   88
    Step One: Review the Project   88
    Step Two: Create a Vision   88
    Step Three: Identify Desired Goals   89
    Step Four: Choose Resources and Partners   89
    Step Five: Create a Timeline   89
    Step Six: Identify Obstacles and Resistance   89
    Step Seven: Evaluate the Success   89

PROJECT MANAGEMENT   91
    Identify the Important Tasks   91
    Identify the Subtasks   92
    Identify the Sub-Subtasks   93

APPLICATIONS   96

5   SKILLS FOR CIVIC EDUCATION   99

READING AND COMPREHENSION   100
    Before Reading   102

During Reading   105
After Reading   108

NOTE-TAKING   109

Note-Taking While Listening   110
Note-Taking While Reading and Researching   111
Note-Taking Formats   112
Reviewing Notes   117

RESEARCHING   117

Steps in the Research Process   118
Sources of Information   118

WRITING   120

Letters   120
E-mail   122
Press Releases   122
Formal Reports   122

APPLICATIONS   124

6 COMMUNICATION AND TEAMWORK   131

BASICS OF COMMUNICATION   132

Communication Model   132
Types of Communication   135
Self-Awareness and Communication   136

EFFECTING CHANGE THROUGH COMMUNICATION   137

Understanding and Empathy   137
Crucial Conversations   137
Negotiation   140
Nonviolent Communication   142

EFFECTIVE TEAMS   142

Why People Join Groups   144
Team Structure and Roles   146
Team Development Stages   146
Characteristics of an Effective Team   147
Virtual Teams   149
Principles of Effective Meetings   150

APPLICATIONS   152

7 LEADERSHIP AND CHANGE   157

CHANGE THROUGH SYSTEMS THINKING   158
   The Individual and the System   158
   Parts of the Whole   158
   Continual Learning   160
LEADERSHIP QUALITIES   160
   Vision   161
   Effective Speaking Skills   161
   Evaluation and Reflection   163
CHARACTERISTICS OF CHANGE   163
   Chaos   164
   Resistance   164
PROBLEM-SOLVING STYLES   166
   Technician   166
   Diplomat   166
   Strategist   167
   Activist   167
CREATING THE ENVIRONMENT FOR CHANGE   168
   Develop Conviction and Courage   168
   Develop an Attitude of Learned Optimism   168
   Nurture Self-Esteem   169
   Take Action   169
   Persevere   170
   Engage Others   170
APPLICATIONS   172

8 AMERICAN DEMOCRACY AND GOVERNMENT STRUCTURE   175

FOUNDING DOCUMENTS   176
   The Declaration of Independence   176
   The Constitution   176
   The Bill of Rights   177

SEPARATION OF POWERS   177
  Legislative Branch   179
  Executive Branch   179
  Judicial Branch   180

VOTING AND THE ELECTORAL PROCESS   180
  Voting Resources   180
  Campaign Finance   182
  The Electoral College   184
  Primary Elections   184

MEMBERS OF CONGRESS   184
  MoCs' Office Staff   185
  Committees   185

HOW A BILL BECOMES LAW   186
  Understanding How Bills Get Started   186
  Understanding the Committee Process   186
  Understanding the Typical Legislative Process   187

ADVOCACY AND LOBBYING   187
  Advocacy   188
  Lobbying   188
  Clarifying Objectives   189
  Working with Members of Congress   192
  Working with the Media   195
  Grassroots Organizing   196

CREATING SUSTAINABLE CITIZENSHIP   198

APPLICATIONS   199

References   202
Index   206

Preface

The purpose of this book is to help you enhance the quality of your life and the lives of others within your communities by sharing the skills necessary to become an active citizen. We welcome you to this exciting journey and commend you for engaging in the process of discovering the unique way that you can help to create a better world! As Albert Schweitzer said, "I don't know what your destiny will be, but one thing I do know: the only ones among you who will be really happy are those who have sought and found how to serve." We all have gifts to bring to this goal, and we hope that, through this text and course, you will come to believe, as we do, that it is entirely possible for you to radically enhance your self-concept and your ability to use the democratic process in pursuit of your vision for a better world.

This book is concerned with bringing about change, with helping you dream powerful dreams and make those dreams a reality for you, your community, your country, and your world. A common set of skills allows us to be effective in all the roles of our lives. The principles and practices presented in this text will enable you to bring the best that you have to offer to each of those roles. As you build the essential skills presented here, your effectiveness as a student and a learner will carry into your role as a citizen. A healthy democracy requires the participation of informed, thoughtful, and skilled citizens. By training ourselves to become more adept thinkers, writers, speakers, and leaders, we not only gather the tools to excel in many areas of our lives but also become more able to participate in our governance and give voice and direction to our priorities.

As you learn more about yourself and develop your capabilities, you may find great satisfaction in serving to uplift others and helping to solve societal problems. This is the great opportunity of democracy. However, we have reached a critical juncture in the evolution of our democratic system. The active participation of citizens is now necessary for our democracy to function and, indeed, to survive. In this book, we distinguish between traditional community service (or direct service) and political advocacy (or activism), which creates systemic change. Direct service, while meeting immediate and important needs, does not change the long-term effects of damaging government policies. Direct service might include, for instance, the necessary work of building houses for Habitat for Humanity. Engaging in advocacy might lead you to try to influence the U.S. Congress to approve affordable housing programs. Changing the policy that creates the social problems creates "systemic" change, or change to the system. In this text, we present skills for critical thinking and systems thinking, which help us understand the larger context within which societal problems exist and how we can create solutions.

How do you know where to engage in society when the problems in all areas can seem equally compelling and as a whole, overwhelming? Start with your heart! People will most likely be able to sustain action only on an issue that they are passionate about. Our emotions give us clues to where our heart is called. Clarifying our values and what we stand for helps us find issues that express these values. This evaluation is important, however, only if we act. Consider your talents, passions, and interests, and go from there. Journalist and humanitarian Coleman McCarthy ended a speech to a grassroots advocacy organization by saying, "I have one word for you—START!" By this he meant don't wait until you are an expert on an issue. Don't wait until you have the time, money, skills or whatever you think you need to make a difference. Just start doing something to serve.

We hope that you come to see your education as the start of a lifetime of learning and civic involvement throughout which you will effect changes to better the communities in which you live. We begin this text by looking within because our behaviors grow out of our beliefs and our beliefs shape the world. By becoming more self-aware, we can learn more effectively and efficiently, participate fully with others, and understand our motivations and desires. Not only are the topics of critical thinking, goal setting, resource management, and the process of change and overcoming barriers to change important for you now, in your role as a student, but the effective use of the principles presented in each of these topics will enable you to contribute effectively as a citizen.

Since working with others is an important component of effecting social change, we also cover working as a team, building relationships, and developing a support system. Although individuals can accomplish large-scale effects—and it is better to do something by yourself than not at all—it is best to find allies and build coalitions to augment your voice. We also address the concept of motivation. Although we are usually taught that motivation precedes action, in fact action also breeds motivation. When we build the skills and find the support to act, we become empowered and more motivated to continue that action. Without skills and support, however, summoning the motivation to act as citizens can be daunting. The ethics of engagement, including nonviolent communication, positive messaging, leadership, and negotiation skills, are presented here as well. We believe, and encourage you to consider, that how you act is equally as important as—if not more important than—what you accomplish.

The text culminates by presenting the structure of our American democracy and how to use it as the tool it was designed to be for effective self-governance. Developing relationships with members of Congress, understanding the election process, and learning how ideas become bills (which become public policy) help demystify the governmental process. We hope that this demystification will encourage you to participate in the process and use it in service to your dreams for the world. Much of the methodology presented here is based on successful field-testing by political advocacy groups. The text highlights real-world relevance by focusing on specific examples of how people of all abilities, interests, personalities, and degrees of participation have effected change.

Martin Luther King, Jr., gave a sermon about activism in 1956 called "The Most Durable Power." In it he said:

> As you press on for justice, be sure to move with dignity and discipline, using only the weapon of love. Let no man pull you so low as to hate him. Always avoid violence. If you succumb to the temptation of using violence in your struggle, unborn generations will be the recipients of a long and desolate night of bitterness, and your chief legacy to the future will be an endless reign of meaningless chaos.

King intuitively understood what the field of systems science is now offering proof for—that the end is inherent in, and inseparable from, the means to that end. If violence is used to create a result, then that result will in effect be violent. If negativity, judgment, or ill will exists in our thoughts, our seemingly good actions will still be party to creating that "endless reign of meaningless chaos." As we think and act with dignity, discipline, and compassion, we are already creating a world that operates with these principles.

On your journey of self-discovery and empowerment, our goal is to help give you the tools to be a mindful and proactive student and citizen. We believe, as 1925 Nobel Prize winner George Bernard Shaw has said:

> This is the true joy in life: being used for a purpose recognized by yourself as a mighty one; being a force of nature instead of a feverish, selfish little clod of ailments and grievances complaining that the world won't devote itself to making you happy.
>
> I am of the opinion that my life belongs to the whole community, and as long as I live it is my privilege to do for it whatever I can.
>
> I want to be thoroughly used up when I die, for the harder I work, the more I live. I rejoice in life for its own sake. Life is no brief candle to me. It is a sort of splendid torch which I have got hold of for the moment and I want to make it burn as brightly as possible before handing it on to future generations.

ACKNOWLEDGMENTS

We offer our sincere gratitude to the professionals who helped, encouraged, and supported us in completing this book. In particular, we extend our special thanks to our editor Sande Johnson, editorial assistant Erin Anderson, and all those at Prentice Hall Publishing who endeavor daily to help students succeed around the world. We'd like to thank Dr. William Niemi, Dr. Jim Westerman, Tonga Cox, Kristi Drexler, and Dr. Charles Beck for their essential contributions to this text. Our gratitude also goes to our reviewers for their insightful advice and thoughtful guidance: Kathryn K. Kelly, St. Cloud State University; Lisa D'Adamo-Weinstein, United States Military Academy; Daniel J. Cook-Huffman, Juniata College; Linda Saumell, Miami Dade Community College; and Sheryl M. Hartman, Miami Dade Community College.

We are inspired by all of the people who have contributed their energy to social movements, demonstrating that individual efforts can create lasting change, including all of the experts we profiled for this text—with special thanks to Eli Pariser, Adam Werbach, Julia Butterfly-Hill, and Carl Safina. Gwen, in particular, would like to thank all those who have modeled for her a very high form of citizen action, with special thanks to Sam Daley-Harris, Lynn McMullen, Laurie Herrick, Dan Zukergood, Marshall Saunders, and all the volunteers and staff of RESULTS who inspire and challenge her daily to make her best even better.

We'd also like to thank the writers, instructors, and professionals who work tirelessly to shape the field of student success and empower students with increased skills and motivation. Kateri would like to extend her everlasting gratitude to Carol Carter, Frank Burrows, and Andrea Worrell for their support and feedback and for the amazing opportunities they've given her.

In addition, we'd like to thank the numerous authors referenced in this book, who are creating a body of knowledge that enhances our understanding of ourselves and inspires us to create a better world.

Gwen would also like to thank her friends—all of you who love and encourage her to keep growing and keep making her dreams come true. You support her in every way possible, and your presence in her life is a profound joy. She would also like to thank her Mom for teaching her the art of writing (even though she hated rewriting all those papers). Kateri would like to especially thank her family, all fifteen and a half of them, for their encouragement and zest for life, and for the inspiration to finish strong.

Self-Awareness and Active Citizenship

1

Things which matter most must never be at the mercy of things which matter least.　　　　　—GOETHE

T he need to make a difference in the world motivates doctors and researchers to spend hours looking for cures for diseases; it drives inventors and business owners to stay up nights trying to find a better idea; it causes artists and novelists to create art; and it leads people to engage as citizens in the hopes of creating a better world. How we choose to use our lives to make a difference, through the process of understanding who we are, is the subject of this chapter.

In his book *Soul of a Citizen*, Paul Loeb states, "Public participation is the soul of democratic citizenship." What leaves many of us on the sidelines, he suggests, is not "an absence of desire to connect with worthy groups that take on wise causes. We need to believe that our individual involvement is worthwhile, that what we might do in the public sphere will not be in vain."[1] In other words, we want to feel like what we do matters.

In practice, participating in our communities almost always gives us a sense of purpose we're not likely to find anywhere else. We also gain a deeper understanding of ourselves and develop new skills. We learn how to work together with others and to act on our deepest values and convictions. Civic service, in essence, often strengthens who we are as individuals.

To make a difference in the world by engaging in civic action, we begin by coming to know our underlying values—our core selves. "Citizenship means more than voting, paying taxes, or obeying laws. It is a powerful expression of self," according to Marianne Williamson, author of *The Healing of America*.[2] If citizenship is an expression of self, self must first be identified. As we become more self-aware and develop more self-mastery, we become more powerful citizens. We become more effective in creating, re-creating, and sustaining our vision for our democracy. We become better prepared to create change for the greater well-being of ourselves, our communities, and our world.

OBJECTIVES

After studying this chapter, you should be able to:

- Formulate a mission statement after identifying your values
- Identify external and internal motivational factors
- Translate values and motivation into goals
- Identify the types of goals
- Set attainable goals
- Identify areas of civic interest
- Identify your problem-solving preferences, skills, and styles
- Apply your style and values to goals and actions

As we grow and transform our own abilities as citizens and leaders, we will more positively influence the growth and transformation of society. When Gandhi said, "We must be the change we wish to see in the world," he gave us profound guidance in our development as citizens. He professed that as we devote ourselves to our personal development, we embody and model the vision we have for our communities. Joseph Jaworski, founder of the American Leadership Forum, has also discovered through his research and experience that personal transformation is the key to societal transformation. In his book with Betty Sue Flowers, *Synchronicity: The Inner Path of Leadership,* Jaworski concludes that attention to our inner lives is integral to effectively shaping our collective future.[3]

The personal journey toward effective citizenship can begin with identifying values, goals, and motivations, and developing a strategy for dealing with challenges. The purpose of this chapter is to help you gain awareness, develop practices, and make choices that will lay the foundation for a lifetime of effective citizenship.

DETERMINING VALUES

Values—
central beliefs and
attitudes that
guide our choices,
either consciously
or unconsciously

Values are our central beliefs and attitudes that guide our choices, either consciously or unconsciously. We all have values, though we may not be aware of what they are. As children, we learn to value the things our parents and communities teach us to value. As we mature, we gain the ability to choose our values based on our own internal guidance and expression of self.

Values can be those things that we are fundamentally committed to, our highest principles; they are the things in life that we consider worthy for their own sake. As you consciously become aware of, and choose, your values, they become an internal guidance system. To make good decisions, set appropriate goals, and manage priorities, it is important to identify the values that are central to who you are today and to who you want to become.

Our values are our guides as to when and how we act to elicit social change. More so than reasoned arguments or gathering the right information, we rely on what we know at the core of who we are. If we trust our convictions, we can take stands whether we have formal credentials or expert knowledge on an issue. Taking the time to define your values and then align your actions with them can significantly impact your ability to achieve what you most desire for your life, community, and world.

Identifying Life Areas

Identifying and defining values is usually a work-in-progress. Since our identities are constantly open to change and redefinition, the values that we hold are also open to change. By practicing self-reflection, you can learn how to be more inten-

M A K I N G   I T   H A P P E N

ADAM WERBACH, SIERRA CLUB

Adam Werbach became president of the Sierra Club shortly after graduating from college. A self-proclaimed mediocre student, who was sent home from grade school for fighting, Werbach channeled his passion into environmental activism in high school.

During one high school summer, he decided to volunteer for the Big Green campaign, a grassroots effort to build voter support for a sweeping state ballot initiative on environmental policy. Within minutes of walking into campaign headquarters, Werbach was appointed to organize high school volunteers for the project. He remembers saying, "Me? I've never done anything like this before. I'm just a high school student!" The organizer in charge replied, "This is your chance. Now is the time to start. There's the phone. Read these papers. Get to work."

Werbach organized more than 300 California high school students that summer to canvass door-to-door and staff phone banks. After failing in their attempt to sway enough votes to pass Big Green, Werbach was extremely disappointed. However, his peers would not allow him to wallow in defeat and pressured him to move on to another project. After calling organizations he had worked with on Big Green, he accepted an invitation from the Sierra Club to come to one of their executive committee meetings to share with them his ideas for student involvement.

Werbach's first project was organizing a summer camp to train student leaders. He then organized the Sierra Student Coalition (SSC), which supported high school and college students in direct lobbying for national environmental policy, and he registered tens of thousands of 18- to 24-year-olds to vote. When Werbach encountered resistance from the Sierra Club board of directors toward the SSC, he decided to run for membership on the board. Any member of the Sierra Club could run for the board, and the national membership of the Sierra Club elected Werbach.

After two years as a member of the board, Werbach proved to be a valuable asset to the organization and was elected president of the Sierra Club by his fellow board members. He was 23 years old. When people ask Werbach if he is too young for his job, he replies, "No, I'm too old. A 15-year-old would get more done." Werbach observes: "As we get older, we begin to accept the unacceptable. We accept that bad things happen. We rationalize. We follow too much advice. . . . We need to rekindle the youth within us. . . . The older we get, the less encouragement we find to experiment and wander beyond the boundaries of a constructed world."

Adapted from *Act Now, Apologize Later* by Adam Werbach. New York: HarperCollins Publishers, 1997.

FIGURE 1.1 *Wheel of Life*

tional in your decisions and actions. You can learn to assess how your actions are expressing the things that are important to you.

The first step in assessing values is to examine how important the various aspects of work and life are to you. Look at the Wheel of Life shown in Figure 1.1, and consider what areas of life might have a particular significance. We may find that some areas are more important than others at varying times in our lives; however, the wheel symbolizes our lives as a whole. Keeping the wheel segments balanced, as demonstrated in our lives, will help us proceed smoothly. Start to identify values in each of the areas. For each category, identify the importance by ranking it from 1 to 10, with 10 being the most important.

> *He who has a why to live can bear with almost any how.*
>
> **NIETZSCHE**

Identifying Values

The following box lists some sample character traits and values that can be used as a starting point in developing a list of personal values. Consider how much you value the following traits, and use these traits to help you distinguish values. For instance, you may value being reliable to your family or being committed to your education. What are traits and values that you would add to your list?

Character Traits and Values

ACCOUNTABLE

Accountability may include being:

Reliable	Trustworthy
Dependable	Responsible
Loyal	Secure

COMMITTED

Committed may mean being:

Participative	Focused
Enthusiastic	Persistent
Energetic	Productive
Faithful	

OPEN

Openness may include being:

Fair	Unbiased
Patient	Open-minded
Tolerant	Joyful

HONEST

Honesty may include being:

Authentic	Genuine
Outspoken	Sincere
Truthful	Frank
Balanced	

RESPONSIBLE

Responsibility entails taking control of our own lives without blame or victimization.

GIVING

Giving may include being:

Dedicated	Compassionate
Accepting	Nurturing
Contributing	Helpful
Cooperative	Generous
Appreciative	Considerate
Forgiving	Respectful
Friendly	

Creating a Mission Statement

One way to clarify the values that guide our lives is to develop a personal mission statement. This statement can help us make choices with clarity and integrity. As we become more and more aligned with our values and purpose, our choices become instant and natural expressions of ourselves. A personal mission statement can help us develop a vision of self, of what we see as our purpose in life, how we want to contribute to life, and where we find meaning and joy.

If you don't know what your passion is, realize that one reason for your existence on earth is to find it. Real success means creating a life of meaning through service that fulfills your reason for being here.

OPRAH WINFREY

A C T I O N !

Creating a Mission Statement

1. By answering the following questions, you can gather information to help you define what is most important to you. Let your emotions guide you. Be aware of when you feel happy, satisfied, and free of personal judgment.

   - Describe a time in your life when you were doing something that felt very satisfying. What are the things that caused you to feel this way? Who were you with? What were you doing?

   - Who has been an influential person in your life? What are the traits of this person that you admire? What qualities of this person would you like to emulate?

   - What do you want to be like in your life? What are the traits and qualities that are most important to you?

   - What do you want to have in life (happiness, friendship, great food, and so forth)?

   - What do you want others to have?

   - What are some of the roles you play in life (for example, family member, community member, student, employee)? Choose a person with whom you interact in a particular role. What would you like that person to say about the contribution you make?

2. Develop a draft of your mission statement. Your statement can be a few words or a few paragraphs. You should be able to use it as a guide to who you want to be as well as how you want to be. Examples of some mission statements include:

   - I have a wonderful life and dramatically contribute to the quality of life on earth.

   - I am a force for loving relationships in my family, and I support my loved ones in being their best selves.

   - I promote beneficial change, and I am a catalyst for sustainability and harmony on earth.

3. Next, reflect on and assess your mission statement. Answer the following questions:

   - Does this mission statement bring out the best in me?

   - Am I excited and happy about the person I am when I use this statement for guidance?

   - Do I feel challenged by, uplifted by, and purposeful about this statement?

   - Does this statement empower me to be of service to others in any way?

   - How do others and/or the greater community or world benefit when I embody this statement?

Acting with Integrity

Webster's New Collegiate Dictionary defines **integrity** as *"the state of being whole or complete; acting with moral soundness."* When our actions are an honest expression of ourselves, we have personal integrity. As we become more intentional about using our values to guide our actions, we develop greater personal integrity.

Integrity— the state of being whole or complete

Each of us must consider our own definition of moral soundness in order to assess the integrity of our actions. Among the widely accepted qualities of morality in our culture are fairness, honesty, service, excellence, patience, and treatment of others with dignity. The U.S. Declaration of Independence speaks to the self-evident value of human dignity: "We hold these truths to be self-evident: that all men are created equal and endowed by their Creator with certain inalienable rights, that among these are life, liberty and the pursuit of happiness."

Acting with integrity is integral to the concept of democracy. It gives direction to our appropriate engagement as citizens.

Congruence

Becoming more self-aware allows you to become more intentional about your choices and how they affect the quality of your life and the lives of others. **Congruence**, which means "to be in agreement or alignment," is another aspect of acting with integrity. To achieve true congruence in your life, what you think, say, and do must be in alignment.

Congruence— to be in agreement or alignment

As philosopher Parker Palmer describes the lives of people who have acted on their deepest beliefs: "These people have understood that no punishment could be worse than the one we inflict on ourselves by living a divided life." And nothing could help them heal that rift like making the decision "to stop acting differently on the outside from what they knew to be true inside."[4]

Congruence is about looking at what you think, say, and do in relation to all the choices you make—from how you dress, what you buy, and how and with whom you spend your time to what kind of lifestyle you have. The actions we take have the power to transform our values into positive, lasting impacts. We may hold generosity as a value, but the act of behaving generously is what creates congruence. When our actions do not align with our values, we experience internal conflict, as well as conflict within our relationships and external world. The consequences of this conflict may include stress, depression, fatigue, anger, or anxiety. These negative feelings can further separate us from our integrity and, in a self-perpetuating manner, create more blocks to self-awareness. Rachel Naomi Remen suggests that "the loss of emotional or spiritual integrity may be at the source of our suffering conscience. . . . Stress may be as much a question of a compromise of values as it is a matter of time pressure and fear of failure."[5]

Conversely, when we act in accordance with what is true for us, we experience positive feelings. These may include happiness, satisfaction, passion, certainty, and abundance. Our feelings give us immediate feedback and are important guides for acting with integrity.

Stephen Covey, in his book *Seven Habits of Highly Effective People*, refers to the concept of congruence as the "inside-out" approach. Covey relates that if you want to create change in some area of your life, focus on what you think and say, and how you act, in that area. For instance, if you want to have better friendships, think about and practice being a more concerned and giving friend. If you want to be a force for peace in the world, notice whether you have aggressive or negative thoughts and how these thoughts might color your actions. Consider how you might change your thinking and, in turn, how you can contribute to peace in your relationships and community. The inside-out approach can support congruence by reminding you to first turn your awareness inside in order to create the alignment of your thoughts, words, and actions.[6]

Congruence is apt to be a lifelong work-in-progress. By continually evaluating our beliefs, choices, and lifestyle patterns for congruence, we can become more powerful agents of change.

Understanding Motivation

Motivation—
the intensity of desire to engage in an activity

Identifying how we are **motivated** can help us determine whether we are acting in accordance with our values or the values of others. Being an effective citizen requires that we develop the ability to think for ourselves, to listen to and be motivated by our own guidance. When we act from our own values and experience self-worth from within, we are internally motivated. When we act to please others or act in alignment with the values of others, we are externally motivated.

External Motivation

External motivation—
the desire to perform an activity to gain the approval of others

Part of human nature is self-protection and the drive to sustain oneself. Many of us have learned to protect and nurture ourselves through gaining the approval of others. We may have learned as children that we gain love by pleasing others or that we can only feel valuable when others approve of us. If we make decisions based on the desire for acceptance from others, we are said to be externally motivated. The danger in **external motivation** is that we may compromise our values and priorities in the pursuit of approval from others. This inevitably produces internal conflict—and the negative feelings that accompany it.

Internal Motivation

Internal motivation—
the desire to perform an activity simply for the pleasure and satisfaction that accompany the activity

An internally motivated person consults his own guidance in decision making. For this person, well-being and self-worth come from within and are not dependent on the validation of others.

Social change usually involves upsetting or challenging an existing system or belief. This necessarily includes attracting the disapproval of others. Developing strong **internal motivation** helps us to engage as potential change agents. When we act on personal values that satisfy and uplift us, we are less likely to be defeated by the disapproval of others. As Eleanor Roosevelt said, "No one can hurt you without your consent."

As citizens trying to effect change, we may encounter the apathy of others. When others don't find passion or meaning in the things that we do, it can cause us to question the validity of our own passion and meaning. However, if we are motivated by a strong internal alignment to our own values and empowerment, we will be less likely to be discouraged by the inaction or lack of enthusiasm of others.

Sam Daley-Harris, founder of a nonprofit group dedicated to ending hunger, describes how a strong identification with the things he valued helped him to become motivated no matter what others did:

> *It is essential that the student acquire an understanding of, and a lively feeling for, values. He must acquire a vivid sense of the beautiful and of the morally good.*
>
> **ALBERT EINSTEIN**

> It turned out that I wasn't hopeless about the technical feasibility of ending hunger, I was hopeless about human nature. I feared *people* would never get it together. That night, however, I realized there was a particular part of human nature I had some influence over—my own. Up to that point, for me, commitment had a certain "I will if you will" quality to it. "I'll recycle if you will," I might have thought. "Oh, you won't? Then I won't either." In that darkened hotel banquet hall, I experienced commitment in a new way, a kind of "I will whether you will or not."[7]

When your self-worth comes from within, things may change in the world, but they cannot compromise your sense of value and empowerment. A study conducted by the University of Rochester's Human Motivation Research Group found, for example, that people whose motivation was internal exhibited more interest, confidence, excitement, persistence, creativity, and performance than those who were motivated by external rewards.[8]

Reflecting

Self-awareness takes time—and intention. Jill Ker Conway, former president of Smith College, reasons that when lives are overscheduled and overstimulated there is no space for people to sit and reflect. This kind of reflective space is what allows us to build the skills of self-awareness and self-determination. Self-determination comes about by knowing ourselves and choosing our experience based on our own preferences and creative impulses rather than on those of others. Conway suggests that we can encourage greater reflectiveness through such activities as journal writing, letter writing, and spending time in quiet and reflection.[9]

In a more effective society, citizens, according to Paul Loeb, "would have time to think and reflect, to be with their families and friends, and to engage themselves in their communities. This would foster a culture that allows us to slow down the pace of global change, challenge mindless consumption."[10]

TRANSLATING VALUES AND MOTIVATION INTO GOALS

Goal—
the end toward
which effort is
directed

No formula exists for determining our optimum lifestyle and appropriate civic engagement; we must each find our own path. We will all likely direct our efforts toward different results. *Webster's New Collegiate Dictionary* defines a **goal** as "the end toward which effort is directed." A goal is a statement of something we want to be, do, or have—for instance, "I want to be a research scientist," or "I want to travel around the world." You already began distinguishing some of your goals during the process of creating your personal mission statement. Goals are our intentions. They provide clarity and focus for our thoughts, words, and actions and guide us to specific outcomes about which we are passionate. Our own unique set of values and motivating factors determines our goals.

Having energy and enthusiasm is crucial, but if that energy and effort are scattered, they are far less likely to create a specific intended result. Concentrated effort is an extremely powerful force. Consider the ability of concentrated light to cut metal. The light energy propelled from a normal 60-watt bulb is traveling very quickly (at the speed of light), but the energy is scattered, or diffused. It is sent out in every direction. If the light from the same 60-watt bulb were concentrated, as in a laser beam, it could penetrate metal. Likewise, if we focus our efforts toward a specific goal, we concentrate our energy on achieving it.

Goals can greatly increase our effectiveness. Our thoughts, words, and actions are energy forces; by focusing them toward specific, intentional points, we intensify their strength. With awareness of our passions and strengths, we can choose meaningful goals. When we choose goals that are in alignment with our values and personal integrity, we access energy that supports our process. If we choose a goal that conflicts in some way with our integrity or personal mission, the conflict dissipates our energies and compromises our strength.

> *The shift from incoherence to coherence can bring dramatic effects: a 60-watt light bulb whose light waves could be made coherent as a laser, would have the power to bore a hole through the sun—from 90 million miles away.*
>
> WILLIAM A.
> TILLER

Types of Goals

When determining goals, it is important to set ones that extend beyond your own needs. Subordinating our personal achievements to something beyond our own immediate self-interests in order to be of service to others or a cause allows us to experience a deeper sense of meaning and self-worth. The commitment to live according to our deepest values not only creates a more stable center in our lives but also helps us to better navigate the challenges we face along the way.

Individual Goals

Individual goals are goals that you set by yourself and for which you alone develop and implement a strategy for achieving. They can be goals that you have for your own development and achievement as well as goals that affect society What makes them individual goals is that you alone are responsible for achieving them.

Collective Goals

Collective goals are set, collectively, by members of a group. Necessarily, each member of the group has a role to play in achieving the goal. In addition, all members will gain something in common by achieving the goal. Collective goals can be initiated by an individual, but if they are intended to benefit a group, they should be formulated and agreed upon by the group.

A collective goal inspires the commitment of all those working toward it.

Short-Term and Long-Term Goals

Having both short-term and long-term goals can be rewarding. Short-term goals are usually less complex and easier to achieve than long-term goals. We build momentum with each goal we complete, so setting short-term goals helps ensure that we'll have frequent victories.

Long-term goals (which take one year or longer to reach) keep us headed in the right direction and can provide a sense of greater purpose. These goals may require longer to achieve their result, so it helps to break down the overarching, or long-term, goal into smaller goals that may be reached in shorter periods of time. Goals that involve a civic interest or challenge are usually longer term. These goals usually involve a collective strategy, and institutions or social systems are generally slow to change. Breaking a long-term goal into smaller, "short-term" goals can provide a sense of accomplishment—and thus motivation—if our ultimate goal requires patience and perseverance over a long period of time.

Prioritizing

Most of us have several goals in different life areas that we would like to achieve. Prioritizing goals can be confusing if you think in terms of which goal is more important. Over the long term, all of your goals are probably important, or they wouldn't be goals. When prioritizing, think in terms of *timing*: "Which goal will I focus on more right now?"

When deciding which goals to focus on first, consider the following:

- Will achieving certain goals first make others easier to achieve?
- Do any of your goals express values that are more important to you than others?
- Which goals will create the greatest impact toward your solution with the fewest resources?

- Which goals will create long-term results?
- Which goals have the greatest chance of success?

Dealing with Conflicting Goals

Because the resources we have to spend on our goals—money, time, and energy—are limited, goals can often seem at odds with one another. Working on one goal can mean slipping on another one. Managing your goals effectively as a group helps avoid frustration.

Some suggestions for dealing with several goals at once include the following:

- **Stay focused.** Don't set too many goals at the same time, and make sure that your goals are in alignment with your most important values.
- **Have at least one simple goal and one difficult goal at any given time.** The simple goals motivate you as you accomplish them rapidly. The difficult goals keep you challenged and growing.
- **Have at least one short-term and one long-term goal at any given time.** As with simple goals, short-term goals help ensure that you'll have frequent victories. Long-term goals keep you headed in the right direction.
- **Be flexible.** Decide which of your goals (and tasks) are most important, but be willing to change a goal or even put it on hold for a while, if necessary.
- **Look for ways to combine goals and tasks.** If you can work on two or more goals at once, you can consolidate your resources.

Goal Setting

Once you have determined your values, set a mission statement, and become aware of the types of goals, you can more easily begin setting goals. The Wheel of Life discussed earlier in this chapter contains various areas of focus in our lives. While these areas appear to be separate, our behavior and choices in any given area affect other areas. Because we are part of society as citizens, our choices and behaviors affect others as well. By using your personal mission statement, and by using self-reflection when setting goals in the different areas of your life, you can ensure that your goals reflect the person that you most want to be. Using the Wheel of Life, begin the goal-setting process by asking yourself what you would like to do, be, or have in each of the categories. For example, if you value financial independence, then you might set a goal of finding a well-paying job or making and sticking to a budget. If you value helping others, you might set a goal of spending several hours a week doing volunteer work. Your goals can also be concrete, such as saving enough money to buy a car, or they can be abstract, such as working to control your temper.

You can set many goals at this point without worrying about spreading yourself too thin because we make a distinction between setting a goal and managing a goal or project. At this stage, think of many goals you would like to shoot for even if you are focused on other things right now. However, also remember the importance of balance. Make sure to set goals across different areas of your life: health, finance, family, relationships, personal growth, career, and so forth. The number of categories in which you should set goals depends on your particular situation. How well-balanced is your life right now? What are your priorities? Are you already strong in some areas but weak in others? Answers to questions like these will give you a sense of where to focus your efforts. In general, expect to focus on a few goals in more than one category at a time. It's okay to set a lot of goals in multiple categories.

Guidelines for Attainable Goals

Most goal-setting theorists suggest that goals should have certain characteristics to make them more easily attainable. In general, goals should be as follows:

Written.   Research has shown that by simply writing down your goals, you increase your odds of achieving them, on average, by 300 percent.[11]

A study conducted by Yale University in 1953 has—despite its age—some telling results about the importance of goals. A survey given to the Yale senior class asked the students several questions, including three that addressed goals. The goal-related questions were as follows:

- Have you set goals?
- Have you written them down?
- Do you have a plan to accomplish these goals?

Only 3 percent of the class answered "yes" to these questions. Twenty years later, the members of this class were surveyed again. The research showed that the 3 percent of the class who had set goals were happier and more successful than those who did not have goals. In addition, the 3 percent who had set goals had 97 percent of the wealth of the entire class. In other words, these 3 percent were wealthier than the entire rest of the class combined. This study illustrates that setting goals can lead to accomplishment and fulfillment.

Realistic.   Believing that your goals are at least possible for you to achieve will more likely motivate you. More important, you—not anyone else—must believe in these goals. However, just because you should believe that a goal is possible does not mean that you must expect it to be easy or even probable.

A goal is realistic if you stand reasonably good odds of accomplishing it, given enough time and effort on your part. You must have some control over the effort in order for goals to be realistic. The majority of the goals you set should be very realistic, or you risk becoming frustrated if you do not accomplish any of them.

Challenging.   Although you will also want to have some easier goals, some of your goals should be challenging. Challenging goals force you to grow. However, limit the number of challenging goals or tasks you set to avoid becoming overwhelmed or frustrated. When our goals are so challenging that we wonder whether they are realistic, it might make sense to break the goals down into smaller, incremental goals.

Measurable and specific. Your goals should be measurable and specific enough for you to know definitively whether they have been completed. Although some goals are ongoing or will likely be works in progress throughout your life and thus may not in themselves be measurable, the individual tasks that you will later assign to these goals should be very specific and measurable. For instance, one of your overall goals may be to end AIDS in Africa. Specific tasks associated with that may be to effect a policy whereby the United States gives $5 billion per year to Africa for AIDS prevention, or to institute a training program that educates 500,000 people per month.

Adaptable. The goals you set now may not be perfect; even if they are, situations can change over time, making them imperfect. The reality is that most people's goals do change over time. In fact, goals usually should change, at least slightly, in response to things that change around you or to new life events.

Although it's important to set goals and to have something for which to strive, once you have set the goals you need to detach from the outcome. "You're not guaranteed specific results as you have defined them, but you gain the satisfaction of living your life for a higher purpose."[12]

Time-sensitive. When considering your group of goals as a whole, many of them should have a concrete deadline. However, some may be ongoing, such as attaining excellent health or creating world peace. Such goals will have no end date, though they should be tracked and monitored; the individual tasks that compose the goals should have deadlines.

Congruous. To be effective, your goals should conform to your value system and be internally motivated. If you set goals to meet someone else's expectations or that do not fit within your values, you will find it more difficult to reach them. Your goals should fit into what you want to do, be, or have in your life. If you find it difficult to develop the motivation to achieve a goal, first look at where the goal fits into your value system and do some self-evaluation. Honest evaluation of why you want to achieve a goal can lead to insights and personal discovery.

For example, your friend may have the goal "to buy a bigger house than my brother's." Asking the question "Why a bigger house?" could reveal that your friend wants to compete with his brother. Maybe there also are other issues to be addressed, such as the need for self-esteem and respect, which owning a larger house will not solve. Perhaps a more congruous goal would be "to earn my brother's respect." Identifying the root goal could have a profound impact on this person's life that could not be achieved with a house of any size.

Positive. Goals are more likely to motivate us subconsciously when stated positively and proactively. You may notice this in advertising messages. Nike says

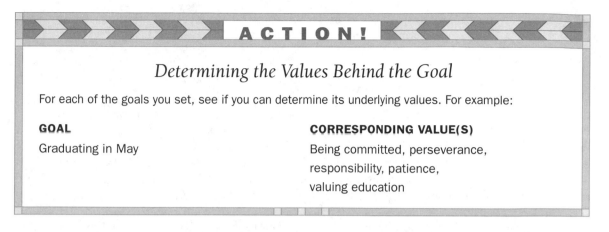

A C T I O N !

Determining the Values Behind the Goal

For each of the goals you set, see if you can determine its underlying values. For example:

GOAL

Graduating in May

CORRESPONDING VALUE(S)

Being committed, perseverance, responsibility, patience, valuing education

"Just Do It" instead of "Stop Sitting There." If your goal is to stop procrastinating, how can you state your ultimate goal, or what you really want, in a positive way? For example, saying, "I want to move with speed and direction in all my tasks and responsibilities" is more proactive. Negatively framed goals require not doing something and thus focus our attention on what we don't want instead of on a positive vision. Positive goals keep us clear and focused on the images of what we want.

CHOOSING WHERE AND HOW TO ENGAGE AS CITIZENS

Choosing where to start engaging as citizens involves observing ourselves and where we experience curiosity and passion for the world around us. "We all have passions if we choose to see them," says Po Bronson, author of *What Should I Do with My Life?* Bronson states: "Most of us don't get epiphanies. We don't get clarity. Our purpose doesn't arrive neatly packaged as destiny. We only get a whisper. A blank, nonspecific urge. That's how it starts."[13]

As a citizen, you may see many areas that need attention in your community and beyond. You have already begun the process of narrowing down areas and issues that interest you. To be as effective as possible in addressing areas of need, it helps to narrow your focus of engagement.

By looking at the life areas that you value most, you can identify how some of these areas are affected by the policies of our government and other influential entities, such as major corporations. For instance, if health is important to you and you find it a challenge to afford health insurance, you may consider how government

> *Where the needs of the world and your talents cross, there lies your vocation.*
>
> **ARISTOTLE**

policies or the policies of insurance companies affect your ability to care for your health. By distinguishing such connections, you may see areas of civic engagement that call to you personally.

Effective Engagement

Landscape of interests—
those items we are concerned about

Frame of action—
those items within our landscape over which we have control

As we look at all of the things that interest us, it becomes clear that there are some things we have influence over and some that we don't. Where do we spend most of our time? What do we think about most often? We find an overall landscape of things that concern us. This **landscape of interests** may be filled with such things as classes, jobs, children, peace, concern for the environment, or finances. Within our landscape of interests, those items that we have control over are our **frame of action.**

By looking at our landscape of interests and our frame of action and determining where we spend most of our time and energy, we can discover quite a bit about our level of efficiency. Effective citizens focus their energy in the frame of action. They work on things they can do something about, and they exhibit energetic, positive qualities.

On the other hand, citizens often become discouraged and blocked if they spend most of their energy focusing on items in the landscape of interests over which they have no control. They may focus on others' faults and the fault of "the system," and thus spend much of their time blaming others and feeling victimized.

Some social problems can seem overwhelming. When we focus on the things we can do, however, we find that we are often empowered to do even more. For instance, providing proper nutrition to every child around the world may seem like a colossal undertaking. However, by looking at what we can actually do, we empower ourselves. For example, we can influence government policy by communicating with our elected officials, we can organize food drives, and we can research the problems and causes and talk to others who share our concerns.

When we proactively look for where we can engage, we become most effective. As we experience success through our efforts, our beliefs about our ability to effect change strengthen. In this way, our frame of action expands to include a larger area within which we can have an influence.

Understanding Our Problem-Solving Preferences

People differ in the ways they prefer to engage as citizens. This is important to understand when determining where you will experience the greatest fulfillment through your involvement. The ability to learn and solve problems is one of the most important skills you can acquire to be effective in your life, and especially as citizens, but we all have a different problem-solving process and unique skills. You will probably recognize that you are better at some of the following skills than others, and that you rely on some more than others when solving problems. As a result, you have developed a unique problem-solving style. The following skills are organized in general categories rather than a comprehensive list of all of the possible skills and styles. Although the categories are not intended to define or limit

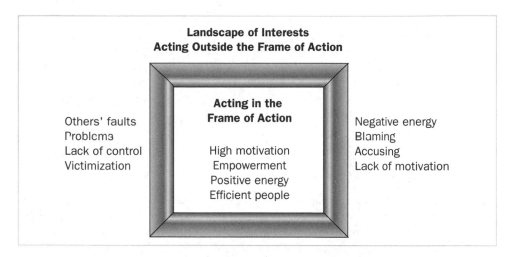

Landscape of Interests
Acting Outside the Frame of Action

Acting in the Frame of Action

Others' faults
Problems
Lack of control
Victimization

High motivation
Empowerment
Positive energy
Efficient people

Negative energy
Blaming
Accusing
Lack of motivation

FIGURE 1.2 *Frame of Action*

you or your style, most people find that they have a predominant style. This guide may help you understand strengths you can use to learn new things or to solve problems. You may also increase your effectiveness as a learner and problem solver by improving on the skills presented here that don't come as naturally.

Problem-Solving Skills

The skills most of us use for learning or solving problems are as follows:

Intuition. This skill involves dealing with people and emotions. People using this skill would tend to rely more on "gut feeling" than on a systematic approach to problems. In new situations, someone with strong intuition skills would be open-minded, sensitive to the needs of others, and adaptable to change.

Observation. This skill entails understanding ideas and situations from different points of view. In a learning situation, people using this skill would rely on patience, objectivity, and listening but would not necessarily take any action. In new situations, observers would rely on thoughts, feelings, and interpretations in forming opinions.

Conceptualization. People with developed conceptualization skills use logic and ideas, rather than feelings, to understand problems or situations. Typically, using this skill would involve relying on systematic planning and development of theories and ideas to solve problems.

Experimentation. Solving problems using this skill incorporates active involvement. Experimenting with approaches to influence or change situations takes place, as opposed to simply watching a situation. People who use this skill value getting things done and seeing the results of their influence and ingenuity.[14]

A person's problem-solving style is a combination of these four basic skills. Because of this, you often may be pulled in several different directions when addressing a problem. Complete the Problem-Solving Inventory in the accompanying box to evaluate the way you solve problems and how you deal with day-to-day situations in your life. We all have a sense that people attack problems, and learn, differently. Combining your scores for each skill can indicate which of the four problem-solving styles best describes you. This inventory may help you better understand yourself and others.

Problem-Solving Styles

Understanding problem-solving styles—and their strengths and weaknesses—can increase your learning power, your ability to get along with others and work in teams, and your adaptability for solving problems. The problem-solving styles are combinations of the four basic problem-solving skills. To get your overall style score for the inventory, add the following columns together:

Column 3 + Column 4: ☐ Technician

Column 1 + Column 2: ☐ Diplomat

Column 3 + Column 2: ☐ Strategist

Column 1 + Column 4: ☐ Activist

Following are descriptions of the four basic styles:

Technician. This style combines the skills of conceptualization and experimentation. People with this style are best at finding practical uses for ideas and theories. If this is your preferred style, you have the ability to solve problems and make decisions based on finding solutions to questions or problems. You would rather deal with technical tasks and problems than with social and interpersonal issues.

Diplomat. This style combines the skills of intuition and observation. People with this style are best at viewing concrete situations from many points of view. Their approach to situations is to observe rather than to take action. If this is your style, you may enjoy situations that call for generating a wide range of ideas, such as brainstorming sessions. You have an imaginative ability and sensitivity to feelings.

Strategist. This style combines the skills of conceptualization and observation. People with this style are best at understanding a wide range of information and putting it into concise, logical forms. If this is your style, you probably are less

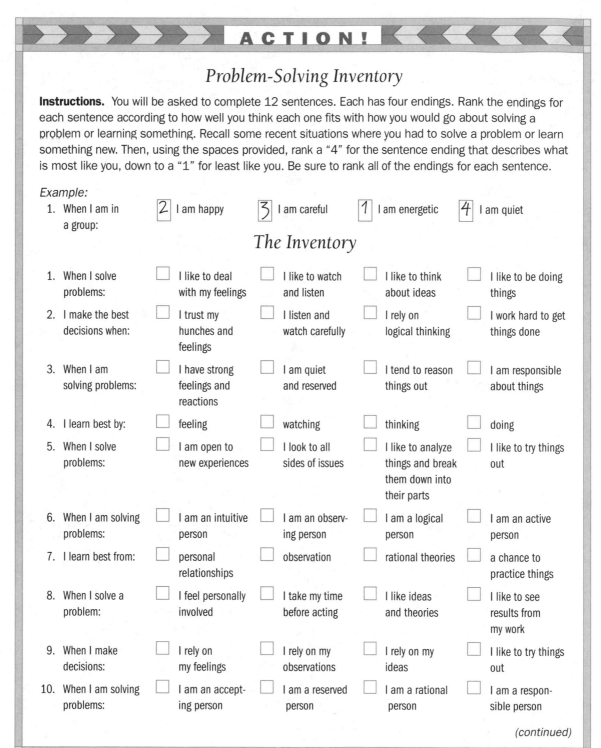

ACTION!

Problem-Solving Inventory

Instructions. You will be asked to complete 12 sentences. Each has four endings. Rank the endings for each sentence according to how well you think each one fits with how you would go about solving a problem or learning something. Recall some recent situations where you had to solve a problem or learn something new. Then, using the spaces provided, rank a "4" for the sentence ending that describes what is most like you, down to a "1" for least like you. Be sure to rank all of the endings for each sentence.

Example:

1. When I am in a group: $\boxed{2}$ I am happy $\boxed{3}$ I am careful $\boxed{1}$ I am energetic $\boxed{4}$ I am quiet

The Inventory

1. When I solve problems: ☐ I like to deal with my feelings ☐ I like to watch and listen ☐ I like to think about ideas ☐ I like to be doing things

2. I make the best decisions when: ☐ I trust my hunches and feelings ☐ I listen and watch carefully ☐ I rely on logical thinking ☐ I work hard to get things done

3. When I am solving problems: ☐ I have strong feelings and reactions ☐ I am quiet and reserved ☐ I tend to reason things out ☐ I am responsible about things

4. I learn best by: ☐ feeling ☐ watching ☐ thinking ☐ doing

5. When I solve problems: ☐ I am open to new experiences ☐ I look to all sides of issues ☐ I like to analyze things and break them down into their parts ☐ I like to try things out

6. When I am solving problems: ☐ I am an intuitive person ☐ I am an observing person ☐ I am a logical person ☐ I am an active person

7. I learn best from: ☐ personal relationships ☐ observation ☐ rational theories ☐ a chance to practice things

8. When I solve a problem: ☐ I feel personally involved ☐ I take my time before acting ☐ I like ideas and theories ☐ I like to see results from my work

9. When I make decisions: ☐ I rely on my feelings ☐ I rely on my observations ☐ I rely on my ideas ☐ I like to try things out

10. When I am solving problems: ☐ I am an accepting person ☐ I am a reserved person ☐ I am a rational person ☐ I am a responsible person

(continued)

A C T I O N !

11. In a new situation: ☐ I get involved ☐ I like to observe ☐ I like to evaluate things ☐ I like to be active

12. I learn best when: ☐ I am receptive and open-minded ☐ I am careful ☐ I analyze ideas ☐ I am practical

TOTAL the scores from each column ☐ Column 1 ☐ Column 2 ☐ Column 3 ☐ Column 4

Each of the totals corresponds to one of the four basic problem-solving skills.

Column One: Intuition

Column Two: Observation

Column Three: Conceptualization

Column Four: Experimentation

Plot your scores on the grid below to get a visual representation of your preferred skills.

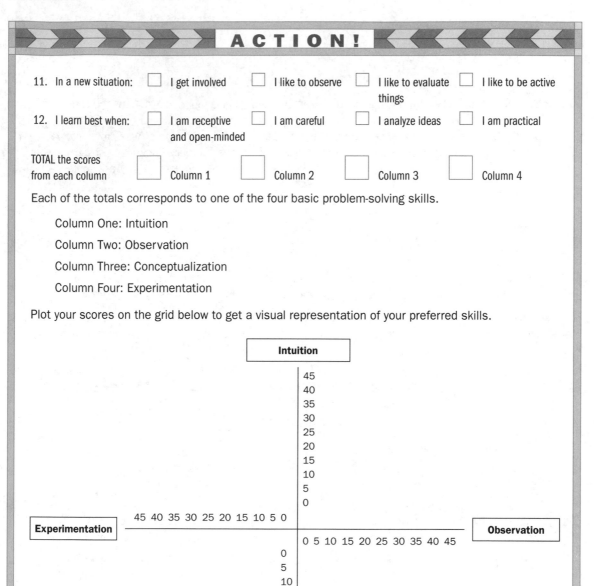

Adapted from "The Learning Style Inventory" by David Kolb, © 1985, McBer & Company.

focused on people and more interested in abstract ideas and concepts. Generally, people with this style find it more important that a theory have logical soundness than practical value.

Activist. This style combines the skills of intuition and experimentation. People with this style enjoy carrying out plans and involving themselves in new and challenging experiences. Your tendency may be to act on "gut" feelings rather than on logical analysis. In solving problems, you may rely more heavily on people for information than on your own technical analysis.

A C T I O N !

Problem-Solving Exercise

In which category of problem-solving style did you score highest? _____
Based on your result, answer the following questions.

1. What do you really like about your problem-solving style? What are your strong points?

   _____

   _____

2. What do others say you could do better in working with them?

   _____

   _____

3. What really stresses you out?

   _____

   _____

4. What kind of activities match your style in terms of creating social change?

   _____

   _____

How can the knowledge gained from the questions above be applied to work situations? Discuss what kind of work situations might best fit each problem-solving style. What are some of the challenges that coworkers who belong to different personality groupings might encounter with one another?

Myers-Briggs Type Indicator® Instrument

In 1921 Swiss psychologist Carl Jung (1875–1961) published the book *Psychological Types*, in which he argued that behavior follows patterns, and that these patterns are determined by the different ways people use their minds. In 1942 Isabel Briggs-Myers and her mother, Katharine Briggs, began to put Jung's theory into practice. They developed the Myers-Briggs Type Indicator instrument®, which after more than 50 years of research and refinement has become the most widely used instrument for identifying and studying personality.[15] Following is an overview of the four temperaments put together by David Keirsey and Marilyn Bates based on Myers-Briggs. They may help you determine your preferences for engaging as a citizen.

Extroversion versus introversion (E/I). This category deals with the way we interact with others and the world around us. *Extroverts* prefer to live in the outside world, drawing their strength from other people. They are outgoing and love interaction. They usually make decisions with others in mind. They enjoy being the center of attention.

Introverts draw their strength from the inner world. They need to spend time alone to think and ponder. They are usually quiet and reflective. They prefer to make decisions by themselves and do not like being the center of attention.

Sensing versus intuition (S/N). This category deals with the way we learn and deal with information. *Sensing* types gather information through their five senses. They have a hard time believing something if it cannot be seen, touched, smelled, tasted, or heard. They like concrete facts and details. They do not rely on intuition or gut feelings. They usually have a great deal of common sense.

Intuitive types are not very detail oriented. They can see possibilities, and they rely on their gut feelings. Usually, they are very innovative. They tend to live in the future and often get bored once they have mastered a task.

Thinking versus feeling (T/F). This category deals with the way we make decisions. *Thinkers* are very logical people. They do not make decisions based on feelings or emotions. They are analytical and sometimes do not take others' values into consideration when making decisions. They can easily identify the flaws of others. They can be seen as insensitive and lacking compassion.

Feelers make decisions based on what they feel is right and just. They like to have harmony, and they value others' opinions and feelings. They are usually very tactful people who like to please others.

Judging versus perceiving (J/P). This category deals with the way we live. *Judgers* are very orderly people. They must have a great deal of structure in their lives. They're good at setting goals and sticking to them. They seldom, if ever, play before their work is completed.

Perceivers are less structured and more spontaneous. They do not like timelines. Unlike judgers they will play before their work is done. They will take every chance to delay a decision or judgment. Sometimes, they can become involved with too many things at one time.

Matching Styles and Values to Action

Choosing activities and causes that are an appropriate match for your personal values and skills helps you engage positively as a citizen. Choosing how and where you engage using the tools and skills outlined in this chapter will help you practice democracy with integrity and efficacy.

> *You can't wait for inspiration. You have to go after it with a club.*
>
> **JACK LONDON**

Using the guidance of your own personal mission statement, you may have already distinguished causes or areas of interest that you want to explore. Once you choose an issue or organization, you must decide *how* you can best be of service.

You are now familiar with different styles of engagement and your preferences for engaging. If your style is that of the activist, you may find that you have a flair for participating in marches, public protests, or public education. If, however, you have more of a technician's style, you may find that you excel in helping favorite nonprofit organizations set up computer databases or Web sites. If you are more of an introvert, you may not choose to engage in fund-raising. You are more likely to be empowered as a citizen if you use your unique talents and are guided by your unique values.

Be creative. If no obvious fit exists between an issue or organization that interests you and what you feel you have to offer, consider inventing a way to engage. As you remain true to your personal gifts and interests and resolute in your desire to make a difference, you will find a way to serve your community and the world.

Applications

IMPORTANT LIFE AREAS. Create a life line to determine what you'd like to see happen during your lifetime. You can even look beyond your lifetime, if you'd like. Start by drawing a horizontal line across the middle of a blank sheet of paper. On the far left end of the line, draw a dot and label it with your date of birth. Estimate how long you'll live and put that dot three-quarters of the way along the line. Next, place a dot for today's date. Along the left side of today's date, place the significant events in your life. Then, set goals for the right side of today's date. Finish the life line by considering what might happen after you die. Think about what you want to occur after your life is done.

1

ATTAINABLE GOALS. Develop a list of short-term and long-term attainable goals using the values you identified.

2

THOUGHTS AND ACTIONS. Think of an issue you care about (the environment, racial issues, freedom of speech, and so forth). What thoughts do you have about this issue on a regular basis? Do you find that these thoughts affect how you act? In what way? What actions do you take on a regular basis that reinforce your hopes regarding this issue? What actions would you like to start taking to achieve more congruence with

3

your values? Do one of these actions this week while applying your problem-solving style and values.

 4   **VALUES AND ACTIONS.** Create a consumption journal for a week. List all purchases you make and how much you spend on each. At the end of the week, reflect on each purchase and the value it represents.

5   **UNDERSTANDING COMMUNITY/FEDERAL CONNECTION.** Choose a service provider in your community (for example, a homeless shelter, youth program, or child care provider), and make an appointment to talk with the director or another staff member. Interview the staff member to find out how the organization is funded and/or regulated by government money and policy. Present your findings.

QUIZ

1. Central beliefs and attitudes that guide our choices consciously or unconsciously are:
   A. goals
   B. motivational factors
   C. styles
   D. values
   E. none of the above

2. Name the ten components of the Wheel of Life:

   _____   _____

   _____   _____

   _____   _____

   _____   _____

   _____   _____

3. What tool can help us make choices with clarity and integrity and develop a vision of self and purpose in life?
   A. values
   B. mission statement
   C. thesis
   D. effective engagement
   E. none of the above

4. The state of being whole or complete and acting with moral soundness is the definition of:
   A. integrity
   B. congruence

   C. internal motivation
   D. external motivation
   E. none of the above

5. Turning awareness inside to create the alignment of thoughts, words, and actions is the concept of:
   A. external motivation
   B. goals
   C. congruence
   D. style
   E. none of the above

6. ☐ True or false: The stimulus response model of human behavior relies on internal motivation.

7. Match the goal with the definition.

   ☐ 1. personal goal   A. A goal that keeps us headed in the right direction and can provide a sense of greater purpose

   ☐ 2. service goal   B. A goal that is set by members of a group

   ☐ 3. long-term goal   C. A goal that subordinates personal achievements to something beyond our own immediate self-interests

   ☐ 4. collective goal   D. A goal that provides a sense of accomplishment and motivation, which produces the patience and perseverance needed to achieve more later

   ☐ 5. short-term goal   E. A goal developed and implemented for one's own development and achievement

8. Attainable goals must be:
   A. realistic, challenging, measurable and specific, adaptable, time-sensitive, congruous
   B. effective, realistic, measurable and specific, engaging, time-sensitive, congruous
   C. congruous, realistic, measurable and specific, engaging, adaptable, time-sensitive, challenging
   D. adaptable, time-sensitive, realistic, effective, engaging, congruous, adaptable
   E. none of the above

9. Fill in the blanks: Those items within our own landscape that we have control over are termed our _____ _____ _____.

10. Give an example of a specific problem and how you could solve it using the following skills:

A. Intuition:

_____

_____

B. Observation:

_____

_____

C. Conceptualization:

_____

_____

D. Experimentation:

_____

_____

ENDNOTES

1. Loeb, Paul Rogat. *Soul of a Citizen*. New York: St. Martin's Griffin, 1999.

2. Williamson, Marianne. *The Healing of America*. New York: Simon & Schuster, 1997.

3. Jaworski, Joseph, and Betty Sue Flowers, eds., *Synchronicity: The Inner Path of Leadership*. San Francisco: Berrett-Koehler, 1998.

4. Palmer, Parker. "The Heart of Knowing." *Shambala Sun*, September 1997.

5. Remen, Rachel Naomi. *My Grandfather's Blessings: Stories of Strength, Refuge, and Belonging*. New York: Riverhead Books, 2001.

6. Covey, Stephen. *Seven Habits of Highly Effective People*. New York: Fireside/Simon & Schuster, 1989.

7. Daley-Harris, Sam, and Valerie Harper. *Reclaiming Our Democracy: Healing the Break Between People and Government*. Philadelphia: Camino Books, 1994.

8. Ryan, Richard M., and Edward L. Deci. "Self Determination Theory and the Facilitation of Intrinsic Motivation, Social Development, and Well-Being." *American Psychologist* 55:1 (January 2000): 68–78.

9. Wilson, Kristen. "Jill Ker Conway: In Her Own Words." *Here in Hanover*, Summer 1998, 7–8.

10. Loeb, *Soul of a Citizen*.

11. Ziglar, Zig. *Success and the Self-Image*. New York: Simon & Schuster, 1995.

12. Williamson, *The Healing of America*.

13. Bronson, Po. *What Should I Do with My Life? The True Story of People Who Answered the Ultimate Question*. New York: Simon & Schuster, 2003.

14. Kolb, David. "Learning Style Inventory." Boston: McBer & Company, 1985.

15. Sherfield, Robert, Rhonda Montgomery, and Patricia Moody. *Cornerstone*. Upper Saddle River, NJ: Prentice Hall, 2005.

Critical Thinking and Problem Solving for Social Issues

2

We often enjoy the comfort of opinion without the discomfort of thought.

—JOHN F. KENNEDY

homas Jefferson once said, "A democracy cannot survive unthinking citizens."[1] One of the most widely accepted objectives of American education today, **critical thinking** is a skill that involves questioning what we read and hear, evaluating information for truth or bias, exploring different sides of an issue, using problem-solving skills to find the best solution, and continually consulting our values, beliefs, and internal wisdom, or intuition. Critical thinking has been defined as "reasonable, reflective thinking that is focused on deciding what to believe or do."[2] Reflective thinking implies that we reflect—or "turn back" and call into question—the assumptions and premises underlying our ideas.[3] Reflective thinkers base their opinions on substantive information and sound logic.

Many people involved in the civic realm spend time using or critiquing analysis done by other people or conducting their own analyses of societal issues. The political arena is full of competing numbers, predictions, evaluations, and conclusions about public policy and its effects. It's important to be able to look at all this information with a critical eye to sort out what is valid from what is not.

Public policy can affect the lives of millions of people in profound and lasting ways. For this reason, it is essential that our decisions be based on accurate information and solid analysis rather than assumptions or half-truths. The more informed and accurate we are on issues, the better advocates we can be. The intent of this chapter is to present a framework for developing critical thinking.

OBJECTIVES

After studying this chapter, you should be able to:

- Use higher levels of thinking to think critically

- Effectively evaluate sources of information

- Recognize false logic and bias

- Distinguish facts and opinions

- Use your values to maintain objectivity and evaluate context

- Define a problem

- Gather information

- Interpret information

- Develop and evaluate solutions to a problem

MAKING IT HAPPEN

STUDENTS TAKE CHARGE

There is a pond by the track at Quincy High School in Washington State. Periodically, the track and field team used to complain about fumes from the pond, but no one else at the high school gave it a thought until Quincy's mayor uncovered a story that the fertilizer companies were using toxic waste as a means of cheaply disposing of their by-products. That waste was dumped into the high school pond and began seeping into the groundwater. Many people in the town worked for the fertilizer company and were unwilling to believe the stories. Some townspeople were even implicated in an attempted cover-up of the story.

When a group of Quincy science students were looking for a research subject for a science class, their science teacher, Rob Stagg, suggested that they study the pond. Through Washington State's Youth Network for Healthy Communities (YNHC) program, the Quincy students were able to talk to university scientists via teleconferencing. They also did a presentation for a panel of experts assembled at the University of Washington by the Center for Ecogenetics and Environmental Health. The panelists asked the students about their project and research, pushing the students to engage in critical thinking. With the help of YNHC, the students were able to research the chemicals involved in the leak, gather documents from state and federal agencies, scrutinize air samples, and determine what the government knew about the health effects. Their research showed that the contamination flowed directly under the high school and that the government knew little of the effects.

Stagg said, "They used to think that environmental issues were just dreamed up by people with an agenda and that if there were a real problem, we would all know about it. Now, they know that these issues involve real data and that most people will never know about the issues unless they look and listen for them." The students concluded that much more research needs to be done about the health effects of the leak, but according to Stagg, they also learned something else that is very important. "They learned that it is within our power to become aware of these conditions, share that understanding with others, and influence actions taken to alter the conditions."

Adapted from "When Youth Lead" by Elise Miller and Jon Sharpe, *YES! Magazine*, Spring 2003.

CRITICAL THINKING

Thinking—
to reason about or reflect on; to ponder

The verb **think** is defined by the *American Heritage Dictionary* as "to reason about or reflect on; to ponder." Although **critical thinking** involves thinking more analytically and reflectively about an issue or problem, knowing facts and figures is also essential for clear thinking. Reflective thought must be grounded on factual knowledge. Critical thinking entails seeking to understand different aspects of an issue and—in deciding what to believe—looking not only at truth and untruth but also at stories that display bias or are incomplete.

Benjamin Bloom created a taxonomy, or scientific classification, for categorizing levels of thinking (see Figure 2.1). At the first level of thinking, we observe and recall information. At the second level, we move into understanding meaning. The third level involves applying the information in some way. At the fourth level of thinking, we recognize patterns and can analyze information, and at the fifth and sixth levels we combine old ideas to create new ideas and recommend action. The lower levels of thinking are the foundation of critical thinking, which takes place at the higher levels in this categorization.

To think critically using the higher levels, you might:

- Evaluate sources of information
- Maintain objectivity
- Identify stakeholders and perspectives
- Separate facts and opinions
- Evaluate the context
- Recognize false logic and bias
- Use your values

Critical thinking— reasonable, reflective thinking that is focused on deciding what to believe or do

Evaluate Sources of Information

Considering the source of the information is crucial to weighing the potential bias of its content. Information can be embedded in a context that manipulates the conclusion in order to serve the interests of a particular group. The higher your level of interest in an issue, the more effort you might want to expend assessing the source. According to the journalist William Greider in *Who Will Tell the People*, corporations routinely push self-serving legislation through Congress by hiring public relations firms to organize lobbying efforts. Greider points out that, "'Responsible Industry for a Safe Environment' is actually a virtual group formed by the National Agricultural Chemicals Association to thwart government regulations of pesticides. The 'Alliance for a Responsible CFC Policy' is a lobbying entity created and paid for by Dow, DuPont and Amoco to oppose banning the ozone-depleting chlorofluorocarbons these companies produce."[4] Sometimes, important issues become driven by misconceptions that take on the power of truth only because they are repeated so often that they become part of mainstream thought.

Media Sources

It is tempting to automatically view what we see in the media—whether in textbooks, newspapers, television, or on the Internet—as factual. The media is our largest source of information. The U.S. Constitution ensures freedom of speech, although it does not ensure the honesty and neutrality of that speech. And, though

Level of Competence	Skills Demonstrated
1. **Knowledge**	Observation and recall of information Knowledge of dates, events Able to: list, define, tell, describe, identify, show, label, collect, examine, quote, name
2. **Comprehension**	Translate knowledge into new context Interpret facts Predict consequences Able to: summarize, describe, interpret, contrast, predict, associate, distinguish, estimate, differentiate
3. **Application**	Use information Use methods, concepts, theories Solve problems Able to: apply, demonstrate, calculate, solve, complete, relate, discover
4. **Analysis**	See patterns Organize parts Recognize hidden meanings Able to: analyze, separate, order, explain, connect, classify, arrange, divide, compare, infer
5. **Synthesis**	Use old ideas to create new ones Relate knowledge from several areas Predict Draw conclusions Able to: combine, integrate, modify, rearrange, substitute, plan, create, design, invent, compose, formulate
6. **Evaluation**	Compare and discriminate between ideas Assess value of theories, presentations Make choices based on reasoned argument Verify value of evidence Recognize subjectivity Able to: assess, decide, rank, grade, test, measure, recommend, convince, select, judge, discriminate, support, conclude, compare, summarize

FIGURE 2.1 *Bloom's Taxonomy*

it is ostensibly the job of the media to track down information and present it in an unbiased way, at times we receive partial or misleading information.

In one instance, Jayson Blair, a former national reporter for *The New York Times*, was shown to have intentionally falsified information for years in his reports.[5] The media may also, at times, report only part of a story. Press releases and promotions portraying tax cuts as a relief for working-class families, for instance, were reported verbatim in the media when President Bill Clinton signed his tax cut bill in 1997, and again in 2003, when President George W. Bush signed a $350 billion tax cut bill. However, when the analysis was done, the cuts did not provide the reported relief for this group. At least half of the benefits went to the wealthiest 5 percent of Americans, with the bottom 40 percent receiving little. Much of the media used the proponents' own words when reporting. In 2003, news reports repeated the Republican National Committee's press releases that stated the tax cut benefited "everyone who pays taxes."[6]

After reporting on a story or policy, the media also may not do any thorough analysis of the effects. In 1999, the Aspen Institute launched a 10-year effort called The Global Interdependence Initiative to better inform and motivate American public support for U.S. foreign policy that is appropriate to an interdependent world.[7] The Initiative's research showed that the media commonly followed by most Americans gives an incomplete view of international events. The research describes mainstream media as presenting events in an isolated context, without discussing many of the long-term causes and accountability of various entities.

Looking at who controls the media reporting is important for assessing the accuracy of the information. According to Peter Mitchell and John Schoeffel, authors of *Understanding Power: The Indispensable Chomsky*, "The large media outlets in America—the largest newspapers, radio stations, TV networks—are megacorporations which are highly profitable. These corporations dominate the country's economy and assert vast influence over government policy making. Through their control of the media they are able to present a picture of the world which perpetuates their economic, social and political agendas."[8]

In June 2003, the Federal Communications Commission (FCC), responsible for overseeing media stations, approved large changes to the nation's media ownership. The FCC wanted to relax more of the restrictions on the ability of broadcast and newspaper conglomerates both to expand into new markets and to extend their reach in the cities where they already have a presence. Owning more stations gives networks more power over what programs to show and what news to broadcast and enables the biggest companies to force out new competition. Responding to public disapproval, Congress later overturned the ruling.

One effect of the control of media reporting was seen on the presidential election night in 2000. Before votes were counted in the very close election, the Fox network made the decision to formally declare George W. Bush the winner, although the Associated Press insisted the race for President between him and Al Gore was still too close to call. After Fox declared a winner, all other networks followed immediately. The man at Fox who made the decision to declare a winner was John Ellis, first cousin of George W. Bush.[9]

Effects of media control were also seen when CBS News attempted to get an exclusive interview with Jessica Lynch, the U.S. Army private who was injured and rescued in Iraq. CBS News belongs to Viacom, which, at that time, also owned Paramount, 39 television stations, MTV, VH1, Showtime, Comedy Central, The Movie Channel, Sundance, Nickelodeon, Simon & Schuster, Blockbuster Video, and the Infinity radio network. When CBS offered Lynch a two-hour CBS News documentary, a TV movie produced by CBS Entertainment, the possibility of co-hosting an MTV special, and a book deal with Simon & Schuster in exchange for her exclusive story, it showed the power that large corporations can yield in media coverage.

> *Criticism is more than a right; it is an act of patriotism—a higher form of patriotism, I believe, than the familiar ritual of national adulation. All of us have the responsibility to act upon the higher patriotism which is to love our country less for what it is than for what we would like it to be.*
>
> **WILLIAM FULBRIGHT**

Media reporting can result in misconceptions among the general public. It is our responsibility to question what we read and hear, even if the source is credible. Although some information we receive from a given source may be factual, that does not mean that all information from that source is necessarily accurate. Learning to assess bias and motivation in our sources of information is an important skill.

Community

Other influential sources of information in our lives are the people with whom we associate most closely. Our families, teachers, business colleagues, friends, church leaders, and others all share information with us that greatly influences our opinions and beliefs. Because of the positions of authority and trust that these people hold in our lives, we may often neglect to fully question or analyze the information they share with us.

In order to do our best thinking, we must put information through our filters. It is often difficult to express an opinion contrary to that of someone close to us. We are taught to be polite and to respect those in positions of authority. Offering a dissenting view need not be disrespectful; indeed, if we are to be effective agents of social change, it is necessary. As Russ Kick says in his introduction to *Everything You Know Is Wrong*, "I believe that dissent is never more needed than when conformity is at an all time high. When the fewest questions are being asked is when they're most needed."[10]

Internet

Reference materials also need to be analyzed with a critical eye. The Internet is a reference that especially warrants the use of critical thinking. Information today is readily available. By using search engines on the Internet, we can retrieve vast amounts of information on many subjects quickly and easily. However, determining the accuracy and reliability of the information is another matter. It may take less time to find information, but we must spend more time verifying the information.

Traditional newspapers rely on editors to determine the accuracy and overall quality of their articles. Many journals also rely on the peer review process. But a great deal of online information does not go through these traditional filters.

When critically evaluating Web sites and their information, consider scrutinizing the following:

Accuracy

- Has the page been rated or evaluated in some manner? If so, who did the evaluation?
- Is the author's point of view clear and sound?
- Is there a bias—political, ideological, or cultural? Does the author hope to persuade you in some way?
- When was the site produced and last updated?

Authority

- Are the qualifications of the site's author or producer indicated on the page?
- Who sponsors the site? Is it a commercial or educational site, or does it appear to be created by an individual?

Completeness

- How well and thoroughly is the subject covered?
- Are the links appropriate, relevant, and comprehensive?

Content

- How many items are included on the page?
- Is a copyright notice indicated on the page?
- Does the site include a bibliography?
- Is the level of detail appropriate for the subject?

Propaganda

- Does the author present accurate descriptions of alternative views?
- Does the author attack other perspectives?
- Is the writing overly emotional?

Maintain Objectivity

Emotions are an inescapable part of our human experience. Our feelings of happiness, excitement, surprise, anger, fear, sadness, and frustration give us the ability to relate to one another's experiences. Emotions may compel us to feel compassion and reach out in times of need or to turn away, ignore, and stop listening to others. We may find that our own emotions, although very important

> *Nothing in this world is bad or good but thinking makes it so.*
>
> **WILLIAM SHAKESPEARE**

in motivating us to act, can negatively affect our ability to think critically if they are so strongly felt that we lose objectivity. If we have an extreme reaction to an issue or topic, we can take that as a clue that our ability to think objectively may be compromised. In this case, it helps to identify our emotions and the personal issues that may be triggering them and to understand the issue from a different perspective.

Identify Stakeholders and Perspectives

Stakeholders—
entities who are
affected by the
policy in question

In the quest for understanding and analyzing information or public policy, identifying the stakeholders is key. **Stakeholders** are entities who have an interest in, or who are in any way affected by, the policy in question, either directly or indirectly. Solutions to social problems are often found in the compromise of legitimate competing interests.

> *Science promised man power . . . But as so often happens when people are seduced by promises of power, the price is servitude and impotence. Power is nothing if it is not the power to choose.*

**JOSEPH
WEIZENBAUM**

Direct beneficiaries. In assessing the value of any given policy or program, the value to the recipient must first be understood. To do this, we must seek feedback and advice from the program recipients. Is the policy helping or hurting? Is it meeting the needs it was intended to meet?

Profiteers. Are there people or groups who will profit financially from the policy in question?

Opponents. Understanding the motivations of those who oppose a given policy or program may provide insight into complexities of the problem or policy that you may not have understood or considered. Identify your opponents' values as compared to your own.

Indirect beneficiaries. If a program or policy directly benefits certain people in society, other members of society often benefit indirectly. For instance, Head Start is an early childhood education program that benefits low-income children and their families. Studies have shown that young people who attended Head Start as children are less likely to commit crimes, which in turn benefits all members of society.[11]

Separate Facts and Opinions

A *factual statement* offers proof from a source that can be verified. Assumptions, or *opinions*, are more often based on emotion and myth.

If a statement is based on facts, it will likely pass one or more of the following three tests:

- Can it be observed?
- Has it been established over the years?
- Can it be tested?

If a statement is an opinion, it will likely meet one of the following criteria:

- It can be argued.
- It will comprise highly descriptive words (for example, *best, tremendous,* or *outstanding*).
- It may include opinion key words (such as *think, believe, assume, imagine, feel, surmise, may, content, conjecture,* or *suppose*).
- It may hint that it is true for everyone by using such words as *all, none, every, no, only, nobody, everybody, always,* or *never*.

Evaluate the Context

Exaggerating a story or taking it out of context is useful when someone intends to mislead or influence others toward his or her own point of view. For instance, in the debate over whether welfare support is a socially beneficial policy, one person may focus on a case in which a welfare mother is living well to demonstrate that welfare is a bad policy. However, you must consider the case in the context of the total issue. One story cannot provide a definitive picture of the problem. Question the stories you hear. Are they representative of the problem, or are they exceptions? Finding out as much information about the topic as possible will help you put the issue into a proper context.

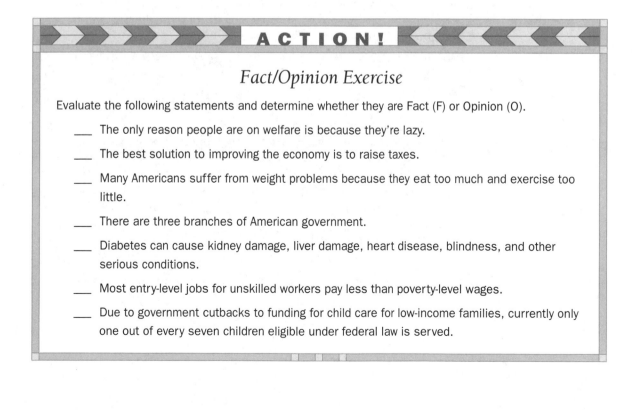

ACTION!

Fact/Opinion Exercise

Evaluate the following statements and determine whether they are Fact (F) or Opinion (O).

____ The only reason people are on welfare is because they're lazy.

____ The best solution to improving the economy is to raise taxes.

____ Many Americans suffer from weight problems because they eat too much and exercise too little.

____ There are three branches of American government.

____ Diabetes can cause kidney damage, liver damage, heart disease, blindness, and other serious conditions.

____ Most entry-level jobs for unskilled workers pay less than poverty-level wages.

____ Due to government cutbacks to funding for child care for low-income families, currently only one out of every seven children eligible under federal law is served.

Recognize False Logic and Bias

By learning to recognize faulty arguments and deceptive logic, you can improve your ability to think critically about issues. Following are some common faulty persuasion techniques:

- **Glittering generalities** say little specifically but convey emotion: "Jim has made this nation a better place."
- **Hasty generalizations** are conclusions based on insufficient evidence: "It turns out that smoking doesn't cause cancer—I saw an article about that."
- **False dilemma** poses only two choices when there are a variety of possibilities and perspectives to consider: "Choose Smith and you'll get inflation; choose Jones and the budget will be balanced."
- **Card stacking** involves presenting evidence in a partial or skewed way to promote the interests of a particular group. For example, saying that "the average income is rising" may be accurate when only the income level of the top 10 percent of the population is rising.
- **Bandwagon** is an approach that encourages people to do something because it is the popular thing to do: "Everybody is doing it!" (This is what your mother was referring to when she said, "If everyone jumped off a bridge, would you too?")
- **Appeals to emotion** summon anger, pity, or fear—including alienation, disapproval, and violence—to entice support. A scare tactic is one use of an appeal to emotion: "If we don't fight crime this way, your children won't be safe." Or: "First they outlaw machine guns, and then they'll take your hunting rifles and impose martial law!"
- **Ad verecundiam** is used when people invoke quotes and phrases from popular or famous people or from those in an authoritative position in order to support their views.
- **False cause and effect** is used to insist that an event is caused by another event just because it took place after that event.
- **Straw arguments** are used when people attack their opponent's argument in the hopes that this will make their own argument stronger (as opposed to focusing on the strengths of their own argument).
- **Ad hominem** is a persuasive technique that involves attacking the person and not the ideas. This is also called *slander* or *name-calling*.
- **Appeals to tradition** look at the past and suggest that because things have always been done one way, they should continue to be done that way.
- **Appeal to patriotism** is a form of persuasion that asks one to ignore reason and critical thinking and to support a school/city/state/nation regardless of the actions of that entity.

Use Your Values

What you know to be true can help guide you no matter how persuasive an argument to the contrary is. In analyzing arguments, we use more than just our intellect; critical thinking also involves tapping into our intuition and values. It is important to access your core values when a good argument attempts to sway you or when you feel intimidated without the facts and figures in front of you. You may find that you sometimes silence yourself or change your opinions in the face of arguments over issues because you're not as prepared. Trust your values to guide you in these instances, and research the needed information.

Critical Thinking Exercise: Christopher Columbus

The history books most students read in grade school tell the story of a heroic Christopher Columbus who discovered the Americas in his quest to prove the world was round. Many Americans idolize Columbus as an adventurer and a heroic thinker. We have a national holiday and celebrate with parades and parties.

Are there other stakeholders with different views? A group of Native Americans wants to ban the celebration of Columbus Day because they contend that Columbus was responsible for human rights atrocities, including the genocide of native inhabitants of America. Their view is that people had lived here for thousands of years before he came and that many were enslaved, displaced, and killed as a result of his actions. To think critically about Columbus and his historic contributions, we can start by gathering more information and looking at his actions from other viewpoints.

In what context did this event occur? Columbus, an Italian, had persuaded the king and queen of Spain to finance his voyage to the other side of the Atlantic. He was attempting to find a sea route to the Indies and Asia for gold and spices. Due to the discoveries of Marco Polo and others, educated people of the time knew the world was round, and Columbus believed he could sail west to reach the Far East.

In *A People's History of the United States*, Howard Zinn relates that Columbus arrived on an island in the Bahamas in the Caribbean, where he and his party were greeted by the Arawak Indians. The Arawaks lived simply but were generous to the newcomers. In his log, Columbus wrote:

> They . . . brought us parrots and balls of cotton and spears and many other things, which they exchanged for the glass beads and hawks' bells. They willingly traded everything they owned . . . They were well-built, with good bodies and handsome features . . . They do not bear arms, and do not know them, for I showed them a sword, they took it by the edge and cut themselves out of ignorance. They have no iron. Their spears are made of cane . . . They would make fine servants . . . With fifty men we could subjugate them all and make them do whatever we want.[12]

Where can we gather more information? The primary source of information on what happened on the islands after Columbus came is Bartolome de las Casas, a priest who participated in the conquest of Cuba. Las Casas transcribed Columbus's journal and wrote a multivolume work entitled *History of the Indies*. In Book 2 of this series, Las Casas tells about the treatment of the Indians by the

Spaniards: "Endless testimonies . . . prove the mild and pacific temperament of the natives . . . But our work was to exasperate, ravage, kill, mangle and destroy; small wonder, then, if they tried to kill one of us now and then . . . The admiral, it is true, was blind as those who came after him, and he was so anxious to please the King that he committed irreparable crimes against the Indians."[13]

When he arrived on Hispaniola in 1508, Las Casas says, "there were 60,000 people living on this island, including the Indians; so that from 1494 to 1508, over three million people had perished from war, slavery and the mines. Who in future generations will believe this? I myself writing it as a knowledgeable eyewitness can hardly believe it."[14]

Is there bias? Samuel Eliot Morison, the Harvard historian and most distinguished writer on Columbus, is also an avid sailor. He retraced Columbus's sail across the Atlantic, and in his book *Christopher Columbus, Mariner,* written in 1954, he extols Columbus's wonderful seamanship abilities but mentions the enslavement and killing in one sentence: "The cruel policy initiated by Columbus and pursued by his successors resulted in complete genocide."[15] Do you need to consult other sources to gather more information?

How do your values affect your viewpoint? After assessing the information you have gathered, consult your values. Perhaps you strongly value patriotism and believe that Columbus Day is a good celebration of American values. However, on closer investigation, you may also have values that persuade you along a different line of thinking. You may come to respect the opinions of others who think differently.

PROBLEM SOLVING

Usually, people use what's most familiar to them to tackle a problem. If they know how to write, they write about it. If they know how to organize, they organize people. If they know how to research, they research, and if they know how to network, they pick up the phone. Each of these tactics may be useful for the problem, or some may be entirely inappropriate or ineffective. A good strategy, like a map for a new travel route, does not rely on the roads you already know. It starts where you are, ends where you want to go, and gives you a way to get there. Without a good strategy, you might get lost and accomplish very little.

To solve a problem using critical thinking, you might engage in the following elements of critical thinking:

- Defining the problem
- Gathering accurate information
- Interpreting the information
- Developing possible solutions
- Evaluating the possible solutions and choosing the best one
- Evaluating success

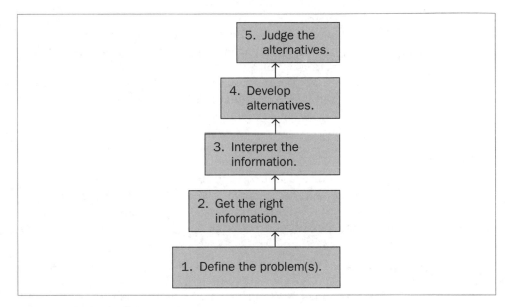

FIGURE 2.2 *Problem-Solving Steps*

The solution to any given problem that involves more than one person must involve compromise, negotiation, and respect for the values and needs of others. Problem solving within groups of people can be a complex process because it includes emotions, opinions, communication challenges, differing values and needs, and so forth. What appears to be a fine solution to one person or group may be a disaster in the eyes of another. Gathering good information, seeking to understand the needs of various stakeholders, and having a large amount of patience are necessary for effective problem solving.

The following steps provide a helpful methodology for problem solving. They will support you in analyzing a problem and choosing viable solutions.

Step One: Define the Problem

By saying that something is a problem, we usually mean that someone is unhappy about a situation. The steps for solving both personal and public problems are basically the same. We must first begin by defining the overall problem.

I need transportation.
Unemployment rates are rising.
Terrorist recruitment is increasing.

Eugene Bardach, a professor at the University of California at Berkeley, says, "It is important not to define the problem in a way that it presumes the solution."[16] In other words, state the problem without giving bias to a certain solution. In the first

The significant problems we face cannot be solved at the same level of thinking we were at when we created them.

■

ALBERT EINSTEIN

example above, the problem could have been written "I need a new car," but that gives a possible solution immediately. It may end up that public transportation is a better option. The second problem could have been stated "More jobs are needed" when the availability of jobs may have been found to be sufficient but there was a growing shortage of child care.

Define the Terms

When considering an issue or a problem, start by defining the terms and seek agreement on the definitions. If, for instance, you are considering whether drug use leads to violent crimes, you might ask the following questions: What constitutes violent crime? What constitutes drug usage?

List the Stakeholders

Some stakeholders in a problem may not be immediately apparent. To identify stakeholders, ask questions of those who hold opinions and beliefs about the problem that are different from your own. Whose problem is it?

Add Details

Once you have stated the overall problem, add some specifics and details to it. When do I need transportation? Why? How many hours a day? What is the unemployment rate? How much has it increased in the last year or last decade?

Step Two: Gather Information

When the problem is defined, you have identified your area of focus enough to begin gathering information. Consider the kind of information you want. You may:

- Get facts and figures on the larger problem.
- Research the history and context of the issue. Understand the underlying causes. Distinguish symptoms from the root cause.
- Look at the problem from the viewpoints of all of the stakeholders. How are different people affected by the problem?
- Distinguish the strategies currently being used to address the issue.

The purpose of gathering information is to more completely understand the problem. It is not necessary to become an expert on the problem in order to take effective action. The need to figure out the perfect solution often blocks us from taking action. Social problems rarely have clear-cut solutions, and often, the best solution is discovered in the process of trial and error. We must be willing to follow our convictions and realize that any apparent "failure" along the way gives us vital information toward a more effective solution; thus it is not a failure but merely an outcome.

Step Three: Interpret the Information

Some of the information you gather may be in the form of numbers and raw data. The challenge is to understand what these numbers and data show. Put yourself in the shoes of the various stakeholders in the problem and assign meaning to the numbers and data from their perspective. The same numbers and data can tell different stories. Other information you gather may be in the form of personal stories. How do these stories make you feel? How might they affect other stakeholders who have a different set of values, needs, and fears?

Interpret information to decide what value it has and how you might use it to help you find a solution to a problem. Check your sources for bias and credibility, and verify the accuracy of information.

Step Four: Develop Possible Solutions

In order to reach a solution, it helps to consider many possible alternatives. There will usually be multiple ways of dealing with a problem. Brainstorm and generate as many alternatives as you can.

Think Creatively

The best problem solvers and decision makers are also creative. **Creativity** is the ability to create something original, be it a solution, a tangible product, a work of art, an idea, a system, a program, or a format—anything at all.

The following techniques can help you improve your creative thinking ability:

Brainstorming. There can be dozens of ways to solve a social problem or answer a question. Brainstorming, the art of considering numerous possibilities from the silly to the practical, allows people to explore a problem or an issue from many different angles. Make brainstorming lists when you are trying to solve a problem, and work with others when possible. Brainstorming will give you practice at keeping your mind open to new possibilities.

Here are some guidelines for successful brainstorming.

- Don't evaluate or criticize an idea right away. Write down your ideas so that you remember them. Evaluate later, after you have had a chance to think about them.
- Even if an idea obviously seems like a bad idea to you, it may help to keep it on your list in terms of considering the views and interests of others.

Brainstorming— the art of considering numerous possibilities

- Focus on quantity; don't worry about quality until later. Try to generate as many ideas or examples as you can. The more thoughts you generate, the better the chance that one might be useful.
- Let yourself consider wild ideas. Sometimes the craziest ideas end up being the most productive, positive, and workable solutions to a problem.[17]

We do well at growing critics and experts, but we do not produce enough people for the responsible roles.

JOHN GARDNER

Thinking through ideas with others. Once you've become comfortable with the process of brainstorming, learn to discuss your ideas with other people and to give and take feedback. Ask permission to give feedback on another's ideas. You may have to encourage the feedback of others as some people are hesitant to give it. The phrase "the whole is greater than the sum of the parts" can apply to the wisdom created by thinking collaboratively.

Looking for the possibilities. See situations in terms of what they can become, not what they are at first glance or what past experience indicates. While learning from past experience can be valuable, it can also place arbitrary limits on what is possible for the future. Don't be afraid to come up with untested ideas.

Making connections. Creative people are good at seeing patterns in seemingly unrelated things. They perceive both similarities and differences and frequently come up with ingenious ways of capitalizing on a trend, a set of circumstances, or an existing need.

Step Five: Evaluate Possible Solutions and Choose the Best One

Once you have identified some possible solutions, evaluate them for viability, value, and whether they will likely achieve the desired result.

Some solutions require resources that don't currently exist or that would be more difficult to acquire or develop, while others employ resources that are readily available. Some solutions may benefit very few people, and some will benefit the majority of stakeholders in the issue. Some solutions may match your values, while others will not. In this step you will want to ask as many questions as possible in evaluating whether a solution is viable. Again, put yourself in the shoes of the various stakeholders in the issue and imagine the questions they would ask. Is anyone harmed by the solution? How do the various stakeholders benefit? What do we want things to look like afterward?

Intuition—
attaining direct knowledge without evident rational thought or inference

Use Your Intuition

On most important decisions, there is an information gap. The art of problem solving rests, in part, on the ability to bridge that gap by **intuition**. In the problem solving process for complex social issues, there may be an absence of information or clear direction in which to proceed. The art of problem-solving rests, in part, on the ability to bridge this gap by using intuition. Intuition is information or direction that we receive from within ourselves without a rational thought process or without the benefit of proven external circumstances or historical precedent.

Trust your feelings when solving problems, and consider your core values. As Robert Greenleaf said in his convocation address at the University of Redlands in 1966: "At the heart of every constructive action are responsible persons, those who reach out to engage with real life issues where the going may be rough, lay out alternatives, assess their relative merits, choose one that accords with virtue and justice—with their own hearts—make the choice knowing they may be wrong and suffer for it, and bear the risk bravely."[18]

Step Six: Evaluate Success

After a solution is implemented to solve a problem, you'll want to assess the effectiveness of the solution. If it did not work, or if there is now a new problem to solve, go to the beginning of the problem-solving process and start again.

Obstacles to Problem Solving

Certain obstacles can hinder the search for good solutions. Watch for these potential stumbling blocks as you work to solve challenging social problems.

The perfect solution. Believing that every problem has one perfect solution can intimidate you. If you come up with several ideas but none seems exactly right, you may want to give up. Refrain from looking for the perfect solution. Instead, look for the best solution, using whatever time frame or resources you have. A step in a positive direction, though it may be only part of an ultimate solution to the problem, is more valuable than no action at all.

> *I have always thought that one . . . of tolerable abilities may work great changes, and accomplish great affairs among mankind, if he first forms a good plan.*
>
> **BENJAMIN FRANKLIN**

The "expert complex." If you run into difficulty while trying to solve a problem, you might be tempted to believe that only an expert on the issue can solve it. This thinking leads to both an unsolved problem and a negative assessment of your abilities. Think positively, and listen to your own internal guidance and intuition. Thinking critically and carefully, any person can contribute to solving a problem.

Attachment to the first choice. We tend to become attached to an initial good idea. Be sure to give each of your ideas equal consideration, even if the first one is good. Evaluate each so you can be sure you have covered every angle. Brainstorm alternatives.

Problem-Solving Exercise: Global Poverty

Let's take a hypothetical situation where we can observe the problem-solving process in action. Carla Ramirez's class has chosen global poverty as a problem, and they would like to generate possible solutions. They watch a video called "341," which was produced by the United Nations in 1999 and shown to international heads of state at the United Nations World Summit for Children.

Step One: Define the Problem

From the video, the students pick out several facts that define the problem. They brainstorm and define the overall problem as follows: "Many people in the world do not have access to basic nutrition, housing, education, or the health care, clean water, and sanitation necessary for preventing disease."

Define the terms. The students define *poverty* as "the inability to adequately feed, house, educate, or clothe oneself, and to avoid preventable diseases."

Differences in construction materials of dwellings can indicate levels of extreme poverty.

List the stakeholders. The stakeholders in this problem are the people living in poverty. The students also determine that everyone is a stakeholder in this problem since they feel it is unconscionable for anyone to starve to death when the resources exist to prevent this tragedy. They feel that the inhumanity of this problem affects everyone.

Add details. The students need to determine what constitutes adequate nutrition, housing, and health care so they call nonprofit organizations working on solutions to hunger and poverty to determine how these are measured. They want to know what is considered "extreme poverty." They are referred to several studies done by nongovernment organizations working to provide self-employment opportunities to the very poor. The studies include the following details:

- No one definition of poverty has been agreed upon. Poverty is a slippery subject that has many sides to it, all of which must be considered to understand it. Besides income or consumption levels, other aspects of poverty include lack of access to education, health, nutrition, markets, and clean water.
- One way that poverty is measured by organizations is through visual assessments of housing construction. A tin roof, for instance, signifies a less extreme level of poverty than a thatched or cardboard roof.
- The World Bank uses an income level of $1 per day or less to designate extreme poverty.

Step Two: Gather Information

The video states that a child dies every two seconds from hunger and disease associated with poverty. But, because it happens every day, it is not news that we hear. The students also learn that the technology and resources exist to eradicate abject poverty on the planet.

The students are curious to find out as much as they can about poverty issues. They do an Internet search of groups working on poverty issues to find resources and books on what is already known. They compile the following pertinent information:

- Approximately 1.2 billion people made less than $1 a day in 1998 (more than one in five people in the world). *Source:* World Bank, *World Development Report 2000/2001* (New York: Oxford University Press, 2000), p. 23.

- Overpopulation is a direct result of poverty. In many developing countries, having many children is seen as a matter of survival. Children help as workers and income generators and are a source of security in their parents' old age. The social conditions that most effectively lead to smaller families include access to improved legal, educational, and economic opportunities for women. *Source:* Lester Brown, *Eco-Economy* (New York: W. W. Norton, 2001), p. 223.

- "Any discussion of 'population' is increasingly understood to include a host of related issues, including the coexistence of extravagant consumption and degrading poverty, and the inability of many governments to meet the basic needs of their people for health care, education, clean water, energy, and shelter." *Source:* Worldwatch Institute, *State of the World 2002* (New York: W. W. Norton, 2002), p. 128.

- One-sixth of the world's population holds 78 percent of its wealth, while three-fifths of the world's people earn just 6 percent of the world's wealth. *Source:* World Bank, *World Development Report 2000/2001* (New York: Oxford University Press, 2000).

- "Extreme poverty in an era of unprecedented wealth is not merely shameful—it is dangerous . . . Poverty and inequality can lead to political instability and social tensions that impede economic growth and spark fanaticism and violence." *Source:* Worldwatch Institute, *Vital Signs 2002: The Trends That Are Shaping Our Future* (New York: W. W. Norton, 2002), p. 149.

- "As pressures to expand food production have climbed, farmers have been forced into marginal areas, plowing land that is too dry or too steeply sloping to sustain cultivation." *Source:* Lester Brown, *Eco-Economy* (New York: W. W. Norton, 2001), p. 63.

- "Two percent of Brazil's landowners have taken control of 60% of the nation's arable land . . . For decades, wealthy land moguls have resisted pressures for more equitable distribution of land . . . In 1985 alone, wealthy landlords and their hired killers murdered over 200 peasants who demanded land." *Source:* Frances Moore Lappe and Joseph Collins, *World Hunger: Twelve Myths* (New York: Grove Weidenfeld, 1986).

- AIDS is contributing to poverty. Some countries could lose more than 20 percent of their gross domestic product by 2020 due to the effect of AIDS on their work force and productivity. The epidemic could easily produce 40 million orphans by 2010, which will overwhelm the resources of extended families. *Source:* Lester Brown, *Eco-Economy* (New York: W. W. Norton, 2001), p. 218.

Step Three: Interpret the Information

The students start to understand that poverty is not a natural occurrence in the world. Rather, it is the human-made result of economic and human rights policies.

They realize that the issues of overpopulation, political unrest, and environmental degradation are tied to the injustice of poverty. When people become self-sufficient and are able to provide the basics of nutrition, safety, and education for their children, population growth stabilizes, societies are more peaceful and stable, and people are free to care for the environment.

The students surmise that while there are adequate resources in the world, these resources are increasingly controlled by large corporations and benefit relatively few people.

Step Four: Develop Possible Solutions

The students decide to brainstorm some ideas for possible solutions to global poverty. They use a flip-chart and have one person write down all the ideas:

- Reduce population growth by starting an educational campaign.
- Educate people by volunteering as teachers and sending more current textbooks to developing nations.
- Lower infant death rates and make sure children don't die of easily preventable diseases by getting more health-care professionals involved.
- Stop the AIDS epidemic by educating people.
- Make more jobs available at wages that keep people above poverty.
- Make sure everyone has access to clean water and food.
- Make land available to poor people so they can grow their own food.
- Reduce consumption by rich nations.
- Make ending poverty a political priority by communicating with officials.

Step Five: Evaluate Possible Solutions and Choose the Best One

In this stage, the students consult their frame of action for solutions that they can implement and control themselves. They realize that for each of the solutions they have listed, it would take government policy to create the largest impact. Each solution would have to be a political priority of leaders.

They discover a grassroots organization, RESULTS, which supports volunteer groups in engaging in political advocacy for solutions to hunger and poverty issues. They decide they would have more of an effect if they form a volunteer group and learn how to communicate with their elected officials about policy solutions to the problem of global poverty.

Applications

Assume you want your local parks to have organized recreation programs for children after school. Hypothetically go through the stages of the problem-solving model and identify what you might do or find in each step.

Critically evaluate a social issue by evaluating sources of information, exploring different points of view, questioning opinions and assumptions, evaluating the context, looking for false logic and bias, and assessing the values that guide your thinking.

Identify the types of faulty persuasive techniques used below:

- Since you do not support the war, you must not love your country.
- Everyone is going to the dance. You should, too.
- He's an alcoholic, lazy and mean. You can't believe a word he says.
- Eight out of 10 Americans believe a tax cut would further stimulate the economy. Therefore, that's what the economy needs.
- A mysterious bright light was seen last night, and this morning the farmer's field had a circular pattern burned into it. Aliens must have landed here.
- Tom Hanks has said that movies are important for our cultural awareness. Support your local movie theatres by seeing more movies.
- My boss is a terrible manager. He plays golf on Sundays instead of going to church. He used to be an alcoholic, and he is a Libertarian.
- If you don't use a good, minty mouthwash, you'll have bad breath, and no one will like you.
- Either people graduate from college or they will not be educated.
- God clearly exists because you cannot prove that He doesn't.
- Sex education in high school will lead to more teenage pregnancies.

Consider the following topics:

- Should the United States take preemptive action on countries that harbor suspected terrorists even if a strong likelihood of civilian casualties exists?
- Is affirmative action reverse discrimination?

- Should marijuana be legalized?
- Does the leadership of the country represent the majority of the country?

Choose one topic, and develop a well-thought-out argument for why you believe what you do. Then, take the opposite viewpoint. Pretend you are someone else, if you need to. Develop a well-thought-out argument for why the *opposite* of your original opinion could be true.

In your group, discuss a social problem and go through the problem-solving steps to determine and evaluate possible solutions.

QUIZ

1. Read the following statements. Then, on the line next to each statement, write an F in the blank if the statement is a Fact, or write an O if it is an Opinion.

    _____A. The Fourth Amendment protects against unreasonable searches and seizures.

    _____ B. About 30 percent of high school seniors are regular smokers.

    _____C. Testing students for tobacco abuse will scare them away from worthwhile activities.

    _____D. Last June, the U.S. Supreme Court approved random drug testing for students in extracurricular activities.

    _____E. Diamond Jim Brady was an upper-class glutton who should have shared some of his food with the poor.

    _____ F. Only one man in U.S. history has served as president of the United States and then chief justice of the United States.

    _____G. An estimated 440,000 Americans die from smoking-related illnesses each year.

    _____H. It will be impossible to reverse the increasing prevalence of overweight and obese people in the United States.

2. Thinking analytically and reflectively about an issue or problem and evaluating bias and half-truths is:

    A. thinking

    B. Bloom's Taxonomy

    C. critical thinking

   D. objective thinking

   E. none of the above

3. Number the levels of Bloom's Taxonomy in ranking order levels 1 to 6.

   _____ A. analysis

   _____ B. evaluation

   _____ C. knowledge

   _____ D. synthesis

   _____ E. comprehension

   _____ F. application

4. Critical thinking involves:

   A. evaluating sources of information for bias and accuracy

   B. questioning your opinions and assumptions

   C. looking for false logic and bias

   D. exploring different points of view

   E. all of the above

5. When evaluating Web sites, consider scrutinizing the:

   1. Content _____

   2. _____

   3. _____

   4. _____

   5. _____

6. Examples of stakeholders include:

   A. direct beneficiaries

   B. allies

   C. shareholders

   D. all of the above

   E. none of the above

7. Rank the steps to solving a problem in order 1 to 5.

   _____ A. Get the right information.

   _____ B. Develop alternatives.

   _____ C. Define the problem.

   _____ D. Judge the alternatives.

   _____ E. Interpret the information.

8. Match the faulty persuasion to the definition:

☐ 1. ad hominem

☐ 2. ad verecundiam

☐ 3. bandwagon

☐ 4. appeal to emotion

☐ 5. false cause and effect

☐ 6. glittering generality

☐ 7. hasty generalization

☐ 8. straw argument

☐ 9. appeal to tradition

☐ 10. appeal to patriotism

☐ 11. false dilemma

☐ 12. card stacking

A. Conclusions based on insufficient evidence

B. Poses only two choices when a variety of possibilities exists

C. Says little specifically but conveys emotion

D. Presents evidence in a partial way to promote interests of a particular group

E. Persuades based on the threat of some type of force

F. Uses the opinions of the majority of people; suggests that because most people agree, it must be right

G. Ignores reason and critical thinking to support school, city, state, or nation

H. Involves attacking a person rather than ideas

I. Suggests that because things have always been done a particular way, they should continue to be done that way

J. Invokes quotes and phrases from popular, famous, or authoritative people to support views

K. Attacks opponent's argument to make their own stronger

L. Encourages people to do something because it is the popular thing to do

M. Insists that an event is caused by another event just because one followed the other

N. Summons fear, anger, or pity to entice support

ENDNOTES

1. Beyer, B. *Critical Thinking*. Indianapolis, Ind.: Phi Delta Kappa Educational Foundation, 1995.

2. Ennis, R. H. "A Taxonomy of Critical Thinking Dispositions and Abilities." In J. B. Baron and R. J. Sternberg (eds.), *Teaching Thinking Skills: Theory and Practice*. New York: W. H. Freeman, 1987.

3. Baldwin, J. M., ed. "Reflection," in *Dictionary of Philosophy and Psychology*. Gloucester, Mass.: Peter Smith, 1960.

4. Quoted in Loeb, Paul Rogat. *Soul of a Citizen*. New York: St. Martin's Griffin, 1999.

5. "Witnesses and Documents Unveil Deceptions in a Reporter's Work." *New York Times*, May 11, 2003 (conducted by a team of researchers and reporters).

6. Krugman, Paul. "Standard Operating Procedure," *New York Times*, June 3, 2003.

7. "2001 Advocacy Manual." Prepared for the National Peace Corps Association by Results Educational Fund, 2001.

8. Mitchell, Peter R., and John Schoeffel, eds. *Understanding Power: The Indispensable Chomsky*. New York: The New Press, 2002.

9. Kurtz, Howard. "Bush Cousin Made Florida Vote Call for Fox News," *Washington Post*, November 14, 2000.

10. Kick, Russ, ed. *Everything You Know Is Wrong*. New York: The Disinformation Company, 2002.

11. Garces, E., D. Thomas, and J. Currie. "Longer-term Effects of Head Start," *American Economic Review* 92 (2002).

12. Zinn, Howard. *People's History of the United States*. New York: Harperperennial Library, 2003.

13. Quoted in Zinn.

14. Quoted in Zinn.

15. Quoted in Zinn.

16. Quoted in Shultz, Jim. *The Democracy Owners' Manual: A Practical Guide to Changing the World*. New Brunswick, NJ: Rutgers University Press, 2002.

17. Coon, Dennis. *Introduction to Psychology: Exploration and Application*, 6th ed. Eagan, MN: West Publishing, 1992.

18. Greenleaf, Robert. *Servant Leadership*. New York: Paulist Press, 1991.

Resource Management for Active Citizenship

Lost time is never found again.

—BENJAMIN FRANKLIN

OBJECTIVES

After studying this chapter, you should be able to:

- Apply the steps of time management in building a weekly schedule

- Determine the usefulness and deficiencies of time management tools

- Assess your beliefs about money

- Create a personal budget

- Identify others who can help you

- Identify areas to improve health and well-being

- Use visioning for one of your goals

A paradox has emerged in our culture: we have enhanced technology, which saves us time and money in many areas of our lives, yet many of us find that we have less time and money than ever. We may find ourselves engaged in activities that aren't totally satisfying or that conflict with our values. As a result, we have fewer resources to accomplish the important goals, and many of us feel that we are too overextended to be active citizens. Defining values and setting goals are important to managing resources, but that importance may not manifest on a daily basis when deadlines loom, e-mails and urgent phone calls interrupt us, and we are forced to respond to one crisis after another. At times, there may seem to be too much distraction at the day-to-day, hour-to-hour level to allow for appropriate focus on the higher goals.

Historically, the concepts of resource management have been presented from the view of scarcity—we have only a finite number of resources to use in accomplishing our goals, be they time, money, or energy. Using this premise, we can find our lives reduced to blocks of allocated time, week after week. David Allen, author of *Getting Things Done: The Art of Stress-Free Productivity,* asserts: "It's possible for a person to have an overwhelming number of things to do and still function productively with a clear head and a positive sense of relaxed control."[1] The key to achieving high levels of effectiveness and efficiency is to recognize that our ability to be productive is directly proportional to our ability to relax. When our actions are congruent with our values and goals, our minds become clear and we can relax with what we are doing in the moment. In this state of clarity, we access the energy to get a lot done.

World-class rower Craig Lambert describes this state of relaxed control:

Rowers have a word for this frictionless state: swing . . . Recall the pure joy of riding on a backyard swing: an easy cycle of motion, the momentum coming from the swing itself. The swing carries us; we do not force it. We pump our legs to drive our arc higher, but gravity does most of the work. We are not so much swinging as being swung. The boat swings you. The shell wants to move fast: Speed sings in its lines and nature. Our job is simply to work with the shell, to stop holding it back with our thrashing struggles to go faster. Trying too hard sabotages boat speed. Trying becomes striving and striving undoes itself . . . Swing is a state of arrival.[2]

Have you ever done something that you love and noticed that time seemed to stand still, or even expand? When you engage fully and consciously in the important activities of your life, you may notice this sense of relaxation as well as heightened efficiency and productivity. This is the principle of resource prosperity. When we commit ourselves to activities that are the most meaningful, resources seem to appear and we can accomplish more than we ever thought possible. The first chapters of this text focused on values, critical thinking, and goals. In this chapter, we will focus on how to manage the resources we have—time, energy, finances, and our relationships with others—to create rich lives that include satisfying participation as citizens.

TIME MANAGEMENT

It's hard to manage time because, in reality, we don't manage time at all; we manage actions within time. Time continues no matter what we do and is a cultural concept that has no absolute meaning on its own. Westerners, for example, think in terms of 24 hours in a day, seven days in a week. Those divisions, however, are arbitrary. In *The Dance of Life: The Other Dimensions of Time*, Edward T. Hall contrasts the way people of American-European heritage think about time with time concepts in other cultures. In summarizing the differences between the Hopi, who "live in the eternal present," and American-European people, Hall writes: "One feels that [for the Hopi] time is not a harsh taskmaster nor is it equated with money and progress as it is with [American-European people] . . . who tend to think that because nothing overt is happening, nothing is going on. With many cultures there are long periods during which people are making up their minds or waiting for a consensus to be achieved."[3]

The real issue in time management is how to make appropriate choices about what action to take at any point in time. When we are making choices that help us move toward greater self-expression and fulfillment, we will naturally use our resources in the best way for us. The challenge for many people regarding time management is to get a sense of clarity and definition about their goals, and what the next action step should be in accordance with their overall mission.

Steps in Time Management

Begin with the End in Mind

Outcome thinking, or thinking to define desired results, is one of the most effective means available for turning goals into reality. After going through the goal-setting process, focusing on those goals can have an unexplainably beneficial effect. Management expert Peter Drucker has written: "There is usually no right answer. Rather, there are choices, and results have to be clearly specified if productivity is to be achieved."[4]

Outcome thinking
—thinking to define desired results

Get It Off Your Mind

There is usually an inverse proportion between how much something is on your mind and how much is getting done. These are open items that pull at your attention and can include everything from "end world hunger" to the more modest "complete term paper" to the smallest task such as "get gas." These open items can take up a lot of attention, adding to the anxious feeling that there is too much to do. Writing down everything you need to do will move it from your mind and make it more likely that you'll get it done.

Do It—The Five-Minute Principle

Discipline yourself to make decisions immediately about all of the tasks you take on so you will always have a plan for actions that you can implement.

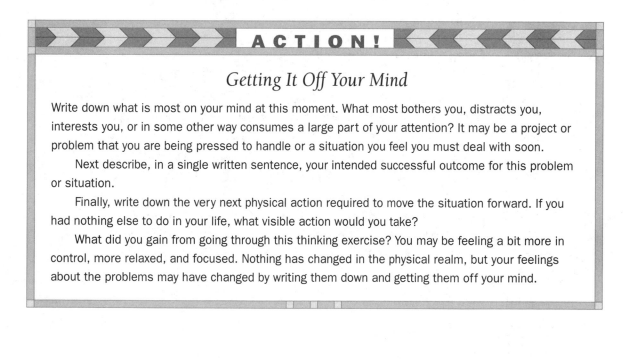

A C T I O N !

Getting It Off Your Mind

Write down what is most on your mind at this moment. What most bothers you, distracts you, interests you, or in some other way consumes a large part of your attention? It may be a project or problem that you are being pressed to handle or a situation you feel you must deal with soon.

Next describe, in a single written sentence, your intended successful outcome for this problem or situation.

Finally, write down the very next physical action required to move the situation forward. If you had nothing else to do in your life, what visible action would you take?

What did you gain from going through this thinking exercise? You may be feeling a bit more in control, more relaxed, and focused. Nothing has changed in the physical realm, but your feelings about the problems may have changed by writing them down and getting them off your mind.

M A K I N G   I T   H A P P E N

MARTIN LUTHER KING JR. AND MALCOLM X—RESPONSES TO A PROBLEM

Consider the problem of racial injustice and the possible solutions that presented themselves early in the civil rights movement. For African-Americans in the 1950s and 1960s in the United States, the memory of slavery and the reality of segregation, lynching, and general humiliation gave way to revolt.

During World War II, the nation maintained segregation in the armed forces and kept African-Americans in low-paying jobs. When the war was over, they began to rise up against the unequal treatment they had endured. President Truman felt he needed to deal with the race issue largely because the Communist Party was making inroads by paying special attention to race equality. Truman appointed a Committee on Civil Rights, which recommended that Congress pass laws against lynching and to stop voting discrimination, and suggested new laws to end racial discrimination in jobs.

However, Congress did not enact the legislation requested by the Committee on Civil Rights. Truman issued an executive order asking that the armed forces institute policies of racial equality "as rapidly as possible." This took over a decade to complete. In 1954, the Supreme Court said that segregated public educational facilities should be integrated; however, in 1965, more than 75 percent of the school districts in the South remained segregated.

Many black people felt that they had to stick up for themselves and fight in order to protect themselves. The philosophy of nonviolence had never been applied in the United States when Martin Luther King came on the scene and professed to a crowd of people in 1956:

> As you press on for justice, be sure to move with dignity and discipline, using only the weapon of love. Let no man pull you so low as to hate him. Always avoid violence. If you succumb to the temptation of using violence in your struggle, unborn generations will be the recipients of a long and desolate night of bitterness, and your chief legacy to the future will be an endless reign of meaningless chaos.

King's stress on love and nonviolence, which he learned from reading about Ghandi's success in India, was effective in building a sympathetic following throughout the nation, among whites as well as African-Americans, and was largely responsible for the successes of the civil rights movement.

Another leader, Malcolm X, belonged to the Black Muslims, who preached hatred against whites. He spoke in 1963 to a Harlem audience with anger:

> You'll get freedom by letting your enemy know that you'll do anything to get your freedom; then you'll get it. It's the only way you'll get it. When you get that kind of attitude, they'll label you as a "crazy Negro," . . . Or they'll call you an extremist or a subversive, or seditious, or a red or a radical. But when you stay radical long enough and get enough people to be like you, you'll get your freedom.

Both Malcolm X and Martin Luther King, experiencing the same frustrations, had different initial ideas of a solution to the same problem.

If there's anything you absolutely must do that you can do in five minutes or less, do it now.

Delegate What You Can

If there's anything that absolutely must get done soon, and you have others who are willing to help, delegate. Delegating is entrusting tasks to others. It is hard to give up control sometimes, but if you delegate properly, it can dramatically in crease your overall effectiveness. Effective delegation is a three-step process:

1. Decide what you want to give to others.

2. Select people with the proper skills.

3. Design a plan for review of the work.

Choose the Most Important Areas

Vilfredo Pareto, a 19th-century Italian economist and sociologist, developed a principle that has since been used frequently. **Pareto's 80/20 principle** implies that about 20 percent of what we do in any given area delivers 80 percent of the results. Going after the "right" 20 percent will get you 80 percent of the results. This is how to work smarter and not harder.

Pareto's 80/20 principle— 20 percent of what we do gives us 80 percent of the results

List Major Goals for the Week

Below, list your important goals according to the important life categories discussed in Chapter 1.

Life Category	Goals

Build a Schedule Framework

Using the template in Figure 3.1, map out what you know you need to do during the week. Include work hours, classes, and all other scheduled activities. On the left-hand side, incorporate the goals you have for the week by life category.

MAJOR GOALS FOR THE WEEK OF			Monday	Tuesday	Wednesday	Thursday	Friday	Saturday	Sunday
LIFE CATEGORY 1:		6:00 a.m.							
		7:00 a.m.							
		8:00 a.m.							
		9:00 a.m.							
LIFE CATEGORY 2:		10:00 a.m.							
		11:00 a.m.							
		12:00 p.m.							
		1:00 p.m.							
		2:00 p.m.							
LIFE CATEGORY 3:		3:00 p.m.							
		4:00 p.m.							
		5:00 p.m.							
		6:00 p.m.							
LIFE CATEGORY 4:		7:00 p.m.							
		8:00 p.m.							
		9:00 p.m.							
		10:00 p.m.							
		11:00 p.m.							

FIGURE 3.1 *Schedule Framework*

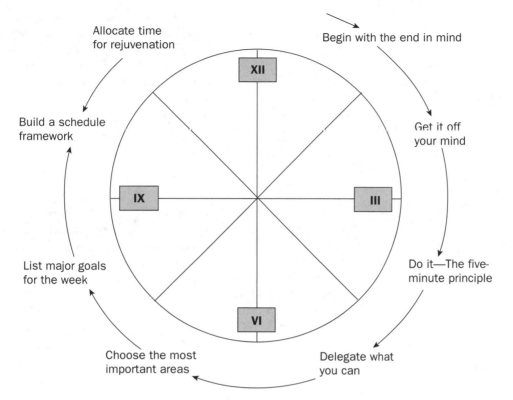

FIGURE 3.2 *Steps in Time Management*

Allocate Time for Rejuvenation

While committing ourselves to our goals is important, if we spend too much time "on task" and not enough time just "being" we may become drained and lose motivation. We need periods of structure as well as unstructured time for rejuvenation. Build into your schedule a time where you can relax, reflect, and discover who you are. Julie Cameron, in her book *The Artist's Way*, describes a useful tool for tapping into the creativity available in times that we allow ourselves for rejuvenation. She suggests scheduling an "artist date," once a week when you spend time by yourself doing something creative, interesting, or fun.[5]

Time Management for Active Citizenship

Active citizenship can begin with as little as 15 minutes a month and go on to become a full-time job. The time each of us devotes will likely fall somewhere in the middle of that range and will depend on our priorities. What is important is that it become a regular part of your life that creates meaning for you. Regardless of whether we're beginners or specialists in effecting social change, our ability to be effective will depend on the systems we create for building time for citizenship into our daily lives.

As the demands of our lives change, we may have more or less time to devote to our role as citizens. But as citizenship becomes an integral part of our lives, we will keep it as a practice no matter what the circumstances of our lives. The following steps may assist you in developing the practice of citizenship in your life.

> *I arise in the morning torn between the desire to improve the world and a desire to enjoy the world. This makes it hard to plan the day.*
>
> **E. B. WHITE**

Level One: Beginner

Beginners may strive to take on at least one action a month by marking a day on their calendars when they can devote 15 minutes or more. Use this time to educate yourself and others by reading about issues. Enlist a friend or two to help you, if possible.

Look at the issues that are most meaningful to you which you may have distinguished earlier in the text. You may wish to begin by educating yourself about these issues and spending time talking to others about them. Decide on a specific activity that you will pursue in your allotted time.

Level Two: Advanced

As you build your practice of citizenship, aim to complete at least one action every week, building on activities and information you have gathered. Set aside a half hour every Monday night, for instance, to write to a legislator or to the newspaper about an issue you care about. Or you might schedule a visit with a local policy maker or social service provider to learn more about how the issue affects your community.

Level Three: Specialist

Keep to a weekly schedule, but broaden and deepen your area of influence. Write an editorial piece for a local paper, or join an organization working on the issue in which you are interested. Start organizing your neighbors and associates to make a difference in your community or communicate with your Members of Congress.

Tools of Time Management

Having some type of scheduling system or calendar is important when managing activities. "ABC" priority codes and daily "to-do" lists are proven techniques to help sort through choices in some meaningful way. What you may have already discovered, however, is that a calendar, though important, can help you manage effectively only a small portion of what you need to organize; it can be inadequate to deal with the volume of things to do and the variable nature of priorities.

E-mail, personal digital assistants (PDAs), scheduling software, and other digital data are becoming increasingly viable means of keeping track of actions. If you've tried to use any of these processes or tools, however, you may have found them also unable to accommodate the complexity and changing priority factors. The ability to be successful, relaxed, and in control requires that we use these tools only to help us, not to limit us. They cannot prioritize for us. They cannot advise us when we need to change our plans due to unforeseen opportunities or responsibilities. They can't remember to add new activities or develop strategies for specific goals. In other words, they can't think for us. However, they can be extremely useful in organizing much of what we need to accomplish.

> *The ancestor of every action is a thought.*
>
> **RALPH WALDO EMERSON**

Time Bandits

Watch the Number of Commitments

Much of the stress people experience comes from inappropriately managed commitments they make or accept. When we intend to do something, or commit to doing something for others, and are not able to follow through, we experience conflict. We run the risk of damaging trust with ourselves and with others. Most of us are almost always juggling commitments in several areas of our lives. A good way to estimate if you have too many commitments is to write them all down and estimate how many hours you'll be spending on them during a week's time.

Saying no is something many of us have a hard time doing. We want to do it all, and we don't want to disappoint others or miss out on opportunities. Determine what you consider most important, and be aware of what will be compromised when you agree to something. When you are clear about who you are and what you are creating in your life, "no" becomes "yes," because you are ultimately saying yes to what you know will be most satisfying to you in the long term. If priorities grow out of a profound sense of values, according to Stephen Covey, we will enjoy a relaxed approach to dealing with important tasks: "Only when you have the self-awareness to examine your values and create a value-centered purpose, will you have the power to say no with a genuine smile to the unimportant."[6]

Develop Good Habits

Good habits replenish energy. These good habits are the activities that are most meaningful to you and help you accomplish your goals. One way to develop good habits is to establish rituals. As Jim Loehr and Tony Schwartz write in their book *The Power of Full Engagement*: "The bigger the storm, the more inclined we are to revert to our survival habits, and the more important positive rituals become."[7]

The television habit. During the past 30 years, Americans have steadily reduced their participation not only in voting but also in traditional forms of community involvement, such as the PTA, the League of Women Voters, unions, mainstream churches, the Boy Scouts and the Campfire Girls, and service clubs like the Lions and Kiwanis. According to Robert Putnam, a Harvard political theorist, this trend does not bode well for American democracy. Putnam argues that the more socially isolated our citizens become, the fewer chances they have for the kinds of civic involvement in crucial public concerns. Putnam examined the causes for this decline and came to the conclusion that regardless of background or current circumstances, the more people watch TV, the less they involve themselves in civic activities of any kind. Putnam also found that the more people watch television, the more mistrusting and pessimistic about human nature they become. They also feel less of a sense of connectedness and common purpose.[8]

Avoid Crisis Management

A certain frenetic energy surrounds managing a crisis that causes an illusion of importance. With this feverish pace of activity, we release such stress hormones as adrenaline, noradrenaline, and cortisol, which may actually be addictive.

Stephen Covey, time management expert, relates that if we are overly externally motivated, we will tend to prioritize the needs of others over our own goals and needs. If you do this, you will find yourself continually dealing with crises and interruptions and not using your time for what is most important. When you live in crisis mode, you attempt to get relief from pressing problems by becoming busy with seemingly urgent but unimportant tasks. However, if you spend your time building relationships, recognizing new opportunities, planning, and preventing crisis, you will be more effective at achieving goals.

FINANCIAL MANAGEMENT

Money is a basic resource, and knowing how to manage your financial life gives you peace of mind and more freedom. When you create financial stability, you are free to give more of yourself as an active citizen. In many ways, money is also a teacher. We learn lessons, have greater self-awareness, and accomplish great deeds through the use of money. How we make it, spend it, share it, save it, and allow it to come in or block it are primary ways we learn about ourselves through money.

Money can be one of the primary tools in achieving great social goals. By learning how to manage your personal finances, you also ensure that you have the necessary financial resources to reach your goals on important issues and help your projects be sustainable. Creating a stable financial base is an important part of effective citizenship.

Assessing Beliefs About Money

Write down the first three or four opinions that come to mind.

What do you think about money?

What did you answer? Share your opinions with your classmates. Do you notice different beliefs? Perhaps you heard "Money is the root of all evil" or "Money is power" or "A penny saved is a penny earned" or "Money is freedom." How might these beliefs affect how a person accumulates wealth? If you believe that money is the "root of all evil," for example, could it be more difficult for you to save or earn a lot, even though intellectually, you think that you should? How might another belief result in your having an easier time accumulating money?

Managing Beliefs

Some people prosper when times are challenging, and some people never do, even when conditions are great. Some people endure serious personal financial hardships and come out stronger than ever; others lose everything. Financial expert Suze Orman believes that "those who do well in both good times and bad times manage their money from a position of power rather than acting out of hope, anger, regret, or fear."[9] Our beliefs are extraordinarily powerful in creating financial well-being.

Fear is something that most people experience in relationship to money: fear that they will lose it, that they won't have enough, that they don't deserve it, that too much is bad, or that not enough is bad. Orman suggests looking over your past for the experiences that created your fears. Do your best to understand your motives and what has created your beliefs about money. Are they based on current reality? The more you understand your fears, the less they will block your ability to use money as a powerful resource in creating what is most important to you.

Many people believe that in order to *be* more, they must *have* more. Orman believes, however, that in order to have more, you have to be more. By living with integrity and staying true to yourself without embellishment or delusion over what you have, you can draw more money into your life.

Budgeting

Budgeting is setting goals with money; it is what permits us to manage the flow of our money. Budgeting begins with what we are creating now as income. We then look at what we want to achieve or create with our money. Effective budgeting

Budgeting— setting goals with money

comes from being as specific and accurate as possible about our current situation and about the situation we want to create. The steps in budgeting include the following:

- Determining how much money you are currently generating
- Determining how much money you are spending on necessary overhead items
- Determining how much money you need to reach your goals
- Determining how you will create the necessary income
- Adjusting your needs and spending habits

Personal Budgeting Tips

Live beneath your means. To live *beyond your means* is to spend more than you make and to create debt for yourself. To live *beneath your means* is to spend less than what you make. When you spend less than you make, you create a surplus of income that can be saved. The savings, however small, will give you a buffer when unforeseen expenses arise.

> *True financial harmony is achieved when your pleasure in saving money equals or exceeds your pleasure in spending it.*
>
> **SUZE ORMAN**

Pay yourself first. When you have extra money left over after your basic expenditures, put it in your savings account. Think of this leftover money as savings, not as "extra." If you include in your budget a payment to yourself that carries equal weight with your mortgage or rent payment, you will honor your commitment to yourself.

Manage your credit cards. Total revolving debt in the United States, including credit card balances, is now a record $721 billion and is increasing. The average American household in 2002 carried an unpaid credit card balance of $8,940. In the past two years, 3 million Americans declared personal bankruptcy, many due to crushing credit card bills.[10] "Americans tend to spend aspirationally—they spend according to the group they aspire to as opposed to their actual income," says Mari McQueen, a *Consumer Reports* editor and consumer debt expert.

Credit card issuers are continuing to aggressively recruit new accounts. Issuers often target clients whom they believe will be late in making payments because that is how they collect big penalties. The average fee for late payments is $30.04—6 percent higher than a year ago.

You can benefit from using credit cards wisely; however, you can run into serious trouble if you use them unwisely. The benefits of using credit cards include:

- Establishing a good credit history
- Handling emergencies when you have no cash
- Keeping a record of your purchases

■ Enjoying the bonuses offered by credit card companies (for example, accumulating frequent flyer miles for air travel)

However, there are some things to watch when using a credit card. For one, you're spending someone else's money until you pay it back. Because you don't have to pay right away, it's tempting to spend more than you should. If your material desires get the best of you, you can wind up with thousands of dollars in debt to credit card companies. Paying the minimum payments, which might look enticing at first, can keep you in debt for decades. For instance, paying off a $3,000 credit card bill with minimum payments would take 30 years.

You're taking out a high-interest loan when you keep a credit card balance. Interest rates on credit cards can range from 11 to 23 percent. Anytime you miss a payment, default on a payment, or in any way misuse your card, a black mark can show up on your credit history, which will lower your credit rating. Sometimes, prospective employers look at credit ratings. If you apply for a bank loan, the bank may refuse the loan if you have a history of missing payments or have overextended your use of credit.

Fix your credit. If you do get into trouble with credit cards, admit it, fix it, and prevent it from going further. Admitting it includes taking responsibility for what happened. Admit your mistake to yourself and your creditors, and arrange payments and a lower interest rate with them. You cannot erase the damage, but correcting the situation quickly and pleasantly can help to minimize problems. Pay more than the minimum payment, and refuse a card issuer's offer to skip a month's payment because you will only remain in debt longer.

Creating a Personal Budget

1. Determine your current personal overhead and how much money is currently being generated. To determine your current **personal overhead**, or what it costs to meet your current needs, consider keeping an expenditure journal for two months. Keep a small notebook with you, and write down everything you spend money on each day. Use Figure 3.3 to group expenses into categories. For some expenses, such as monthly bills, you will be able to fill out the amount immediately. For others, such as entertainment, you may be surprised at the actual amount revealed by keeping your journal. Write down all your current sources of income, and calculate a total. Does your income cover your current overhead?

    Personal overhead— what it costs to meet your current needs

2. Determine how much money you need to reach your goals. Look at the goals you have for different areas of your life. For instance, you may have a goal of attending a specific workshop for communication skills training that costs $250. You may want to attend a graduate school program that will cost $3,500 per semester. You may want to travel to Washington, D.C., to attend a protest march, which could cost $350.

Expense	Monthly Expenditure
Rent or mortgage	
Utilities (electric, gas, water)	
Food	
Telephone	
Loan payments (student or bank loans)	
Credit card payments	
Car expenses (repairs, insurance, payments)	
Gasoline	
Additional transportation	
Tuition	
Clothing/personal items	
Entertainment (eating out, books/magazines, coffee)	
Child care	
Taxes (if employer withholds no taxes or not enough taxes from paycheck)	
Medical care	
Gifts	
Miscellaneous/unexpected	

FIGURE 3.3 *Budget Chart*

3. Determine how you will create the necessary income. Can you work more hours at your job? Do you have time to take on a second job? Is there a special project you can take on for more short-term income? Do you have personal items you can sell?

4. Adjust your needs and spending habits. By restructuring your needs and spending less, you may be able to make a significant difference in reaching your needs for specific goals and for meeting your basic needs. Search every

current expenditure for places to "trim the fat." Your rent or mortgage and loans are your fixed costs. Even they can be altered, if need be, by moving or sharing your home. Loans can be refinanced (restructured so that your payments change), or cars can be sold. Everything is fair game.

PERSONAL RESOURCE MANAGEMENT

In addition to time and money, other important resources are available to us. If we nurture and develop the relationships we have with others, as well as our own personal strengths, we can extend our energy levels and accomplish many more of our important goals.

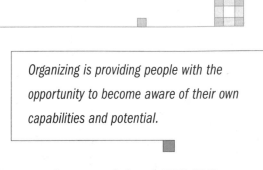

Organizing is providing people with the opportunity to become aware of their own capabilities and potential.

Other People

Assess the resources you have in other people with whom you interact. Other people are often our greatest assets. Historically, people used to share resources

FRED ROSS

because it was a necessity. One person might have had the plow while another had the horse. Relationships with others in which we experience this give and take can make our lives richer. By sharing our talents with others and allowing them to share theirs with us, the whole becomes greater than the sum of its parts. There are likely many people with the same goals who can help you. Energy attracts energy, and if you are energetic about an issue, you will attract others to your mission.

One way to increase your access to resources through others is to broaden your sphere of acquaintances and connections. Learn about organizations in your community that will put you in touch with new networks of people. Join associations, teams, and clubs. Also remember to nurture existing relationships.

Effectively organizing others requires a mix of ingredients: strong people skills, to bring people together and keep them inspired and working well; capable structure, to ensure that the work involved actually gets done; and strategic savvy, to pick the right objectives and the right public actions to interest the people. Learning how to mix these ingredients is an important component in organizing people.

The most critical component in organizing others, regardless of the style you use, is relationship building. To build solid, work relationships, you should be genuine, have a good sense of self-awareness, and involve people in decision making and strategy. As an organizer, you will want to acknowledge and appreciate those who add to your cause and to recruit additional people who may have a personal stake in the issues.

The people in our communities are among our greatest assets and resources.

A C T I O N !

Identifying Helpful People

Write down five major people in your life. What resources do they add to your life?

1. _____

_____

2. _____

_____

3. _____

_____

4. _____

_____

5. _____

_____

Health and Personal Well-Being

Health—
the condition of being in sound mind, body, and spirit

One of our greatest resources is our own health. *Webster's Dictionary's* primary definition of **health** is "the condition of being in sound mind, body and spirit." When we maintain this kind of balance in our lives, we experience energy and resilience. It is this energy and resilience that allow us to handle the pressures and challenges of life and remain whole and healthy. How we use our other resources, such as time and money, in the service of our health and well-being is crucial to having the energy to reach our goals and to experience joy.

Biological Rhythms

The concept of maximizing performance by alternating periods of activity with periods of rest was first advanced by Flauvius Philostratus (A.D. 170–245) when he wrote training manuals for Greek athletes.[11] No two people have the same biological rhythms. Author Flora Davis shares the conclusions that she reached in *Living Alive!* on how to use energy highs and lows:

> Every system in the body, whether you're talking about the pulse, or the temperature, or the functioning of the endocrine glands, goes through twenty-four hour cycles.

There's a time when it peaks, and these are predictable periods. When the body temperature is low, you are at your lowest in terms of efficiency and alertness. Most people probably don't have to take their temperature to know when that time is for them. Most people know if they're an afternoon or a morning person. But what a lot of people don't know is that it's a physical phenomenon, and there are real reasons for it."[12]

Sleep and Rest

Everyone differs in terms of their ideal amount of sleep. Most people function best on six to eight hours of sleep. Sleep deprivation causes significant damage to the immune system.

Davis and others refer to the *postprandial dip*—the period, sometimes after lunch and in the afternoon, when someone "just runs out of steam," as Davis says. Psychologists studying this phenomenon have found that 50 percent of their subjects experienced postprandial dip. If you experience a dip in energy in the afternoon, plan your activities accordingly. As athletes who use interval training understand, when we stretch ourselves beyond our normal limits and then rest in order to create the growth, we can endure more and exceed our initial limitations. This same concept tolds true in many areas of our lives.

Exercise

You may want to reduce fatigue and stress by making time in your schedule for strenuous exercise. Dr. Kenneth H. Cooper, a former Air Force medical officer, is credited with popularizing the type of exercise known as aerobics. Aerobics are strenuous activities, such as running, sports activities, or even brisk walking. As little as 20 minutes a day is said to bring positive results. Tiring our bodies through physical activity increases our ability to rest more deeply. Try to avoid exercising close to bedtime, however, because exercise can be stimulating.

> *More men are killed by overwork than the importance of the world justifies.*
>
> **RUDYARD KIPLING**

Choose exercise that you enjoy, that allows you to learn something, or that interests you. This will make it fun and something you look forward to.

Nutrition

Eating well is one of the most profound ways you can positively affect your well-being. Experiment with your diet to create more energy. Make sure you are getting enough lean protein, whole grains, and fruits and vegetables, which create more stable energy. Excess sugar and refined foods tend to intensify blood sugar "crashes" and their accompanying fatigue, mood swings, and lack of concentration.

Balance

When we are committed to a project, it is sometimes easy to neglect other important areas of our lives. However, we have the greatest level of vitality to give to our goals if we experience life balance, particularly in four areas: physical, emotional, mental, and spiritual.[13] Reflect on your daily activities, and adapt your schedule to include each of these areas.

Spiritual Practice

It is now widely accepted that experiencing good health and well-being entails achieving integrity in mind, body, and spirit. Renowned physician and author Andrew Weil has said that any program intended to improve health must address all of these areas. Weil states: "It is possible to lead a spiritual life and explore the influence of spirituality on health whether you are religious or not."[14]

Elizabeth Lesser, author of *The New American Spirituality*, states:

> *They may be strikeouts to some people, but to me, every one of them was nearly a home run.*
>
> **MICKEY MANTLE**

Inviting spirituality into your life is like packing for a long journey. As you search for your own definition [of spirituality], here are some of the most important things to pack: an openness to things you may have been conditioned to reject, a comfortableness with the unknown, and fearlessness . . . One thing we can confidently say is that spirituality is fearlessness. It is a way of looking boldly at the life we have been given, here, now, on earth, as this human being. Who am I? How should I live my life? What happens when I die? Spirituality is nothing more than a brave search for the truth about existence.[15]

Meditation. In our increasingly hectic lives, carving out time to simply be still can be of great benefit. Although meditation is traditionally a spiritual practice, it has been shown to create great benefits in overall health and well-being. Buddhist teacher and author Pema Chodron says, "We don't sit in meditation to become good meditators. We sit in meditation so that we'll be more awake in our lives."[16]

Being active citizens requires that we become more aware of the world and how we relate to it and to those with whom we share it. Meditation can be a powerful tool with which to access our internal guidance and truths.

> *The soul never thinks without a picture.*
>
> **ARISTOTLE**

Meditation is a simple process involving the following elements as a foundation:

- Find a quiet space free of distractions.
- Sit in a comfortable position with your spine aligned in good posture.
- Still your thoughts by focusing on a positive phrase or on your breathing.
- Use a timer to set a specific period of time for your meditation.

Influences

Consider the people with whom you spend the most time. How do these people—what they think, say, and do—influence what you think, say, and do? Do the people in your life bring out the best in you? Do they reinforce your values? Do your conversations focus on positive, uplifting themes, or are they more negative? How can you affect this?

Emotions

Positive emotions can give us energy and renew us. Training ourselves to guard our emotional state and feel positive can significantly impact our well-being. Throughout the day, we have ongoing internal conversations with ourselves. We are constantly evaluating what is happening around us and giving meaning to events. The internal conversations we have lead us to feel particular emotions. Other people don't make you mad or sad. Your evaluation of events is what creates the emotion you feel. When faced with the same circumstances, 10 people could have 10 different emotional responses. Once you've created emotions, you have only two options: You can act on them or be acted on by them.

If you feel that your emotions are both justified and accurate, you will likely make no effort to change or even question them. However, anything that causes you to overreact can control you—and often does. For instance, responding inappropriately to e-mail, projects, unread textbooks, thoughts about what you need to do, a boss, or an instructor will lead to less effective results. Emotions and our automatic responses to them endanger our well-being and our ability to function optimally. How do we take ourselves from an automatic response state into one that puts us back in control?

When we add meaning to the action we observe, we tell a story about the action. Is there an intermediary step between what someone does or says and how we feel? When we begin to feel a strong emotion, it helps to be completely present. Focus energy only on what you're feeling. Think critically and analyze the story you're telling yourself that results in the emotion.

Applications

Create a schedule of activities using the principles in this chapter for one week. Using a chart such as the one below, keep a journal of what happens with your time during this test week by jotting down a few notes about how the schedule is working for you. What do you like? What is not working?

Monday	
Tuesday	
Wednesday	
Thursday	
Friday	
Saturday	
Sunday	

Choose one of your easier goals to begin practicing visioning. Relax and, as vividly as possible, imagine yourself achieving the goal. What did you imagine? What were the details?

3 For a week, keep an expense journal. Using the chart provided, write down how much money you spend in each category. Create a budget.

Expense	Daily Expenditure						
	S	**M**	**T**	**W**	**Th**	**F**	**S**
Rent or Mortgage							
Utilities (electric, gas, water)							
Food							
Telephone							
Loan payments (student or bank loans)							
Credit card payments							
Car expenses (repairs, insurance, payments)							
Gasoline							
Additional transportation							
Tuition							
Clothing/personal items							
Entertainment (eating out, books/magazines, coffee, etc.)							
Childcare							
Taxes (if employer withholds no taxes or not enough taxes from paycheck)							

Expense	Daily Expenditure						
	S	M	T	W	Th	F	S
Medical care							
Gifts							
Miscellaneous/unexpected							

What are three things you can do to improve your health and well-being?

QUIZ

1. ☐ True or false: Effective time management strategies include delegating tasks to others.

2. ☐ True or false: Crisis management can help you in time management by giving you energy to accomplish important tasks.

3. ☐ True or false: When you are feeling a lot of stress, strenuous exercise can reduce it.

4. ☐ True or false: When we feel a strong emotion, it indicates that we are usually right.

5. The 80/20 principle refers to:
   A. 80 percent of people can manage time effectively
   B. 20 percent of people can manage time effectively
   C. 20 percent of what we do delivers 80 percent of the results
   D. 80 percent of what we do delivers 20 percent of the results

6. Beginners in the active citizen realm should do all of the following except:
   A. devote at least 15 minutes a month
   B. enlist friends to help
   C. educate themselves about the issues
   D. write an editorial piece for a local paper

7. Tools of time management:
   A. can effectively manage priorities for you
   B. include calendars, PDAs, and scheduling software
   C. can develop strategies for specific goals
   D. all of the above
   E. none of the above

8. Budgeting is defined as
   A. checking your account balance weekly
   B. reconciling your bank statement
   C. setting goals with money
   D. paying your bills

9. The average American household in 2002 carried an unpaid credit card balance of:
   A. $549
   B. $254
   C. $8,940
   D. $1,250

10. Rank the following steps for creating a personal budget in order from start to finish (1 to 4).
    _____ Adjust needs and spending habits.
    _____ Determine how to create the necessary income.
    _____ Determine personal overhead.
    _____ Determine how much money you need to reach your goals.

ENDNOTES

1. Allen, David. *Getting Things Done: The Art of Stress-Free Productivity*. New York: Penguin USA, 2003.

2. Lambert, Craig. *Mind over Water: Lessons on Life from the Art of Rowing*. New York: Mariner Books, 1999.

3. Hall, Edward T. *The Dance of Life: The Other Dimensions of Time*. Garden City, NY: Anchor Press/Doubleday, 1983.

4. Allen, Quoted in *Getting Things Done*.

5. Cameron, Julie. *The Artist's Way*. New York: Jeremy P. Tarcher/Putnam 1992.

6. Covey, Stephen. *Seven Habits of Highly Effective People*. New York: Fireside/Simon & Schuster, 1989.

7. Loehr, Jim, and Tony Schwartz. *The Power of Full Engagement*. New York: Free Press, 2003.

8. Putnam, Robert, "Bowling Alone," *Journal of Democracy*, January 1995.

9. Orman, Suze. *The Laws of Money, The Lessons of Life: Keep What You Have and Create What You Deserve*. New York: Free Press, 2003.

10. Loeb, Marshall, and Alicia Ferrari. Newsletter, April 29, 2003, www.CBS.MarketWatch.com.

11. Loehr and Schwartz, *The Power of Full Engagement*.

12. Davis, Flora. *Living Alive!* Garden City, N.Y.: Doubleday, 1980.

13. Loehr and Schwartz, *The Power of Full Engagement*.

14. Weil, Andrew, M. D. *8 Weeks to Optimum Health*. New York: Alfred A. Knopf, 1997.

15. Lesser, Elizabeth. *The New American Spirituality*. New York: Random House, 1999.

16. Chodron, Pema. *When Things Fall Apart: Heart Advice for Difficult Times*. Boston: Shambhala Publications, 1997.

Action Strategies and Project Management

A vision without a task is but a dream, a task without a vision is drudgery, a vision and a task is the hope of the world. —FROM A CHURCH IN SUSSEX, ENGLAND, C. 1730

OBJECTIVES

After studying this chapter, you should be able to:

- Develop an action strategy for an issue or problem

- Implement the steps of an action strategy

- Identify ways to overcome discouragement

- Identify actions to take to overcome procrastination

- Design a basic project plan

- Draw a Pert chart

Written historical accounts of important social change sometimes focus only on the conclusions and omit the process by which ordinary citizens have repeatedly brought about major shifts that benefit society. We see the end result but may not receive information on the often lengthy process of social change, with all its passion, frustration, perseverance, sense of congruence, and purpose.

As we explore the process of planning strategies for change and implementing projects, you will see how developing these plans becomes a source of motivation to follow them through.

The French theologian Phillipe Vernier offers this perspective: "Do not wait for great strength before setting out, for immobility will weaken you further. Do not wait to see very clearly before starting: one has to walk toward the light. Have you strength enough to take this first step? You will be astonished to feel that the effort accomplished, instead of having exhausted your strength, has doubled it—and that you already see more clearly what you have to do next."[1]

The first three chapters of this text have laid a foundation for taking civic action. Virtuous intentions and clear thinking are certainly valuable in and of themselves, but when they are put into action, their value exponentially increases as we use them to improve systems that dictate the quality of life. Once you become aware of your priorities and passions in life, identify areas of your life where you would like to see improvement, define problems in these areas, and think about possible solutions to them, you are ready to plan your strategy. You will likely find that as you gain more personal mastery over your own life, you will gain more ability to serve the needs of your community and society.

Foundational skills can help you thoughtfully and strategically choose a course of action. In this chapter, we will cover how to develop an action strategy for creating and successfully managing a project from beginning to completion.

CREATING AN ACTION STRATEGY

Tackling large social issues requires breaking the process into manageable pieces and working strategically. To develop a successful action strategy, whether for a personal or a community problem, it helps to use a planning process to guide your activity. One of the most common mistakes in project planning is incomplete planning and rushing into action. Time spent in the planning process more than makes up for itself in the ultimate efficiency and flow of the project and in creating the desired result.

The best way to predict the future is to create it.

PETER DRUCKER

We can use the principles of project planning in small or large, personal or civic projects. These principles become more valuable when we have a lot of resources dedicated to a project or when the results are highly important. As you build these skills, you will become more effective in handling any kind of problem or challenge you encounter.

In creating an action plan, you should:

- Review the issue or project
- Create a vision
- Identify desired goals
- Choose resources and partners
- Create a timeline and a plan
- Consider possible obstacles and resistance
- Allow for change
- Evaluate the outcome

Review the Issue or Project

The first step in creating an action strategy is similar to that in the problem-solving process covered earlier in this text. Before goals and objectives can be set effectively, it is important to go through the process of thoroughly understanding an issue or problem and coming up with a solution based on research, reflection, and perceived benefit. Review the research and critical thinking you have done on the problem or project you have chosen. Will the benefits of the project be worth the costs of doing the project?

The beginning is half of every action.

GREEK PROVERB

Ask for the input and feedback of others. Who are the stakeholders? It is critically important to get the input of those whom your project is meant to benefit. Knowing their needs and wants is necessary in deciding upon your objectives. Also consult anyone who may be adversely affected.

M A K I N G   I T   H A P P E N

ROSA PARKS

Rosa Parks was born in 1913 in rural Alabama. She picked cotton as a child as young as six or seven. She married civil rights activist Raymond Parks in 1932, when she was still a teenager. Her husband encouraged her to pursue her high school diploma, which she received in 1933, when fewer than 7 out of 100 blacks had a high school education.

As one of two women members of the local National Association for the Advancement of Colored People (NAACP), Parks tried to register to vote in 1943. Harassment and random local registration rules discouraged blacks from voting; NAACP members sought to change this. She tried several more times before succeeding in 1945 at age 32. As a volunteer, she served as secretary of the Montgomery branch of the NAACP and helped organize petitions and training workshops. She contributed to many of the legal efforts to keep black men from being executed for unproven crimes. These efforts were rarely successful, and Parks said, "Sometimes it was difficult to keep going when all our work seemed to be in vain."

In 1949, while working during the day as a seamstress, she became an adviser to the NAACP Youth Council. "We didn't have too many successes in getting justice," she recalls. "It was more a matter of trying to challenge the powers that be, and to let it be known that we did not wish to continue being treated as second-class citizens."

In the summer of 1955, at age 42, Parks attended a 10-day workshop on desegregation strategies at the Highlander Folk School in Tennessee. The school offered workshops and classes to train citizen leaders to work for change in their own communities.

On the evening of December 1, 1955, while riding the bus home from work as usual, she decided not to give up her seat when the driver asked her to move so that a white person could sit down. Parks stated, "I was not old. . . I was not tired. . . the only tired I was, was tired of giving in." Three days later, after the morning of her trial, she was back to her volunteer duties answering phones and preparing for a meeting that night at a local church to start a new activist organization. The organization, the Montgomery Improvement Association, elected Martin Luther King Jr. as its president the day of Parks's trial. At the meeting on the night of the trial, King spoke. His speech included the line: "One of the great glories of democracy is the right to protest for right."

Parks's action spurred the first organized activism by large numbers of blacks in the civil rights movement—the Montgomery bus boycott—and ultimately led to desegregation and the signing of the Civil Rights Act in 1964. Parks shares: "There was a time when it bothered me that I was always identified with that one incident. Then I realized that this incident was what brought the masses of people together to stay off the buses in Montgomery."

(continued)

(continued)

After almost a year of violence and challenge to the Montgomery bus boycott, the action produced results. In November 1956, the U.S. Supreme Court declared bus segregation unconstitutional and boycotters returned to buses in December. After Parks and her family received threatening phone calls and harassment, they decided to move to Detroit.

African-Americans continued to have trouble registering to vote, and the desegregation process was marked by violence and resistance. In March 1965, Martin Luther King Jr. and other activists organized the Selma to Montgomery March. At age 52, Parks participated in the march. In August 1965, the Voting Rights Act passed, guaranteeing blacks access to all registration and voting privileges.

Parks worked for African-American U.S. congressman John Conyers from 1965 until 1988, when she retired at age 75, and she continues to speak publicly and attend national demonstrations and marches. Parks concludes her autobiography with the following statement:

> It seems like we still have a long way to go . . . I try to keep hope alive anyway, but that's not always the easiest thing to do. I have spent over half my life teaching love and brotherhood, and I feel that it is better to continue to try to teach or live equality and love than it would be to have hatred or prejudice. Everyone living together in peace and harmony and love . . . that's the goal that we seek, and I think that the more people there are who reach that state of mind, the better we will all be.

Adapted from *Rosa Parks: My Story* by Rosa Parks with Jim Haskins, New York: Dial Books, 1992.

Choose Your Target Audience

Primary target— an entity who makes the desired political decision

Identify who has the power to implement the change you desire. If you desire that a political decision be made, determine the individual, group, or institution who has been given the authority to make it. This might be a school board, a city council, a CEO of a company, Congress, or the U.S. president. This entity is called your **primary target**. Other groups of people—such as the media or their supporters or constituents—will influence your primary target; these entities are referred to as **secondary targets**.

Create a Vision

Before developing the project plan, create a clear vision of what the project will create. This vision is what you will use in developing the "message" of the project.

Messaging

The message that your vision conveys will keep you excited and inspired about the project. It will also allow you to describe your project to others in a way that generates enthusiasm and understanding to further support the project.

Your vision should communicate the answers to the following questions:

- Who will directly benefit from the project?
- How will the greater community benefit?
- What is the project trying to achieve and how will these results be measured?
- How is it in the self-interest of your primary target to implement your solution?

Especially with large and complex problems, you need to be able to articulate a solution in a way that not only provides you with clarity but also allows you to easily explain the solution and its benefits to others. It helps to practice reciting a "laser description" of the problem and solution you have chosen. Imagine a short conversation, such as the length of an elevator ride, for instance. What words and statements convey your message best? Do your words help others to understand and be moved by your vision? When you speak of your vision, does it excite you?

Project Name

If appropriate, you may want to invent a project name or slogan. This is another way to distill your vision into a message that energizes your project. You can use this message on everything connected to the project, including flyers, posters, and signs.

Identify Desired Goals

Developing a strategy for implementing solutions to problems requires that we focus our efforts on specific goals and objectives. Getting from point A to point B requires knowing what point A and point B are. What is the current situation, and where do you want to end up? As you gather more information and distinguish more concerns and needs, your goals and strategies may shift. But in order to decide on a place to begin, you must have these goals and objectives in mind.

Social problems are complex and often have many differing interests to weigh. Slow-moving bureaucracies or institutions may be involved, and entrenched systems and beliefs may need to be addressed. In developing objectives for engaging with social problems, it helps most to have both long-term objectives that are exciting enough to keep you motivated over the long haul, and short-term objectives that are clear, specific, and attainable. When the long-term, ideal goal is the only focus, it is easy to become overwhelmed or discouraged by what it will take to achieve it. Short-term objectives give us the feeling of movement toward a greater end.

Choose Resources and Partners

As the scope of your project becomes clearer, you should consider the resources you will need to accomplish your goals.

Working with Others

The most important assets to the success of most projects are other people. Partners can offer skills that complement our own. They can inspire us if we are feeling frustrated or low, and they can share in the victories along the way and make the project more fun and satisfying. Sam Daley-Harris describes finding others to work with as the culminating step in a process of taking action:

> *Coming together is a beginning; keeping together is progress; working together is success.*
>
> ■
>
> **HENRY FORD SR.**

So you've (1) gotten in touch with your commitment to serve, (2) faced a problem that concerns you, (3) faced the hopelessness you feel about the problem, (4) looked for solutions, and (5) connected with your courage. That logically leads to Step 6: Find others to work with, both locally and, if it's a national or international problem, with an institution and people that are working at that level. In other words, don't do it alone. If you try to do it alone, you'll never make it.[2]

It may help to look for the following in potential partners:

- People you enjoy being with
- People you can learn from
- People with skills and resources that you don't have
- People who have passion for the project

As people begin to work with one another, it is important that everyone agrees on the vision and goals for the project. If you develop a project committee, or core group of partners, the group should agree on a collective vision. If the vision you originally created for the project is one that every partner can get behind, then you can agree to adopt that as your collective vision. If not, you must allow the group to adapt the vision to one they can all agree on. Each person involved in the project must feel "ownership" of the collective vision. This must be a voluntary and thoughtful choice.

Another element of successfully working with others is to develop clear agreements for communication and accountability. It helps to know what you can expect from one another and what you can't. If it is important to you that your partners return your phone calls or e-mails promptly, agree on this process at the outset. Encourage one another to agree only to actions on which each will follow through.

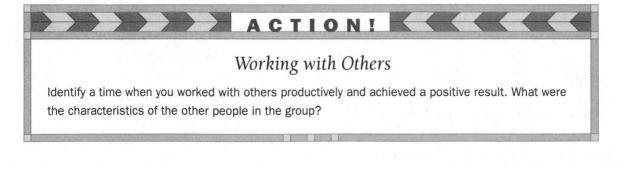

A C T I O N !

Working with Others

Identify a time when you worked with others productively and achieved a positive result. What were the characteristics of the other people in the group?

Doing what you say you will do builds a crucial level of trust within your group. Being part of a team with this kind of integrity brings out the best in everyone and often inspires partners to go beyond what they thought was possible.

Brainstorming Resources

Once you have found partners, work together to distinguish the other resources you will need. Look at your goals, and brainstorm all the material and nonmaterial things you will need to complete your project. These resources may include the following:

- Skills
- Additional partners
- Knowledge and information (research)
- Funding
- Material needs (office space, computer)

Goals are an integral part of any action strategy.

Make a specific plan for who will work to procure each of the resources you will need.

Create a Timeline and a Plan

An action strategy includes a timeline for when the project will begin and end, with landmarks along the way to track progress. It can help to work backward from the achievement of each goal to create your timeline. For instance, if you had the goal to enroll 50 people to call their Member of Congress about an issue, you might want to start with the date for the action to take place. You and your partners would then decide how long it would take to contact and get commitments from 50 people, taking into account the resources you have, then set a date for when you would need to begin action on that goal.

Evaluate Necessary Activities

What activities and tasks must you complete to do the project? Include such things as:

- Descriptions of meetings
- Necessary research
- Outreach to experts, government officials, and other potential project partners
- Budgets and fund-raising

- Action alerts
- Petitions
- E-mail
- Newsletters
- Fact sheets
- Public service announcements/press releases
- Follow-up

Plot each of these activities and tasks into your timeline.

Consider Possible Obstacles and Resistance

If you anticipate obstacles and decide ahead of time that they will not be a test of your commitment, they will be easier to handle when they appear and far less likely to throw you off course. You have already considered some of the stakeholders in the problem. Who are the stakeholders who stand to lose something in your solution to a problem? What are they likely to say about it? What resources do they have? What kind of counteractions might they take?

Try to understand their position. People in adversarial positions are much more apt to be open to you if they feel respected and considered. Are their fears justified? Are there possible benefits that you could point out that they may not be seeing?

You may also encounter material obstacles. A common obstacle is lack of funding. By anticipating the resources you will need up front and creating a plan for gathering them, you may avoid having your project derailed by unexpected material obstacles.

Allow for Change

Although an action strategy involves careful planning and a clear vision for what is to be accomplished, it also helps to remain unattached to the outcome and to your plan for getting there. Be open to changes in direction along the way.

Social problems often exist within a complex network of causes and possible solutions. Even with careful research and the best of intentions, we cannot always know the best outcome or what would create the largest benefit to the community. It is important to stay open and to listen along the way for what may be a new direction to take. Rather than viewing this change in direction as a failure of your plan, recognize it as a positive opportunity to adapt your plan in order to create more value.

Evaluate the Outcome

It may be somewhat difficult to evaluate the effectiveness of an action plan within the social arena. However, you can certainly determine whether you met your goals and objectives and, if so, how that is working. Did meeting your objective advance your cause? What else might you need to do? When you get to this question, the process of solving problems begins again.

Even losing battles in the social sphere, however, are opportunities to strengthen your cause by learning new political skills, building on your base, or building coalition with new allies. We're never promised that getting involved is going to lead to specific results as we define them. We go through this problem-solving process because it gives us some structure. It helps to remember how many changes there have been because of others' struggles that in the beginning stages seemed fruitless. So, even if our problem or objective is not entirely solved, by looking at the education we provided, the debate we kept alive, the impact we likely made on others with our dedication, and the inroads we made into the problem, we can more accurately assess the effectiveness of our efforts.

STAYING ON TRACK

At times in the process of attaining worthwhile goals you will feel discouraged. The most worthwhile accomplishments are, by their nature, uncommon and likely to be challenging. The resistance you face may come from others, from circumstances, and from what may be the most difficult obstacle: yourself. When you feel discouraged, consider the following approaches.

Revisit Goals

There may be times when you will not be motivated to follow through. It is at moments like these that you let your vision call forth the best in you and carry you forward. When you lose energy or motivation, or you experience other possible negative mental states, focus on your vision. Are your goals worthwhile and in alignment with your values and vision? What will help you see positive results from your efforts and endure any struggles that lay ahead is a clear vision of your goals.

Erin Brockovich, whose real-life triumph against the Pacific Gas and Electric Utility Corporation (PG&E) in Hinkley, California, was made into a movie, is an example of someone who overcame personal and external obstacles. As a single mother of three young children, with no legal experience, she was instrumental in crafting and winning a multimillion-dollar lawsuit against PG&E for polluting the town's drinking water with carcinogenic chemicals. Brockovich says:

> Not everything you or I will do will be as newsworthy as the Hinkley case became, and there may not be as huge a monetary reward at the other end, but if you are true to yourself, and your moral and spiritual foundation remains strong and intact, you will enjoy a different and far more valuable reward. You will discover, among other things, there is no obstacle you cannot surmount, no challenge you cannot meet, no fear you cannot conquer, no matter how impossible it may sometimes seem.[3]

Break large, difficult goals into smaller, manageable goals. If your goals are too large, difficult, or complex, it can be both overwhelming and discouraging if progress does not come quickly. By shelving some of the pieces until later, you can avoid feeling overwhelmed or discouraged. If you think of any goal as requiring a finite number of tasks, then each one completed is a step closer to completing the goal.

Recognize partial accomplishment. Acknowledging partial success is especially important in the process of attaining challenging goals.

Consider the alternatives. You are the only one who can decide if it's time to move on to something different. Goals will change, as will the underlying motivations for individual goals.

Use a personal support group. When appropriate, call on trusted family and friends to help if they can, even if it means just lending encouragement. Discuss your goals and get these people's input.

Face the Fear of Failure

One of the biggest obstacles for most people in taking action as citizens is the fear of failure. Often, we use the belief that our actions won't make a difference as a reason to remain passive as citizens. In reality, we may be using this excuse to mask our underlying fear of the sadness, humiliation, or wasted resources that we imagine having to endure if we were to take an action that failed.

Our fear of failure may reflect a societal agreement that failure is bad. However, it is just as easy to value failure as a positive learning tool and a natural part of the process toward manifesting solutions to problems. Dr. E. H. Land, former CEO of Polaroid, reframed the value of failure in a 1959 speech to the company's employees:

> In the physical sciences, in chemistry and physics and in mathematics, when you work in the lab, you fail, fail, fail. When you've failed enough times, you have 3000-speed film. If you want color film, you have to fail 10 times as many times. Failure here is the very essence of progress. The secret of science is that it has learned to fail without emotion and embarrassment. A scientist is a person who is a continuous failure . . .
>
> But in the social sciences, we start an experiment . . . and we fail the first week and everybody laughs. They say, "Well, he should have known better" or "He didn't have the background" or "You can't change human nature" or some such nonsense.
>
> The trouble with experimentation in the social sciences is that we are always guilty about failure . . . I want to end up with a company which, socially, is nothing but failure. I want failure all over the place, people failing all day long in some social experiment, so that when we look back five years from now and say, "We have 700 people who never dreamed they could handle languages; another 500 who can handle mathematics; we have made inventors out of people who thought they could never do anything; and we are still failing."[4]

If you are prepared to fail and are prepared to learn from the experience, you can look forward to failure as a valuable way to gain information for the success of your project.

Face the Fear of Success

Although it may appear counterintuitive, many of us actually fear living up to our dreams. Perhaps we feel that we are not worthy of them or that we might have to give up too much to achieve them. We may sabotage our goals if our self-esteem doesn't match the image of who we believe we must be to be successful.

Marianne Williamson addresses this tendency in her book *A Return to Love:*

> Our deepest fear is not that we are inadequate. Our deepest fear is that we are powerful beyond measure. It is our light, not our darkness, that most frightens us. We ask ourselves, Who am I to be brilliant, gorgeous, talented, fabulous? Actually, who are you not to be? You are a child of God. Your playing small doesn't serve the world. There's nothing enlightened about shrinking so that other people won't feel insecure around you. We are all meant to shine . . . And as we let our light shine, we unconsciously give other people permission to do the same. As we're liberated from our own fear, our presence automatically liberates others."[5]

If you notice a tendency to doubt your abilities, avoid risks, or give less than you may be capable of, consider that you may be afraid to succeed. In this case, it may help to share your feelings with your partners and ask them to encourage you to give your best to the project.

Put Off Procrastination

Most of us are familiar with procrastination. When we have an important project to complete, we may suddenly find all kinds of other things to keep us busy. We know what we need to do but do not take action to move ahead. As we continue to put off the tasks at hand, we may become increasingly paralyzed by fear or anxiety.

Procrastination can be a symptom of fear of failure or fear of success, fear that doesn't even have to be significant. Remind yourself of your vision and how you will feel when you accomplish your goals. Imagine the positive impact on the lives of people who will benefit from your project. This will help you to access your commitment in the face of an ingrained habit.

Take one action. When you are experiencing serious procrastination, it often helps to take a single, simple action related to what you need to get done.

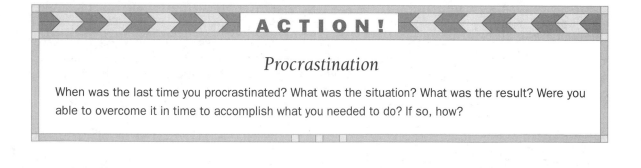

ACTION!

Procrastination

When was the last time you procrastinated? What was the situation? What was the result? Were you able to overcome it in time to accomplish what you needed to do? If so, how?

Ten-minute approach. Another approach is to take 10 minutes a day to look at your project. Look at the project for only 10 minutes, and then walk away. If you need to, follow the 10-minute approach the next day.

Reinvent the Standard

One of the biggest blocks that we may encounter in our quest to effect change are the standards of perfection that we may believe we can't live up to. We may tell ourselves that unless we are as committed as Gandhi or as brilliant as Martin Luther King Jr., we might as well not even try. Holding these great leaders up as examples of what humanity is capable of helps only if it inspires us.

Many of us feel that whatever we embark on has to be outstandingly worthwhile. We feel that we have to accomplish our task better than anyone ever has, would, or could. We idealize people who have made significant changes and compare ourselves to them. If we don't measure up, we are seriously tempted to quit before we get started. **Pressure,** a form of stress, occurs when we feel compelled to reach higher standards of performance. This internal pressure may be either constructive or destructive. It may motivate us to learn to play a musical instrument, do extraordinarily well in classes, or work hard to achieve social change. However, it may erode our self-esteem if we allow a fear of failure to paralyze us from taking action.

> **Pressure—**
> a form of stress that occurs when we feel forced to reach higher standards of performance

Consider the responses a student may have to an assignment to complete a big project, assuming that there are few guidelines given by the instructor and that the instructor has a reputation of never giving good grades. One student may be tempted to not put much effort into the project because she knows she cannot achieve the perfect grade. Other students may approach the project by offering their best and learning for learning's sake, no matter what the final grade.

The desire to achieve this standard of perfection is another significant barrier to acting on social concerns. We have the mistaken belief that anyone who takes a public stand has to be perfect or an expert. They have to have absolute knowledge about every aspect of the issue at hand. They have to devote all day, every day, to causes and be unshakably committed to their vision. We believe this, in part, because as a culture we tend to idolize our heroes. Our textbooks focus on the outcomes of their actions but rarely mention the very ordinary human processes of pain, doubt, and failures that occurred along the way.

Developmental psychologists look at the factors that influence personal changes by looking at individual characteristics versus shared human traits. **Shared human traits** are common patterns in human development. One such shared trait is the ability to lead. While this trait may be encouraged in some people more than others, we all have it. When we give up the mythology that we must be perfect before we can act, we acknowledge the learning process that change is. We then may engage in the process of change knowing that failure is not something to fear but is an integral part of learning necessary lessons for deep and lasting change.

Examples of ordinary citizens who were never perfect but who took actions for change include the following:

- Martin Luther King, Jr., who headed into Montgomery as a 26-year-old preacher unaware of what, if anything, he might achieve
- Lech Walesa, who was a shipyard electrician before he was thrust into the leadership of Poland's Solidarity movement
- Wei Jingshen, who was a technician at the Beijing Zoo who placed an essay on a public wall about China's need for democracy and whose long imprisonment helped inspire the Tiananmen Square protests
- Lois Gibbs, who was an ordinary housewife until she organized her neighbors at Love Canal and founded the Citizens Clearinghouse for Hazardous Waste
- the three sixth-grade girls Barbara Brown, Kate Klinkerman, and Lacy Jones, who began the "Don't Be Crude" oil recycling program
- Rachel Carson, who was a marine biologist for the U.S. Fish and Wildlife Service before she published *Silent Spring*, the book credited with starting the environmental movement

We highlight these people not to use them as a basis of comparison to your achievements but, instead, to encourage the use of their stories as sources of inspiration. They all likely believed, at one time, that their voices were too small to be heard, but they shouted anyway. As Nelson Mandela says: "Each of us can be great. We cannot all be famous, but we can all be great." Letting go of the idea that we must be perfect and famous allows us to be great citizens.

Delay Gratification

Another hurdle we must overcome in our quest for social change is our need for instant gratification. As our advertising culture has indoctrinated us to expect the "quick fix" or the overnight transformation, we have lost some of our capacity for patience and perseverance. If our efforts don't instantly achieve dramatic results, we may be quick to criticize ourselves or doubt that our efforts matter. We may believe that we are not destined for this—that we "don't have what it takes." Consider the student who studies chemistry for an hour and gives up any hope of ever understanding it, or the dieter who gives up after a week by rationalizing his extra weight as his body's natural state. For social change, we must practice the discipline to stay with the process of change long enough for the change to manifest.

> *I venture to suggest that patriotism is not a short and frenzied outburst of emotion, but the tranquil and steady dedication of a lifetime.*
>
> **ADLAI E. STEVENSON**

If we are to effect change within the burgeoning institutions and governments that have been established over many decades, or centuries, we must accept that the process of change may take longer than we might like. Lynn McMullen, former executive director of a grassroots advocacy group, describes the process as "dirt work, dirt work, dirt work . . . MIRACLE!"[6]

SAMPLE ACTION PLAN

Most social change efforts require funding and thus include some type of fund-raising activity. Many ways to raise funds exist. One common practice is to bring people together, educate and inspire them about your efforts, and ask for their financial support. Such an effort has many details to think about, even when organizing a small event.

Step One: Review the Project

In this example, we will look at a fund-raising project for community youth in which our plan is to raise $5,000. The money will be used to send five at-risk youth to a summer program that specializes in counseling and has been successful with previous participants. Our fund-raising project will entail holding an event where speakers will present the benefits of the summer program.

A common fund-raising error is to underestimate the cost-to-income ratio of carrying out the fund-raising event or activity, so we will make sure we choose an activity that costs little to implement by finding a space to hold the event for free and having refreshments donated.

Choose Your Audience

You may also think about who your audience is or who you will be asking for money. Who will be helping with the project, and who do they know? Who can you reach out to? In this example, we will target specific groups in the area, including the Rotary Club, Kiwanis Club, and Elks Club as well as the general public.

Step Two: Create a Vision

This step involves creating a message that will explain your project clearly and succinctly to others. In our example, the message might be:

> Community youth supporters will hold a fundraiser to raise $5,000 to allow five at-risk youth in our community to attend a summer counseling program. The event will be open to the community, and guests will learn about how those who have attended this successful and inspiring program have positively benefited their communities.

Step Three: Identify Desired Goals

Your goals may be concrete, such as:

- Raise $5,000
- Have 60 or more people attend

    You may also have other goals, such as:

- All guests leave the event inspired and uplifted
- All volunteers on this project are supported and satisfied by their participation

Step Four: Choose Resources and Partners

Now list the resources you will need for the project. These might include the following:

- Three people to be on the planning committee
- Ten people to help invite guests
- A venue in which to have the event
- Refreshments for the event
- Printed invitations and a printed program
- Audiovisual equipment
- Someone with fund-raising experience to act as a consultant

Step Five: Create a Timeline

Next you will want to create a timeline to guide your activity. Decide how much time you will need to plan your fund-raiser and to invite the necessary number of guests. In this example, we decide that we need three months, so we pick a date three months in the future for the event and start working backward from there.

Step Six: Identify Obstacles and Resistance

One obstacle we may encounter is that this event falls at the end of most companys' fiscal years, which means that they may have less money to give. The economy may also pose a problem in that some people are feeling strapped. Another obstacle we may face is that a big community fund-raising event was held last month. An event can face many obstacles; however, if you can identify each of these, you can develop a strategy for dealing with them. We may find that we need to invite more people than we originally thought, for instance.

Step Seven: Evaluate the Success

We will schedule a meeting after the event to celebrate and debrief with the partners. It is generally a good idea to review your goals and to what degree you achieved them. Make a list of what worked and what you could have done better. Make a plan for any follow-up activities that need to be handled, such as sending thank-you notes to people who donated, and special thank-you letters to everyone who helped put on the event or invited people to attend.

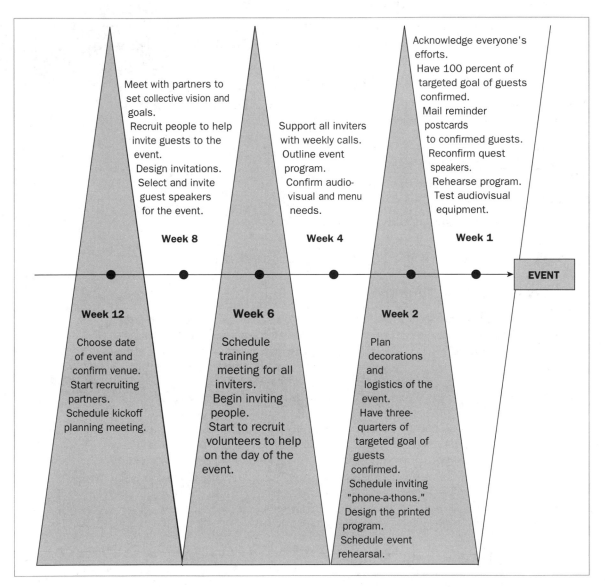

FIGURE 4.1 *Timeline for Sample Action Plan*

PROJECT MANAGEMENT

With the project clearly defined, you can also develop a project plan, which is a detailed breakdown of what needs to be done to accomplish the project. The project management tools you use, and the extent to which you use them, should depend on the importance of the project. If the success of the project is very important, and if errors will be costly, you would want to consider using project management. Developing the project plan means thinking about the "big picture" of the entire project as well as thinking about all the details. It involves identifying each big goal of the project and breaking it down into specific tasks.

Project management software packages on the market today can make the detailed part of the planning process easier. As with all other forms of technology, the software can be used as a tool to help in the work, as a hammer aids in the building of a house. But the software can no more manage the project than the hammer can design the house. Critical thinking skills play an important role in project management.

Identify the Important Tasks

After defining the problem, identify the important tasks. In our fund-raising example, these might be as follows:

1. Decide on a location and date for the event

2. Recruit partners

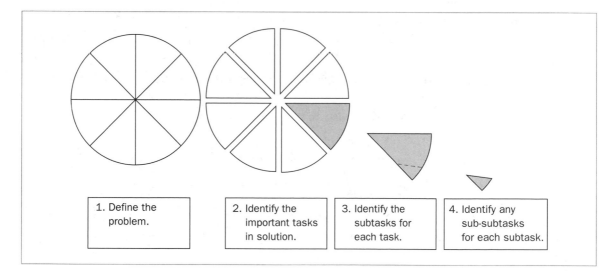

FIGURE 4.2 *Project Plan Development*

3. Schedule and plan kickoff planning meeting

4. Design invitations and information on the youth program for inviters to use

Identify the Subtasks

Identify the steps that will make up each of your important tasks. In our example, these might include the following:

1. Decide on a location and date for your event
   1.1 Call event centers to determine open dates
   1.2 Check with the Chamber of Commerce to find out about conflicting community events
   1.3 Check with partners on scheduling conflicts
   1.4 Make sure the facility for the event is accessible and has ample parking before making a decision

2. Recruit partners
   2.1 Ask teachers we know
   2.2 Make a presentation on the youth program at the next church group meeting
   2.3 Invite friends over to watch the youth program video, and ask them if they want to help with the fund-raiser

3. Schedule and plan kickoff planning meeting
   3.1 Check with key partners for a good date and place for the meeting
   3.2 Schedule meeting with fund-raising consultant friend to get ideas for the meeting
   3.3 Work on vision and goals for the event to present to the partners at the meeting
   3.4 Invite the partners to attend
   3.5 Hold the meeting

4. Design invitations and information on the youth program for inviters to use
   4.1 Ask graphic designer friend to help with the invitation design
   4.2 Get picture from the youth program brochure to use for the invitation
   4.3 Get testimonials from past youth participants, and make a flyer for inviters to use
   4.4 Take design to have printed
   4.5 Get a box of youth program brochures for the inviters to use

Identify the Sub-Subtasks

Identify any additional steps for each of the subtasks. In the fund-raising example, these might include the following, expanding on certain items in the list above.

1.1 Call event centers to determine open dates
    1.11 Call Elks Club
    1.12 Call Community Center
    1.13 Call Conference Hotel
    1.14 Ask friends about other options

2.2 Make a presentation on the youth program at the next church group meeting
    2.21 Schedule presentation
    2.22 Do PowerPoint presentation
    2.23 Rehearse presentation

3.1 Check with key partners for a good date and place for the meeting
    3.11 Call partners for ideas
    3.12 Confirm location
    3.13 Call partners back with definite time and place

4.3 Get testimonials from past youth participants and make a flyer for inviters to use
    4.31 Call participants for quotes
    4.32 Develop the flyer

After you have identified all of the tasks, subtasks, and sub-subtasks, you can assign time estimates for each. Project management software allows you to do this easily. You can also assign task dependencies (or predecessors) in the software, or tasks that must be completed before another task can begin. You can automatically enter this information as you go, and the software will keep track of the total time.

Figure 4.3 shows how the time estimates might look for the project.

The chart in Figure 4.4 visually represents the project and makes it clear that the most time-consuming part of the project is recruiting partners. To complete a chart such as that in Figure 4.4, sometimes referred to as a Pert chart, begin with all activities that have no predecessors. These can be started at the same time as soon as the project begins. Then continue filling in boxes with the activities that follow those you have already filled in. You can also write the time it takes to complete each of the activities within the boxes. Some will take longer than others.

As a general rule, for a legitimate project, tasks should have a time frame of two weeks or less. Task dependencies should be identified as well as the person who will be responsible, the start date, the end date, and all additional resources (equipment, money, and so forth.) that will be used per activity.

Task	Estimated Time	Predecessors
1. Decide on a location and date		
1.1 Call event centers	1 day	
1.11 Call Elks Club	1 day	
1.12 Call Community Center	1 day	1.11
1.13 Call Conference Hotel	1 day	1.12
1.14 Ask friends about options	1 day	1.13
1.2 Check w/Chamber of Comm.	1 day	
1.3 Check re: scheduling conflicts	1 day	2
1.4 Check facility parking	1 day	1.1
2. Recruit partners		
2.1 Ask teachers we know	2 days	
2.2 Make a presentation		
2.21 Schedule presentation	1 day	
2.22 PowerPoint	1 day	2.21
2.23 Rehearse presentation	1 day	2.22
2.24 Set date and do it	1 week	2.23
2.3 Invite friends to watch video	1 day	
3. Schedule and plan kickoff meeting		
3.1 Check re: date and place	1 day	2
3.11 Call partners for ideas	1 day	2
3.12 Confirm location	1 day	3.11
3.13 Confirm w/partners	1 day	3.12
3.2 Meet w/consultant	1 week	
3.3 Work on vision and goals	1 day	
3.4 Invite partners to attend	1 day	2
3.5 Hold meeting	1 day	3.1, 3.2, 3.3, 3.4
4. Design invitations and information		
4.1 Ask graphic designer for help	1 week	
4.2 Get picture from brochure	1 day	
4.3 Get testimonials and make flyer		
4.31 Call participants for quotes	1 day	
4.32 Make flyer	1 day	4.31
4.4 Take design to have printed	1 day	4.3
4.5 Get a box of flyers together	1 day	4.4

FIGURE 4.3 *Fund-raising Project Tasks*

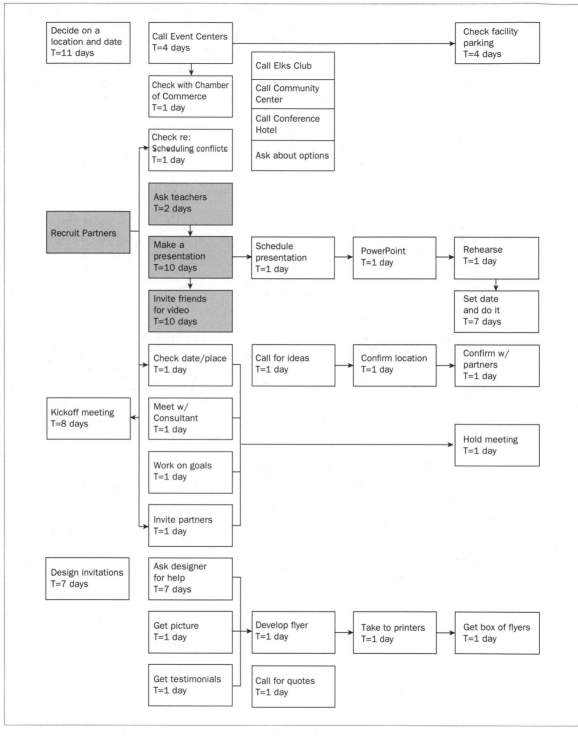

FIGURE 4.4 *Pert Chart*

Your chart headings will look like the following:

Task	Estimated Time	Predecessors	Person Responsible	Start Date	End Date	Additional Resources

If you are using project management software, these categories are built in, and you can fill them in as you go.

Applications

1   In a group, choose a social problem and go through the action planning process. Identify which of the steps you can take and implement those.

2   For the same social problem, identify the associated tasks. Choose one of the tasks and identify all of the subtasks and sub-subtasks. Draw a Pert chart of the project.

3   Choose a source of discouragement to which you are most susceptible. Compile a list of things you can do to overcome this challenge when it happens. Compile a second list of supportive actions to ask for from others to help you overcome the challenge.

4   Form a group of three students. Think of a small project you could undertake that would benefit an individual or group in your community. Develop a project plan for the project.

QUIZ

1. In creating an action plan, you will want to:
   A. create a vision
   B. identify desired goals
   C. create a timeline and plan
   D. evaluate the outcome
   E. all of the above

2. In creating an action strategy, the first step is to review the issue or project. This means it is important to go through the process of thoroughly

understanding an issue or problem and coming up with a solution based on research, reflection, and perceived benefit. What else does reviewing the issue involve?

A. asking for feedback

B. knowing the needs of the stakeholders

C. consulting those adversely affected

D. A and B

E. A, B, and C

3. When reviewing an issue or plan, entities who do not make the desired political decision but who will have influence, such as the media or their supporters or constituents, are referred to as:

A. secondary targets

B. obstacles

C. primary focus

D. goals

4. Developing a strategy for implementing solutions to problems requires that we focus our efforts on specific _____ and _____ (getting from point A to point B).

A. causes and effects

B. goals and solutions

C. do's and don'ts

D. apples and oranges

5. When choosing resources and partners, it is important to:

A. continue independently

B. push your vision for the project above all other concerns

C. take full control of the project

D. work with others

6. ☐ True or false: In creating a timeline and plan for your project, it often helps to work backward from the achievement of each goal.

7. When you lose energy or motivation, you need to focus on your vision and goals. Which of the following can help you get back on track?

A. breaking large goals into more manageable goals

B. starting from scratch and redesigning the entire project

C. working aggressively and independently

D. using a personal support group

E. both A and D

F. both B and C

8. Which of the following is a challenge one must overcome in order to take action?
    A. facing your fears of failure and success
    B. having too much energy
    C. expecting miracles
    D. striving for immediate gratification

9. To effectively manage a project, you must:
    A. define the problem
    B. identify the important task
    C. identify subtasks for each task
    D. all of the above

10. A Pert chart is a way to view a project. With a Pert chart, you can see all of the following *except*:
    A. which tasks need to be completed before others begin
    B. which tasks can be worked on at the same time
    C. the critical path
    D. a bar graph in which each task is represented by an individual bar that varies in length according to the task time

ENDNOTES

1. Vernier, Phillipe, and Dorothy Berkeley. *The Choice Is Always Ours*. San Francisco: HarperCollins, 1989.

2. Quoted in Williamson, Marianne, ed. *IMAGINE: What America Could Be in the 21st Century*. Daybreak, 2000.

3. Brockovich, Erin. *Take It from Me: Life's a Struggle But You Can Win*. New York: McGraw-Hill, 2002.

4. Quoted in Daley-Harris, Sam, and Valerie Harper. *Reclaiming Our Democracy: Healing the Break Between People and Government*. Philadelphia: Camino Books, 1994.

5. Williamson, Marianne. *A Return to Love: Reflections on the Principles of "A Course in Miracles."* New York: HarperCollins, 1996.

6. McMullen, Lynn. Results International Conference, Washington, D. C., 1999.

Skills for
Civic Education

It's too hard, and life is too short, to spend your time learning something because someone else has said it's important. You must feel the thing yourself.

—ISIDOR I. RABI

P olicy change at the local and national level is often implemented because of the results of studies, complaints, or proposals citing compelling reasons for change. To understand how these policies affect us and our communities, we need to comprehend the sometimes complex information and arguments being presented. Even the basic act of voting requires that we read carefully and understand and process a large quantity of information.

As active citizens, our input—in the form of letters to our elected officials, letters to newspapers, e-mail alerts, reports, and even proposed drafts of legislation—often involves research and writing. The ability to research and integrate information helps us offer input based on critical thinking and sound evidence. We need skills to research and study information so that we can identify key factors and missing pieces. Large quantities of reading material can be effectively handled with the proper strategy. You don't need to be an expert on the subject you are researching in order to distinguish and evaluate the facts that will help you build a specific argument or understand the value of a specific policy. Focusing techniques can help you select appropriate facts and relevant material from your readings.

An understanding of the basics of how an argument is constructed and the ability to respond critically as a reader also help make you a better writer, note-taker, and researcher. Developing these skills can help you understand how government policy and our civic systems work and how best to adapt them when necessary. This chapter will help you develop the comprehension, note-taking, writing, and research skills necessary for effective involvement as a citizen.

OBJECTIVES

After studying this chapter, you should be able to:

- Define functional literacy and mature reading ability
- Apply the comprehension process during reading
- Use new vocabulary
- Compare note-taking methods and use two of the methods presented
- Identify the steps in the research process
- Conduct an interview and evaluate the type of information received
- Write a letter to a Member of Congress

READING AND COMPREHENSION

Functional literacy—
the level of learning at which one is able to read well enough to negotiate life's everyday activities and demands

The different levels of reading skills range from very basic functional literacy to comprehension of complex material. **Functional literacy** is the level of reading ability at which one is able to negotiate life's everyday activities and demands (for example, reading signs, bills, and menus). Based on results of the 1992 National Adult Literacy Survey (NALS), nearly half (47 percent) of Americans scored in the lower two levels of a five-category test assessing functional literacy. One-fifth, or approximately 20 million people, were considered functionally illiterate. Considerable progress has been made in this area since 1992, however. The *Chronicle of Higher Education* reported a recent survey compiled by the National Center for Public Policy and Higher Education that states: "American [high school] students are better prepared for college now than ever before."[1]

Building a healthy, democratic society requires citizens to be more than just functionally literate, however. We have complex issues to understand, and more of us need to become mature readers in order to fully understand them. **Mature readers** can read the lines, read between the lines, and read beyond the lines. A recent study of college students estimated that about 20 percent are in this optimal achieving category.[2] Mature readers question the validity and acceptability of what they read, and they determine how the information affects their understanding of the world.

Mature readers—
readers who can read the lines, read between the lines, and read beyond the lines

There is no one particular way that everyone learns to read and comprehend.[3] Much depends on the learning style, attitude, background, purpose, and desired outcome of the reader. Some students may assume that when a passage is confusing or counterintuitive, the fault lies with them, as the readers. However, certain "rules of the game" can help you analyze a writer's work, and if there is a deficiency, to determine whether it is yours or the writer's. Research indicates that these differences in critical reading ability among students may have as much to do with their level of self-confidence from previous learning experience as it does with their latent ability.[4]

As we discuss reading and comprehension, we will focus on academic reading as opposed to fiction. Academic reading includes texts, reports, discussions, articles, essays, proposals, and prepared presentations. These are unlike fiction in that they are not linear and do not have to be read in order, from page one to the end. They do not use characters and plots to tell a story but include facts and ideas to present an argument or relate information.

When reading an academic piece, you can choose what information to focus on and how to assimilate it. As an independent thinker, you are in control of the framework within which you evaluate, test, accept, and reject assertions and information. Critical thinking will help you distinguish between facts and writers' opinions and make links between the known and what is speculation.

Comprehension—
the act of thinking and constructing meaning before, during, and after reading, and integrating information from the author with the reader's background knowledge

Comprehension is the act of thinking and constructing meaning before, during, and after reading, and integrating information from an author with the reader's background knowledge.[5] It is an interactive process that involves understanding

ELI PARISER

Eli Pariser is a graduate of Simon's Rock College of Bard. In the days following September 11, 2001, he was concerned about perpetuating a violent cycle and wondered what he should do. He didn't know what he could do, but he knew how to create Web sites, so he decided to put his skill to use and launched an online petition calling for a peaceful response to break the cycle of violence. This petition was quickly signed by more than 100,000 people in the United States and almost half a million worldwide. He did not market the site—the petition was signed by people who had heard about it from others. Eli learned through this experience about the power of word of mouth for citizen involvement.

Following this experience, Eli joined forces with MoveOn and is now the international campaigns director. MoveOn is an international network of more than 2 million online activists that has built electronic advocacy groups on such issues as campaign finance, environmental and energy issues, gun safety, and nuclear disarmament. Once a group is assembled, MoveOn provides information and tools to help each individual have the greatest possible impact. MoveOn's grassroots advocates help Congress understand the depth of public opposition to unfavorable policies.

Eli has been involved with numerous projects, many of them unsuccessful. He is challenged by the unsuccessful projects, believing that he can learn from his mistakes and that "people don't hit home runs if they don't swing." Dedication and persistence are the most important qualities to have. While other skills, including strategic thinking and communication are very important, it is crucial to begin, envision the outcome, and persist.

The number of Americans engaging as citizens has been steadily increasing, and this gives him hope. One of Eli's goals is to educate others as to how easy it is for them to make a difference. He says: "Write an e-mail or letter to a congressman. They get very few of these, and when they start to receive more than 200, they pay attention because others are paying attention to them." Eli believes that we are at a turning point for our country: "The time to wring our hands has passed. This is very serious. There will be devastating consequences for our kids if we don't sit up and assume responsibility."

To begin the process, he suggests digging into a subject of interest, learning the players, reading the news, and finding out information about decision makers. According to Eli, much of the time big decisions are made with swing votes, and you just have to know people's pressure points. The people who are making policy decisions are just people with personalities you can get to know. You can understand the way they think and communicate with them on that level. Then, you should try to create an environment where the issue of concern is known publicly. You do this by using the media, e-mails, phone calls, and letters to the editors. Although no foolproof strategy exists, and often it is "hit and miss," there are also times of outstanding success. The important thing is to learn from your mistakes and just be involved, using the skills that you have.

From a phone interview with Eli Pariser on June 11, 2003. Photo courtesy of MoveOn.org.

and applying information rather than simply reading to be able to repeat information. In the comprehension process, proficient readers may do the following:

- Activate prior background knowledge about a topic
- Set a purpose for reading
- Preview the reading
- Make predictions
- Construct images during reading
- Self-question
- Identify main ideas and supporting details
- Analyze the structure of the reading
- Determine meanings of new words
- Critique the quality of the information
- Summarize
- Reflect
- Review
- Apply new information[6]

The aspects of comprehension can be done as pre-reading, during-reading, or after-reading activities (see Figure 5.1). **Pre-reading activities** include activating background knowledge, determining the purpose, previewing and predicting, and skimming for new vocabulary words. **During-reading activities** include constructing images, questioning, identifying the main ideas and supporting details, analyzing, and critiquing the reading. **Post-reading activities** include summarizing, responding, reflecting, comparing ideas, and applying the information.

Before Reading

Activating Background Knowledge

J. Dewey and L. Rosenblatt, in their article on the reading experience, determine that "meaning isn't received through the act of reading; it is experienced through the prisms of our perspective, which in turn is shaped by context."[7] The elements of context—the people, places, history, and events—belong only to the individual and are the filters through which all information passes. This context determines the reader's perception and understanding of the material.

The more background information and experience a reader has, the more that reader will be able to comprehend a wide variety of reading topics. Reading in and of itself will not automatically lead to comprehension. Twenty percent of functional literates are "voracious readers, but their capacity to think may be limited by their narrow knowledge of many subjects in which they proclaim no interest and pursue no continuing self-instruction."[8] **Inferencing** is the process by which a reader is required to use his background knowledge to make connections regard-

Inferencing—
the act of using background knowledge to make connections within reading material

Before Reading: Preview	During Reading: Critiquing	After Reading: Reviewing
What I already know about the topic:	Main ideas and supporting details:	Questions about the important ideas:
What I want to learn and/or predict I will learn:	Structure of the reading:	What I learned:
New vocabulary words to look up:		What else I need to know:

FIGURE 5.1 *Aspects of Reading Comprehension*

ing what he is reading. Many readings require that the reader use inferencing to understand the material, an ability that depends on the reader's general knowledge and background.

Multiple literacies are one's level of acquired knowledge in different areas or topics. This is illustrated with such terms as *math literacy*, *computer literacy*, or *financial literacy*. To have a meaningful discourse on an issue, we need literacy in the issue. We need to be able to use the proper set of meanings and terms that are specific to the issue, and we need to have enough background knowledge to make inferences when necessary. Illiteracy in a topic can make it difficult to understand written or spoken discourse on an issue. For instance, to understand a report on farming issues, one would probably need to understand the meaning and usage of such terms as *crop*, *irrigation*, *harvest*, and *yield*.

Multiple literacies— one's level of acquired knowledge in specific areas or topics

The more varied your experiences and prior knowledge of diverse topics, the greater will be your reading comprehension. One way to acquire more background knowledge is to read on a variety of topics and to choose challenging material to read. Readings that are too simple do not readily provide the opportunity to stretch your understanding and critical thinking about an issue. However, if the reading is at a level that makes comprehension too difficult, it may reduce self-confidence and motivation. Expanding literacy and knowledge of diverse issues is also a critical asset to our ability to govern ourselves as citizens.

Determining Purpose

A reader may have several purposes when approaching material, including to gain a detailed and comprehensive understanding of the material and to find the answers to particular questions. Critical readers may intend to do the following with the information:

- Absorb
- Analyze
- Summarize
- Identify specific issues
- Question
- Understand for discourse
- Critique

If you have a particular purpose in mind for the information you are reading—such as taking a test on it, preparing an essay, writing a letter to an elected official about an issue, or constructing an argument—you may be better able to determine how to approach the information and how best to use it.

Previewing and Predicting

The purpose of previewing is to motivate your interest in what you're about to read, to activate your background knowledge, and to choose whether information is relevant to your needs. **Previewing** may include reading the introduction, conclusions of chapters, chapter headings, subheadings, and introductory and final paragraphs of more specific sections. If you need further information, you can read the first and last sentences of paragraphs or read intensively in appropriate sections. You can also look at pictures, diagrams, figures, or tables, and search for key words.

During the preview process, you should determine:

- What you already know about the reading
- What you want to learn
- What you predict the reading will be about

During Reading

Vizualizing events, questioning, and determining the reading structure can help you become a more active reader.

Imaging

Imaging—the ability to visualize or turn words into images—is a reading strategy that helps with comprehension. When reading the words, imagine the real-life scenarios they may describe. To get a visual image of the reading, consider using the mapping technique presented later in this chapter.

Self-Questioning

Self-questioning, or reflective, learners are active, creative, engaged, strategic thinkers. They set goals for their learning process but remain open to new directions that their learning may reveal. They pose questions about the topic before, during, and after reading.

Identifying Main Ideas and Supporting Details

Determine who or what the topic is about and rephrase it using fewer than 10 words. Name the most important idea about the topic. Identify areas the author covers that support the main idea.

Determining Structure

Information is usually structured in a way that can increase your ability to use and understand it. Ideas and information are structured in specific ways. Three structures typically found in academic material are cause and effect, compare and contrast, and time order.

Cause and effect. Cause and effect shows that something has happened and that someone or something made it happen. If this is the reading structure, the reading will likely answer some or all of these key questions:

> What has happened?
> What will happen?
> Why has it happened?
> Who or what made it happen?

Compare and contrast. In this structure, facts and ideas are presented that are similar or different. The reading will likely answer some or all of these key questions:

> What is being compared and why?
> What facts or ideas are similar?
> What facts or ideas are different?

Time order. Details of a topic in this structure are presented in the chronological order of their occurrence to show the way something happened or will or should happen. The reading will likely answer some or all of these key questions:

> What events happened in what order?
>
> What events will or should happen in an order?

Key Words

To determine structure, predict outcomes, consider counterarguments, and test reasoning, consult the language and grammar of the reading passage. For instance, a colon followed by two or more commas or semicolons signifies that to the left of the colon is the main point (e.g. "The structure of a sentence might include: a noun, a verb . . . "). A new paragraph indicates a topic change, and the first and last paragraphs usually highlight the topic. Words such as *is, cannot be,* or *must* suggest absolute certainty and can be challenged by the reader if the statements are not fully supported by the author's reference to authority. Use of the word *claim* when reporting another's work usually means the writer intends to be critical.

Cause and effect. Certain cue words can indicate if you are reading a cause-and-effect structure. They will tell you who, what, or why. Look for the following:

so	because
so that	because of
the cause	as a result of
in order to	therefore
it follows that	consequently

Compare and contrast. Certain cue words will tell you if something is the same or different. These may include the following:

both	but
the same as	different from
on the other hand	still
alike	unlike
as	similar to
better	best
different	more
less	compared to
in contrast to	similarly
however	although

Time order. Certain cue words that indicate a time order structure include the following:

first	next
then	finally

second	third
before	after
during	while

Monitoring Vocabulary

The ability to identify or decode unknown words rapidly and accurately is an important prerequisite for reading fluency and comprehension. By the time most people graduate from high school, they have encountered more than 88,500 word families, with many of these words learned in the course of wide reading.

The rate at which students learn new words varies substantially.[9] The more vocabulary words with which you are familiar, the better able you will be to rapidly comprehend text. Specialized vocabulary occurs in every discipline, and we are bound to run across words we don't understand if we are extending ourselves and increasing our knowledge base. To become familiar with more words, seek out more difficult material and new topics. Tips for deciphering the meaning include:

- Skim the passage for unknown vocabulary words and look them up in a dictionary before reading.
- Reread the sentence with the word you don't understand.
- Read before and after this sentence looking for clues.
- Read the sentence without the word. What would make sense in its place?
- Look for a prefix or suffix in the word.
- Look for any graphical illustrations.

When you know its meaning, use the word as soon as possible in a new sentence, and use it frequently thereafter.

Critiquing

The skill of analyzing arguments in texts can be learned. We can critique what we read by looking at three areas:

What
How
Why

What refers to the topic being covered. Look at the information content, and answer the following questions:

- Does what I'm reading make sense?
- Is this what I expected?
- Are statements supported by full reference to sources? Are they acceptable and trustworthy?
- Are references up to date and accurate?

How refers to the organizational structure and how the writer signals this to the reader. Is it cause and effect, compare and contrast, or time order? Distinguishing the type of structure will allow you to look for the effectiveness of this structure in communicating what is being presented. Answer the following questions:

- Do the facts selected illustrate the points made?
- Are the examples well-chosen and typical?
- Is another explanation possible?
- Is the structure clear and easy for the reader to follow?
- Does the layout make logical sense?
- Are there paragraphs, subheadings, and clear punctuation?
- Is the sentence structure clear and direct?
- Do statements in one part of the document contradict statements in another?

Why refers to the author's intention, which is revealed through the language and structure used. Answer the following questions regarding the viewpoint:

- Does the author primarily describe, evaluate, suggest, compare, justify, criticize, or discuss?
- Does the author accomplish the purpose?
- Does the author make emotive appeals in place of solid argument?

After Reading

Summarizing

Within 30 minutes of reading, summarize what you have read. Close the text or put away the material, and write or tape-record what you remember. Ask yourself these questions:

- What were the most important points?
- Which sections supported these points?
- What is my opinion?
- How do I feel?
- What new information did I learn?

Reflecting

It's important to give yourself the time and space to reflect and consider new meaning and ideas in light of the reading. Reflection allows you to connect key ideas within the reading and integrate them with personal experiences. In this way, new meanings and ideas are generated.[10] You may determine that you need to read more, reread, or seek more information. In this process, you may also come up with more questions about the topic.

Reviewing

Review the material once more, along with any notes you took during reading, highlighted areas, and vocabulary words. Again, determine whether you have any questions that have not been answered.

It often helps to review with another person or a group, if possible. The group members can benefit by comparing thoughts and questions and can help one another remember the material. The group can brainstorm solutions, ideas for research, projects, future study, or exam questions. Discussing the material with others can help you formulate new ideas or opinions and make connections you may otherwise not have considered.

Applying Information

What do you need to do with the information you read? Do you need to take a test, write an essay, make a presentation, or prepare an argument or supporting information? Did you gather the information and understanding necessary for your application?

NOTE-TAKING

Taking notes is a useful way to organize your thoughts, focus on structure and key ideas, and help commit important information to memory. There are different reasons to take notes, and note-taking techniques may differ accordingly. We may take notes in order to:

- Brainstorm
- Explore ideas and gather more information
- Synthesize ideas
- Focus on a topic's details
- Present information

Several different formats for taking notes exist, including the two most common forms:

- Reading and researching
- Listening to a lecture, presentation, or interview

The note-taking techniques used for purposes and formats discussed in this section include:

- Mapping
- Tabular
- Journaling
- T-format
- Index cards
- Outlining

Primary Note-Taking Purpose	Primary Note-Taking Techniques
Brainstorm	Mapping, journaling
Explore ideas and gather more information	Tabular, journaling, T-format
Synthesize ideas	T-format, mapping
Focus on a topic's details	Index cards, outlining
Present information	Outlining, index cards

FIGURE 5.2 *Note-Taking Techniques by Purpose*

Note-Taking While Listening

When taking notes from a lecture, presentation, televised news event, interview, or other source for which it may be difficult to have the content repeated, it helps to have previously determined what information you want to gather. Since this format places the note-taker in the position of getting content down as quickly and as efficiently as possible, knowing what you are looking for in the presentation will help you be selective. It is not possible to write down every word or detail while listening to someone speak. Taking notes in these instances requires concentration and a system of shorthand. You should also go through the notes later to analyze and synthesize. No matter what system you use for taking notes, the following suggestions apply to taking notes during a lecture, presentation, or interview:

> *Anxiety is caused by a lack of control, organization, preparation, and action.*
>
> **DAVID KEKICH**

- Review any previous notes and readings to provide context and continuity for new information.
- Date the session, and title the notes with the subject of the lecture or presentation.
- Write down the full name of the person lecturing or being interviewed and/or the channel you're watching or listening to.
- Highlight any actions that you need to take.
- Keep notes legible. Handwriting should be clear enough to comprehend when reviewing.
- Skip lines after crucial points.
- Use bullets.
- Summarize important points.
- Quickly review your notes before the end of the lecture or presentation, and ask the lecturer to clarify anything you're unclear about.
- Be an effective listener. Concentrate on the message and listen for key words and main ideas.

- In your notes, distinguish between a main idea and an example or illustration.
- Distinguish between what is said and your commentary on it. You might put your personal thoughts and commentary in brackets.
- Be selective in the information you take time to write down.
- Write in a shortened form that you understand. Use abbreviations, numbers, and symbols as long as you know what they represent.
- Ask for clarification of ambiguous statements and answers to questions you have noted, if possible.

Knowing what you are trying to get out of a lecture will help you listen for the information you need.

Adapting to Different Styles

You can adjust your note-taking techniques according to the varying styles and personalities of lecturers. If your lecturer can be characterized as primarily using one of the styles shown in Figure 5.3, use the associated tips for taking notes.

Note-Taking While Reading and Researching

Although taking notes during reading and researching allows you the luxury of going back to passages for further understanding, you may have to do more synthesizing of multiple ideas and topics.

No matter which technique you use to take notes while reading, consider the following suggestions:

- Note any terms and definitions given. You can check the definitions of unfamiliar terms as well as names, events, dates, steps, or directions.
- Wait until you read the document at least once before marking the text. If you mark text as you are reading it for the first time, you may tend to overmark. Wait until you've finished a section; then go back and highlight the key points.
- Highlight key terms and concepts, if you're able to mark the document. Mark the examples that explain and support the important ideas. You might try using more than one highlighter color to differentiate definitions or ideas from examples.
- Highlight figures and tables, if you're able to mark the document. Whatever information you need from the tables and figures should be highlighted along with any tables that summarize the concepts discussed in the text.

Lecturer Style	Tips for Note-Taking
Organized lecturer	Copy all material from the board or slide.
	Understand the definition of all key words and phrases.
	Be prepared by doing background reading.
Entertaining lecturer	Predict what an outline of the topic would look like, and write this down before the lecture.
	As you listen to the lecture, remind yourself to ask these questions: • "What is the point?" or "What am I learning?" • "What is this story an illustration of?" • "What is this example demonstrating?"
Questioning lecturer	Ask questions to clarify.
	Record your own responses to the instructor's questions, even if you don't voice your response.
	Note when the lecturer affirms an idea (for example, "Yes, that's right," or "Exactly, that's an important point").
	Note when the lecturer summarizes or paraphrases an idea.

FIGURE 5.3 *Note-Taking by Lecture Style*

- Write notes in the margin, if you're able to mark the document. Comments such as "main point" or "important definition" will help you locate key sections later. Also note in the margins any questions you may have about the document's validity.
- Review your highlights, and organize them into notes. Be an active reader. You will not necessarily learn from what you highlight unless you review it carefully.

Note-Taking Formats

T-Format

If you don't have much experience taking notes from lectures or interviews, you should begin by using some form of double-entry system to gain practice in recording both content and your personal response. This format is referred to as the **T-format** and may take the form shown in Figure 5.4.

Cornell system. The **Cornell system** is a more advanced T-format. Divide the page into two parts, as shown in Figure 5.5, with a line drawn one-third of the way in from the left side. The smaller left side is used later to synthesize main ideas, while the wider right side is used to gather details.

This system is similar to a box score for an athletic event, which might include the most important players, plays, scoring events, and team totals. Similarly, you can keep track of the most important information from the lecture, presentation, interview, or reading using this method.

As you take notes using the Cornell system, leave space between details, usually one inch for every two inches of notes taken. This allows for clearer notes and for returning to interject related information presented later. If the presentation is interactive and you're able to ask questions, you can note the areas you would like to ask about with a question mark and later fill in the responses.

The Question or Topic	
Content summary (what it says)	Personal response
	Tie to previous content
	Why this is enlightening
	Why this is important
	A new question generated

FIGURE 5.4 *The T-Format for Notes*

Subject: Date:	
	Details
Main idea	
Inferences	
New Questions	
Summary: Include here a brief abstract of the information's meaning to you, your judgment on the quality of information, and any additional support evidence or clarification needed.	

FIGURE 5.5 *The Cornell System of Note Taking*

Mapping

Mapping is a visual technique that can be used many ways. To take notes on a topic using mapping, take a blank piece of paper and follow these instructions:

- Identify the main topic, and place it at the center
- Identify subtopics and ideas, and put them into surrounding boxes
- As information becomes available about each of the subtopics, attach that information to the appropriate subtopic

This creates a map, or web, of information and related facts that can be used for making connections or identifying where gaps in knowledge exist. It can also be used to brainstorm or explore an idea and to synthesize ideas. To use mapping in this way, put the main topic in the center and follow these instructions:

- Brainstorm words that are associated with the main topic
- Group these words into broad categories
- Provide labels for the categories
- Generate words or subcategories
- Determine the interrelationships of categories and subcategories

Once you have identified the structure of reading or research material, you can organize and reorganize information and ideas into a map or chart. This will help in managing a large amount of information so you can select the important information, identify and clarify relationships among ideas, relate information from different sources, and link it all to your prior knowledge. These maps, when used for note-taking during reading or researching, can be concrete representations of complex concepts. Figure 5.6 is an example of a map of the branches of government.

Tabular Format

Using a **tabular format** when taking notes during reading enables you to compare different views, ideas, and interpretations horizontally (see Figure 5.7). This allows you to generate and record ideas or questions on the left and research each of those questions and record information on the right.

Index cards

Index cards (see Figure 5.8) can be used for detailed information that comes from specific sources. The information noted on these cards is readily accessible and easily organized, and it can be used when preparing presentations and reports.

Politics should be the part-time profession of every American.

DWIGHT D. EISENHOWER

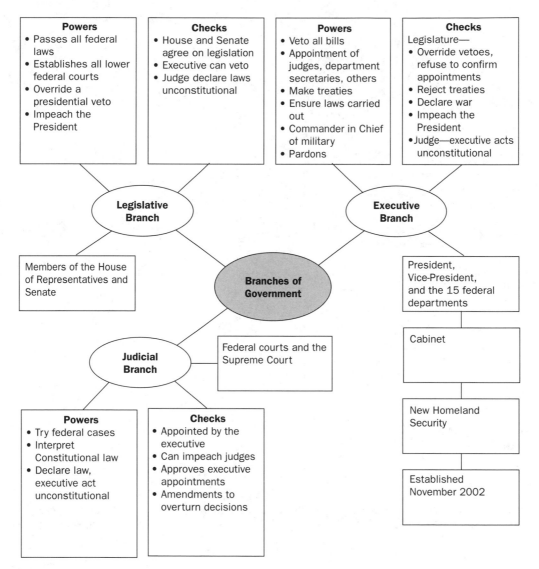

FIGURE 5.6 *Branches of Government Using Mapping Technique*

Outlining

An **outline** is a structure to help organize your thoughts, lectures, or readings. It generally takes the following form, though it does not have to be as exact and formal when used for taking notes.

I. First main idea
   A. First subdivision of main idea
      i. First reason or example
     ii. Second reason or example
       1. first supporting detail
       2. second supporting detail
   B. Second subdivision of main idea
II. Second main idea

Summary of Topic:	
Purpose or Question 1	Sources and abbreviated notes:
Purpose or Question 2	

FIGURE 5.7 *Tabular Format for Note Taking*

Number of Source or Author's Last Name and Date	Rating System for Value of Information	Key Word for Subtopic or Question
Most important facts:		
Paraphrased specific information:		
Summary:		
Direct quote:		
Primary source of info:		

FIGURE 5.8 *Index Card Note Taking*

ACTION!

Note-Taking Exercise

Using the map for the branches of government shown in Figure 5.6, put the notes into two other note-taking formats: outlining and T-format.

Reviewing Notes

Responding to notes soon after you write them helps reinforce what you've learned, provides an orientation for future information, helps you study from your notes, and helps you logically structure ideas so you can further reflect on the topics.

Simply recopying notes is not the best use of time, but analyzing and reorganizing them can be very beneficial. If you can find someone else who attended the lecture or presentation, watched the same media program, or read the same material, discuss it with each other. Go over the main points, and explain the information to each other. Often, others may have noted what you did not and can fill in missing pieces. Talking to others will also help you form new ideas or connect ideas with other topics and experiences.

After taking notes while listening, it helps to free-write a one-page summary of the lecture or presentation. When you are finished taking notes while reading or researching, review the notes and answer the following questions:

- What is the most important idea I learned?
- What are three important terms I learned to define or understand?
- What question do I want to answer to help me better understand the material?

RESEARCHING

To fully understand the issues with which we deal as citizens, we often need to do some research, which requires the highest levels of thinking. We may use research skills to find information or discover facts. However, the larger goal of research is to tell a story associated with those facts—a story that has not been told before. With the proper research tools and reference skills, you can go to the library or search the Internet to find information. You can also go beyond this by collecting information and then weaving it together to form conclusions that increase people's knowledge and understanding.

Research is the systematic process of collecting and analyzing information in order to increase our understanding of the phenomenon about which we are concerned or interested. The act of researching can lead you into new territories. You may wish to further explore unexpected or contradictory findings or challenge findings that are not what you would expect. Using critical thinking will help you look at

Research—
the systematic process of collecting and analyzing information in order to increase our understanding of the phenomenon about which we are concerned or interested

previous research studies and scrutinize them for faulty assumptions, questionable logic, weaknesses in methodology, and unwarranted conclusions.

Steps in the Research Process

The steps in the research process may include:

- Exploring
- Determining your question or problem
- Dividing the principal problem or question into subproblems, if necessary
- Deciding what information you might need
- Determining sources of information
- Selecting key words
- Searching the literature
- Organizing information
- Drawing conclusions
- Presenting information

The research process begins with an orientation phase in which you being to learn about a theme. You may do this by perusing general material related to the issues at hand. You then narrow that theme into a specific interest of inquiry and focus on preliminary questions that interest you the most.

Sources of Information

You may use one or more sources of information in your research on social issues, including the following:

Public libraries	Interviews with experts	Advocacy groups	Professional conferences and agendas
Committees	Business groups	Diary or journal	Think tanks
Professors	Letter	Museum	Dictionary
Encyclopedia	Political cartoon	Survey	Online database
Photograph	Atlas	Autobiography	Television
Almanac	Policy journals	Internet	
Newpapers	Corporations	Biography	
University libraries	Offices of political officials	Magazines	
Government agencies			

By typing key words into a library terminal using any of the databases, you will see abstracts of articles or texts. Scan these references, and read intensively around the key words. Note the information you need, and ignore the rest.

In research, we refer to two types of information: (1) that from primary sources, and (2) that from secondary sources.

Primary information, or data, is often considered the most valid and the most illuminating. **Primary data** is collected for the purpose of the research. You will gather this data if you hold an interview. **Secondary data** consists of already compiled research and information. You will gather this type of data when doing a literature review.

Primary data— data collected for the purpose of the research

Secondary data— data consisting of already-compiled research and information

Interviews

You will likely conduct many interviews in the course of your citizenship work. These can yield a great deal of useful information. The interviewer can ascertain:

- Facts
- Beliefs
- Feelings
- Motives
- Present and past behaviors
- Standards for behavior
- Conscious reasons for actions or feelings

> *True democratic community requires an educated, informed citizenry. But people only become informed if they actively seek out information.*
>
> **CHRISTOPHER LASCH**

Interviews can be open-ended (one without a preset plan), or structured (in which only specific questions are asked and answered). An open-ended interview is advantageous in that it can yield information that the interviewer had not expected. The primary disadvantage is that the researcher gets different information from different people and does not have a basis of comparison. The researcher should take good notes during the interview.

Following are some suggestions to make interviews as productive as possible:

- Have a clear reason for interviewing the person.
- Find a quiet place for the interview.
- Take a few minutes at the beginning to establish rapport.
- Get written permission from the participant.
- Take care to let interviewees speak without concluding too early what you think they will say.
- Record responses verbatim.
- Keep your reactions to yourself.
- Remember that you are not necessarily getting the facts.

> ► ► ► ► **A C T I O N !** ◄ ◄ ◄ ◄ ◄

Interviewing Exercise

Interview two classmates using open-ended and structured formats, and give a report to the class on your findings. How did the interviewing styles of your classmates differ? How did the information received differ?

WRITING

Much of what we wish to communicate to Members of Congress, the media, and other people needs to be in written form, so good writing skills are important. It helps before writing to use the outline or mapping techniques described earlier to organize your thoughts. You will use writing skills for active citizenship when you write letters to Members of Congress or other elected officials, letters to the editor, e-mail messages, press releases, and formal reports.

Letters

General letter writing tips include the following:

- Keep the length to one page, if possible.
- Use 3/4- to 1-inch margins.
- In the first sentence, tell readers what you expect of them.
- Keep the tone informal. Use words such as *I*, *we*, *you*, and *us*.
- Use short paragraphs.
- If you have extensive information, write a short letter with an attachment. The short letter clarifies the reader's role and summarizes the attached information.

Educate and inform the mass of people . . . Enlighten the people generally, and tyranny and oppressions of body and mind will vanish like evil spirits at the dawn of day.

THOMAS JEFFERSON

- An attachment to a letter may be a list of instructions, a proposal, a progress report, an outline of pros and cons for a coming decision, minutes of a meeting—almost any kind of document. The reader may use the attachment as a handout at a staff meeting, post it on a bulletin board, or create a new letter and send copies to others.
- Letters contain the date, the name and address of the recipient, and the salutation.
- The letter ends with a closing and a signature. Other information may appear after the signature, such as carbon copy, attachment, and initials of the typist, if appropriate.

- The letter format may be full block, modified block, or semiblock.
- Letters should be checked for spelling and grammar and proofread by another person.

Letters to Elected Officials

The most effective letters are those that are obviously personal and individually written, as opposed to form letters. A short, passionate, handwritten letter shows a legislator that you are serious enough about an issue to take the time to understand it and communicate about it to them. Politicians know that if you take the time to write an original letter, then you probably care enough about the issue to have it influence your support at the polls.[11]

Writing letters with others allows us to stay motivated and receive feedback.

Guidelines for writing to your elected officials include the following:

- State why the issue is important to you and your reasons for opposing or supporting the specific legislation in four or five sentences. Include the bill number of the legislation you are writing about.
- Be personal. If you have personal experience or expertise with the issue, be sure to include it. Share your feelings and passion.
- State that you are a constituent. Always include your full name and mailing address.
- Be positive and constructive. It is more effective to focus on what you want and why it is beneficial than on what you don't want and the negative aspects.
- Make a clear request. Ask for a response to your letter indicating whether the legislator will take the action you are requesting.
- Share your letter with others to generate more letters to the legislator.

Letters to the Editor

Suggestions for increasing the chance that a newspaper will print your submitted letter include the following:

- Use the guidelines given in your chosen paper. The editorial section will list guidelines for length and to whom you should send your letter.
- Stick to facts about an issue, and give your sources. Do not make assumptions.
- Refer to another letter or recent news story that relates to your issue.
- E-mail your letter, if possible. If not, send a neat, typed letter.

> *Communication is not a technical science, but a personal expression.*
>
> **MARK ALBION**

- Include your full name, address, and phone numbers. Most papers will call you to confirm that you wrote the letter before printing it.

E-mail

Since most computer screens are smaller than the typical page of text, e-mail messages tend to be shorter than memos. Readers can respond more quickly to an e-mail if they can see the entire text. If they must scroll down too much while reading, they tend to lose the train of thought. Tips for sending e-mail messages include the following:

- Proofread e-mail before sending it. Errors occur more easily in e-mail messages than in printed documents.
- Be certain that you want to send the message. Once you hit the "send" key, you cannot change your mind. Therefore, it is a good idea not to write e-mail messages when you are angry or emotional.
- Be careful when using humor or sarcasm in e-mail, as these are sometimes difficult for others to interpret in this context.

Press Releases

A **press release** (see Figure 5.9), which announces new information about an issue or an event or concern, should include:

- When it should be reported
- Your contact information
- Today's date and the location from where you're sending the release
- Introductory summary statement
- Wording that can be read or printed exactly as is
- Brief description of your organization

Formal Reports

A formal report sends information to decision makers or others who need the information. The structure of a formal report can be a variation of the following:

a. Letter explaining the purpose of the report (list the report itself as an attachment to the letter)
b. Title page
   Title of the report
   Author
   Submitted to
   Date
c. Abstract or summary of the report
d. Table of contents
e. List of visuals (figures and tables)

   f. The report text, including
      Page numbers centered at bottom
      Headings and subheadings
      References with author, title, and date
      Appealing page layout
   g. Bibliography/references (last main heading of the report)
   h. Appendix/appendices

FOR IMMEDIATE RELEASE:
June 3, 200x
CONTACT:
Jane Jones
(202) 222-2222 x110
cell: (202) 222-2222

Executive Director Objects to House Head Start Bill

WASHINGTON, D.C.—Marian Wright Edelman, executive director of The Children's Defense Fund, voiced strong objections to the Head Start legislation (H.R.2210) considered at a hearing today in the House Education Reform Subcommittee. "The first reports talked about a demonstration project involving only a few states. That was wrong. It is clear that this bill could completely dismantle the Head Start program," Edelman said.

Today, local Head Start centers are funded directly by the federal Department of Health and Human Services (HHS), bypassing state governments. The House bill to reauthorize Head Start would allow state governments to take control of Head Start within their states.

"Head Start is one of the most closely scrutinized of all federal programs," Edelman noted. "It prepares disadvantaged children for school addressing all of their needs in a comprehensive way. While we encourage efforts to strengthen Head Start's academic focus, a hungry, sick or trouble child cannot learn. It's also tough to succeed if your parents have multiple problems."

The array of services might be lost, Edelman suggested, if management of the program is taken over by cash-strapped states. "The temptation to water down a strong mix of services will be hard to resist," she asserted. The bill says that states would have to acceptable standards in place to qualify, but the power to approve state proposals would rest with the secretary of education and the secretary of HHS. "The standards for states [contained in H.R. 2210] are too vague," Edleman added.

The bill could move quickly through the full House Committee on Education and the Workforce. The Senate Committee on Health, Education, Labor and Pensions has not yet scheduled action on Head Start reauthorization.

FIGURE 5.9 *Sample Press Release*

Applications

 Choose an article from a magazine you would normally not be interested in. Take notes on it using one of the methods described in this chapter. Hypothetically determine your purpose in taking notes. Identify the relationships of ideas, find cue words, and ask questions. Compare your notes with those of a classmate who chose a different purpose. How do your notes differ? Discuss why your notes may differ according to the purpose.

 With the class broken into two groups, have each group plan a meeting on the topic of their choice. Each group is given five minutes to role-play their meeting in front of the other group, and the groups give each other feedback.

 Set up a 10-minute interview with a parent. Find out as much as you can about their favorite memories of your childhood.

4 Find a letter to the editor in a recent newspaper that intrigues you. Using the tips in this chapter, write a letter to the editor of that paper responding to the letter.

5 **READING EXERCISE.** In the following reading exercise, perform the following before, during, and after reading functions:

Before Reading
- *Activating background knowledge*. Skim the text of the article. What do you know about this topic?
- *Determining purpose*. For what purpose(s) are you reading this article?
- *Previewing and predicting*. What do you predict that this article will say?

During Reading
- *Imaging*. Write down the images you create as you read the passage.
- *Self-questioning*. Write down the questions you generate while reading.
- *Identifying main ideas and supporting details*. Write down the main idea and supporting details as you read them.
- *Determining structure*. Which of the following structures does the article follow? What key words can you identify that help you determine the structure?
  Cause and effect
  Compare and contrast
  Time order
- *Monitoring vocabulary*. Write down the vocabulary words you don't know.
- *Critiquing*. Write down your analysis of the article while you are reading it.

After Reading

- *Summarizing.* In summary, what does the article say?
- *Reflecting.* Is there any new information you would like to have? What conclusions can you make? Does the article give you insight into a topic that you had not yet considered?
- *Reviewing.* Look up the meanings to the vocabulary words.
- *Applying information.* What are some possible applications for what you have read?

Reading

Op-Ed for *Newsday* (New York), August 26, 2003
By Carl Safina, president of the Blue Ocean Institute, Cold Spring Harbor, NY. His books include *Song for the Blue Ocean* and *Eye of the Albatross.*

Since the late ocean explorer Jacques Cousteau titled his 1950s book and documentary film "The Silent World," the ocean has spoken up, and it is complaining.

Like swells from distant storms suddenly surging upon a crowded beach, waves of new ocean studies are reporting the depth of overfishing, failures of ocean management, fish-farm contamination, invading species and new diseases, coastal crowding and pollution, dying coral reefs—and what could be done to ease such problems.

But despite the news flood, none of the political bodies seem to be moving their beach blanket. They've applied more sun-block and rolled over. They've heard the wake-up call and hit the snooze button.

The veritable tsunami of recent scientific studies—originating from weighty ocean-science centers such as Duke, Stanford, British Columbia and Dalhousie universities, the Scripps Institution of Oceanography and elsewhere—have shown:

The numbers of large fishes we prefer to eat, such as tuna, cod, swordfish, shark and grouper, have declined roughly 90 percent since 1950.

Consequently, fishing boats are scouring lower in the food chain, catching even jellyfish for human consumption.

One quarter of all sea life caught is unwanted and discarded dead, endangering sea turtles, albatrosses and certain fishes. Shrimp boats discard 10 pounds of unwanted marine life for each pound of shrimp.

Invading species transported by seafood farmers and, especially, in ships' ballast water are spreading new problems and diseases to our waters.

More than half the world's 6 billion people live near coasts, creating pollution from pesticides, sewage, factories and other sources.

Climate warming is stressing coral reefs and melting polar ice, increasing coastal flooding, and threatening food supplies of penguins and polar bears.

Having spent a lifetime in intimate contact with the sea around us, I'm sorry to say these findings ring true. But take heart: Some problems have been solved. Turtle drownings have been reduced by putting escape doors in nets. Seabirds can be protected with devices designed to scare them from industrial fishing lines, or by fishing at night or setting nets deeper.

The United Nations successfully eliminated the 40-mile-long "curtains-of-death" drift-nets in the 1990s. Some whales recovered enough to support whale-watching ventures. Even certain fish are recovering due to tougher regulations. This should inspire hope and a new ethic of ocean stewardship, spurring more vigorous, widespread application of solutions.

But we have a long way to go. The capacity of fishing fleets—fishing power—must be roughly halved. In a world facing still-increasing human populations, this will be challenging. Alaska and several countries reduced fishing power by setting allowable catches and then letting boats buy and sell shares of the total.

This system enables some marginal operators to make money by selling out their shares while other marginal operators increase profitability by buying shares. For this to work economically, fish landings must be well capped and enforced, thus maintaining fish populations. To benefit fishing communities, share limits must safeguard smaller operators and prevent corporate accumulation. Alaska's system does both.

We need new ocean governance. U.S. fishing falls under the National Oceanic and Atmospheric Administration. There, buried deep in the Department of Commerce, it plays Cinderella to favored siblings like the weather service, space program and others.

As the independent Pew Oceans Commission recently affirmed, a separate oceans agency is needed, focusing on stewardship of ocean wildlife rather than exploitation. President George W. Bush has appointed a National Ocean Commission; its findings are due this fall. They could chart a course toward recovery of the fish and habitats relied on by coastal communities, recreational ocean lovers and the seafood industry—and let the administration claim one victory for the environment.

New Zealand, Australia, the Philippines and several other countries have established ocean reserves, closed to fishing. Fish grow and breed more successfully in reserves. But, as on land, we cannot rely solely on wildlife refuges. Users must also receive guarantees that they stay in business. What is needed is not just closed reserves, but ocean zoning.

Zoning would explicitly allow a range of activities in a range of designated areas, while setting aside sensitive habitats and breeding grounds. Zoning would accommodate commercial and recreational users, plus establish strategic "no-take" reserves.

We need international cooperation. The frontier mentality must yield to a high seas enclosed in law, acknowledging the public trust and our ethical responsibilities to other creatures.

The United Nations must vigorously implement its recently enacted high-seas fishing treaty and its "Plans of Action" for depleted sharks and seabirds. And we need public concern. Consumers can play a large role in improving fishing and ocean farming practices. Environmental organizations publish evaluations of menu choices seafood lovers can enjoy with a clear conscience.

Answers to ocean recovery lie in fishing at a pace slower than fish can breed, farming seafood less destructively and giving consumers information to vote their conscience with their wallet. So, yes, there is hope.

Used with permission of the author.

QUIZ

1. Reading comprehension is:
   A. the process of researching and note-taking in order to understand a conceptual theory
   B. taking notes while reading
   C. considering alternative viewpoints from that of the author
   D. the act of thinking and constructing meaning before, during, and after reading

2. Before reading, you should do which of the following to help in comprehension?
   A. activate background knowledge
   B. determine purpose
   C. preview and predict
   D. all of the above

3. Imaging is used:
   A. in diagnosing a problem
   B. in researching a solution
   C. during reading
   D. while questioning

4. The structure typically found in academic material dealing with similar or different facts and ideas being presented is:
   A. cause and effect structure
   B. time order structure
   C. compare and contrast structure
   D. factual structure

5. After reading, you should:
   A. review the material
   B. put the material away and not think about it again
   C. summarize the material
   D. A and C

6. The best note-taking system to use for presenting information is:
   A. mapping
   B. journaling
   C. T-format
   D. index cards

7. When taking notes during reading, it helps to:
   A. highlight key terms and concepts
   B. read through the material at least once before marking
   C. check definitions and unfamiliar terms
   D. all of the above

8. Which of the following note-taking methods is a common T-format?
   A. index cards
   B. journaling
   C. mapping
   D. Cornell system

9. Research is defined as:
   A. the systematic process of collecting and analyzing information
   B. the process of organizing information
   C. discovering new sources of information
   D. critically thinking about research studies

10. The most effective letters to Members of Congress are:
    A. businesslike
    B. form letters
    C. accompanied by a summary memo
    D. personally written

ENDNOTES

1. Quoted in Margulies, J. "Grading the States," *School of Library Journal* 47 (October 2001): 16.

2. Manzo, A., U. Manzo, A. Barnhill, and M. Thomas. "Proficient Reader Subtypes: Implications for Literacy Theory, Assessment and Practice," *Reading Psychology* 21 (2000): 217–232.

3. Du Boulay, Doreen. "Argument in Reading: What Does It Involve and How Can Students Become Better Critical Readers?" *Teaching in Higher Education* 4 (April 1999): 147.

4. Du Boulay, "Argument in Reading."

5. Snider, V. E. "Reading Comprehension Performance of Adolescents with Learning Disabilities," *Learning Disability Quarterly* 12 (1989): 87–96.

6. Asselin, Marlene. "Comprehension Instruction: Directions from Research," *Teacher Librarian* 29 (April 2002): 55+.

7. Dewey, J. *Experience and Education*. New York: Collier Books, 1993; Rosenblatt, L. *The Reader, the Text, the Poem: The Transactional Theory of the Literacy Work*. Carbondale, Ill.: Southern Illinois University Press, 1978.

8. Manzo, et al. "Proficient Reader Subtypes."

9. Nagy, W. E., and R. C. Anderson. "How Many Words Are There in Printed School English?" *Reading Research Quarterly*. In Diane Bryant,

Nicole Ugel, Sylvia Thompson, and Allison Hamff, "Instructional Strategies for Content-area Reading Instruction," *Intervention in School & Clinic* 34:5 (May 1999).

10. Rhoder, Carol. "Mindful Reading: Strategy Training That Facilitates Transfer," *Journal of Adolescent & Adult Literacy* 45:6 (March 2002): 498+.

11. Halperin, Samuel. *A Guide for the Powerless—and Those Who Don't Know Their Own Power; A Primer on the American Political Process.* Washington, D.C.: American Youth Policy Forum, 2001.

Communication and Teamwork

6

We are all dependent on one another, every soul of us on Earth.

—GEORGE BERNARD SHAW

B ecause social change generally occurs through the coordinated efforts of many people, it requires that we become more skilled in working and communicating with others toward the achievement of goals. Near the end of World War II, President Franklin Delano Roosevelt recognized the importance of this when he said, "We are faced with the preeminent fact that, if civilization is to survive, we must cultivate the science of human relationships—the ability of all peoples, of all kinds, to live together and work together in the same world, at peace."[1] Communication skills can be very important in determining the results of a group's efforts. Several researchers have found that the way team members communicate with one another helps determine the overall effectiveness of the team.[2]

Effective communication involves presenting our views and listening to others in a way that fosters empathy. Active citizenship is as much learning how to listen with empathy, especially to those who disagree with us, as it is learning how to voice our beliefs. Sociologist Todd Gitlin argues that this type of listening often takes place precisely when we enter "that difficult, rigged, sometimes impassable territory where arguments are made, points weighted, counters considered, contradictions faced, and where honest disputants have to consider the possibility of learning something that might change their minds."[3]

Communication is the method with which we interact with others. In the healthiest communities, people find a way to engage in dialogue. They talk through important issues. In contrast, communities that fail to improve do so largely because of an absence of healthy dialogue. This kind of social health, illustrated by effective groups and communities, is interrelated with physical health. Dr. Janice Kiecolt-Glaser and Dr. Ronald Glaser have studied immune systems and found that people who routinely

OBJECTIVES

After studying this chapter, you should be able to:

- Identify the steps in the communication process
- Recognize crucial conversations
- Compare typical compromise with synergistic compromise
- Use the NVC model in a conversation
- Assess your motivating factors
- Identify team structure, stages, and roles
- Understand how to negotiate
- Identify the principles of sending e-mail
- Define groupthink

failed in conversations had far weaker immune systems than those who found a way to resolve them well.[4]

The stresses and pressures most people experience have rapidly increased in pace with our changing world. This charged atmosphere makes it important that we nourish our relationships and develop teamwork tools and skills, and the enhanced capacity to find synergistic solutions to problems.

This chapter focuses on human relationships in two specific areas integral to creating change and interacting in effective groups and communities: communication and teamwork.

BASICS OF COMMUNICATION

The word *communication* is derived from the same Latin root, *communis*, as is the word *communion*, which implies mutual participation. For communication to take place, whereby information is shared, the mutual participation of two or more parties is necessary. Even with active, mutual participation, however, there may at times be a gap in the communication process between what someone intends to communicate and what is actually heard.

In the childhood game "Telephone," a child starts with a message that is whispered sequentially down a line of successive children until the last child receives the message and announces aloud what is invariably a different message from the original. Because each of us hears and considers information though our own set of intellectual, emotional, and physical filters, what is intended can differ from what is received.

Communication Model

Communication is best understood as a system in which a sender and a receiver interact. This system comprises different parts, including programming, intention, method, reception, and feedback. It is an interactive process in which each person reacts simultaneously to all of the variables that affect the interaction.

Programming

Communication begins with who we are. We each have a family history, an ethnic and cultural background, educational experiences, and other characteristics that have played a role in creating our mental and behavioral patterns. What we have experienced in our lives shapes the expectations and assumptions we bring to any communication. We may see or hear what we expect rather than what was intended by the sender of the communication, and we may tune out what doesn't fit our preconceptions.

Self-awareness helps us decide whether our past conditioning and present influences are in alignment with who we choose to be and what we want to create in the world. For instance, if we choose to expect the best from others, we may experience more positive communication.

Intention

Effective communication involves having a clear purpose. We are much more apt to successfully transmit our message, and to avoid distracting the receiver with irrelevant information, if we think through our intentions before communicating. Without this intention, we may say things we don't mean or share information that is counterproductive to creating empathy, compassion, or clarity.

Before we speak, we can choose to consider what we want to say and what we want to achieve by saying it. We can choose to have our words and actions reflect the person we most want to be.

Method

After we have considered our intention, we select a method of communication that may take the form of a personal meeting, a telephone call, a meeting involving others, formal speech, a written letter, e-mail, voice mail, a sticky note, a chat room, or a video or telephone conference.

In choosing an appropriate method, consider what will support you in communicating a clear message and how it will be best received. For instance, if you fear that you might be intimidated, get emotional, or lose your train of thought, you might choose to write down your remarks. However, if your communication is likely to lead to compromise, you might choose to meet in person or talk on the phone.

Reception

After some preparation, we produce something that a receiver can experience. At this point, the communication becomes mutually participative. The outcome of the communication is now a collaboration between the sender and the receiver.

Feedback

After we present our message, the process of effective communication continues with the solicitation of feedback. We examine the outcome to ensure that our intended message matches what our audience interpreted and that it resulted in what we intended. We may ask the individual or group to repeat what we've said, or we may ask questions to check for mutual understanding. An outcome that matches our intentions is successful communication. An unexpected outcome means that we may need to reevaluate and continue the process by examining our programming or revisiting our intention and choice of method.

MAKING IT HAPPEN

MARSHALL ROSENBERG AND THE NONVIOLENT COMMUNICATION MODEL

Marshall Rosenberg, the developer of the formal nonviolent communication model known as NVC, uses the technique to help bring understanding and peace to areas of extreme conflict in the world. He was presenting NVC in a mosque at Deheisha Refugee Camp in Bethlehem to about 170 Palestinian Moslem men. Attitudes toward Americans at that time were unfavorable. As he was speaking, he noticed a wave of muffled commotion fluttering through the audience. "They're whispering that you are American!" his translator alerted, just as a man in the audience leapt to his feet. Facing him squarely, he hollered at the top of his lungs, "Murderer!" Immediately, a dozen other voices joined him in chorus: "Assassin!" "Child-killer!" "Murderer!"

Rosenberg turned his focus to what the first man was feeling and needing. On the way into the refugee camp, he had seen several empty U.S. tear gas canisters that had been shot into the camp the night before. He knew that the refugees harbored a lot of anger toward the United States for supplying tear gas and other weapons to Israel.

Rosenberg addressed the man who had called him a murderer:

Rosenberg: Are you angry because you would like my government to use its resources differently? [He didn't know whether this guess was correct, but what was critical was his sincere effort to connect with the man's feelings and needs.]

Man: You're right I'm angry! You think we need tear gas? We need sewers, not your tear gas! We need housing! We need to have our own country!

Rosenberg: So you're furious and would appreciate some support in improving your living conditions and gaining political independence?

Man: Do you know what it's like to live here for 27 years the way I have with my family—children and all? Have you got the faintest idea what that's been like for us?

Rosenberg: Sounds like you're feeling very desperate and you're wondering whether I or anybody else can really understand what it's like to be living under these conditions.

Man: You want to understand? Tell me, do you have children? Do they go to school? Do they have playgrounds? My son is sick! He plays in open sewage! His classroom has no books! Have you seen a school that has no books?

Rosenberg: I hear how painful it is for you to raise your children here; you'd like me to know that what you want is what all parents want for their children—a good education, an opportunity to play and grow in a healthy environment, and so forth.

Their dialogue continued, with Rosenberg listening to the man's feelings and needs for nearly 20 more minutes. Once the man felt understood, he was able to hear Rosenberg explain his purpose for being at the camp. An hour later, the same man who had called him a murderer was inviting him to his home for a Ramadan (Muslim observance) dinner.

Adapted from *Nonviolent Communication: A Language of Compassion* by Marshall Rosenberg. Encinitas: PuddleDancer Press, 1999.

Types of Communication

Verbal Communication

Verbal communication is the expression of something in words or language, whether spoken, written, or thought.

Virtual communication. **Virtual communication** is a form of verbal communication that is prevalent in our society today and has had significant social effects.

Jody Williams received the Nobel Peace Prize in 1997 for her work on banning land mines. She faced great opposition from governments around the world, but she organized 1,000 human rights and arm control groups on six continents. When asked about this accomplishment, she said her secret weapon was e-mail. Through this new technology, opponents of land mines had a direct, global impact that would have been unthinkable previously. Individuals, both those with great intentions and those with sinister motives, can now individually effect change on a massive scale.

The two categories of virtual communication are:

- **Synchronous communication**, which takes place at the same time—real-time interaction. This includes telephone and video conferencing, electronic display (whiteboard), and chatting.
- **Asynchronous communication**, which takes place at different times—delayed interaction. This includes e-mail, voice mail, group calendars and schedules, bulletin boards and Web pages, and file sharing.

Synchronous communication— virtual communication taking place at the same time

Asynchronous communication— virtual communication with delayed interaction

A study by Lisa Tidwell and Joseph Walther investigated how much and how quickly people reveal information about themselves and the overall impressions people make of one another when using the computer to communicate. They found that people reveal much more information online than they would in a face-to-face interaction and even develop more socially rich relationships than people who interact face to face.[5] Developing relationships with others may take longer using virtual communication, but it does occur.

Using e-mail for messages, however, can hinder understanding. It may contribute to greater polarization of opinions; group members may take more extreme positions when putting information in writing than when communicating orally.[6]

Nonverbal Communication

Nonverbal communication is communication that does not rely on written or spoken words. This includes body posture and movement, eye contact, facial expression, seating arrangement, spatial relationships, personal appearance, response time, and tone of voice.

As I grow older, I pay less attention to what people say: I just watch what they do.

ANDREW CARNEGIE

We also send messages with our actions. For instance, the people with whom we spend time, what we spend our money on, how we care for our health, and how we care for others are all ways in which we communicate nonverbally.

Nonverbal communication also includes internal conversations and thoughts. Our internal thought processes create emotion and energy. Even when we don't give voice to these feelings, they may influence others around us.

Self-Awareness and Communication

The **Johari window** is a simple model that can give insight into how communication works. The premise behind this model is that some things are known by us, some by others, and some by both. As shown, the window gives us four selves: the open, the hidden, the blind, and the unknown.

Open self	Blind self
Hidden self	Unknown self

The open self. The open self includes all of the information, behaviors, attitudes, feelings, desires, motivations, and ideas that we know about ourselves and that others know about us. The types of information may vary from name, color of skin, and sex, to age, political affiliations, and the car we drive. The smaller this quadrant (the less we and others know), the poorer communication we have with others. Communication depends on how much we open up ourselves to others. If we do not allow others to know us, we keep the open self small, making communication between them and us more difficult.

The hidden self. The hidden self consists of all that you know of yourself and of others but which you keep to yourself. This area includes all of your successfully kept secrets about yourself and others. In relating with others, some people are overdisclosers. They keep nothing hidden about themselves or others. They do not distinguish to whom such information should or should not be disclosed, nor do they distinguish what types of information should be disclosed. The underdisclosers tell nothing. They talk about you, but not about themselves. Most people fall in between—they are selective disclosers.

The blind self. The blind self represents all of the things that others know about us but that we do not know. Such things may include the rather insignificant habit of saying "you know" or raising your eyebrows when you get angry, or it may include having a body odor or a defense mechanism. Some people have a very large blind self and are oblivious to their own faults and virtues. When we open ourselves to other people and accept their feedback, we move information from our blind selves to our open selves.

The unknown self. The unknown self represents truths that exist but that neither we nor others know. Sometimes the unknown is revealed through temporary changes induced by drugs, hypnosis, dreams, or projective tests.

EFFECTING CHANGE THROUGH COMMUNICATION

The nature of change is social. It occurs through the interaction and communication between people. Margaret Wheatley, author of *Turning to One Another*, describes this process:

> Nothing has given me more hope recently than to observe how simple conversations give birth to actions that can change lives and restore our faith in the future. There is no more powerful way to initiate significant social change than to start a conversation. When a group of people discover that they share a common concern, that's when the process of change begins. To make important changes in our communities, our society, our lives, we just have to find a few others who care about the same thing we do. Together we can figure out the first step, then the second, then the next. Gradually, we grow powerful. But we don't have to start with power, only with passion.[7]

Eric Utne, founder of the *Utne Reader*, describes the value of communication to active citizenship: "Communication is an activity, a process. It is based on people's experiences, relationships and common learning. The only way to have a truly informed citizenry, an active and motivated citizenry, is through live, personal discussion and debate."[8]

Important communication concerns for active citizenship include understanding and empathy, crucial conversations, negotiation, and nonviolent communication.

Understanding and Empathy

The most effective communications are based on mutual understanding. By giving of ourselves through listening to others and endeavoring to understand their point of view, we create the conditions of empathy. Peter Senge describes this process: "We are used to thinking of compassion as an emotional state, based on our concern for one another. But it is also grounded in a level of awareness. In my experience, as people see more of the systems within which they operate, as they understand more clearly the pressures influencing one another, they naturally develop more compassion and empathy."[9]

The more we are aware of others' points of view, the more we are able to approach communication in a way that will be meaningful for them. Empathy is distinct from sympathy. Sympathy implies agreement, whereas empathy does not require that we

Listening with an open mind involves being willing to change our minds in response to new ideas and viewpoints.

agree with another. Empathy is a process of understanding how another thinks and feels. The Dalai Lama states: "This technique involves the capacity to temporarily suspend insisting on your own viewpoint but rather to look from the other person's perspective, to imagine what would be the situation if you were in his shoes, how you would deal with this. This helps you develop an awareness and respect for another's feelings, which is an important factor in reducing conflicts and problems with other people."[10]

Being willing to temporarily suspend our point of view is difficult because it puts us in a vulnerable position. We are necessarily opening ourselves to thinking differently about an issue or scenario. This is when strong identification with our values and personal mission is very important. We may find that we can think differently about an issue while remaining true to our integrity, or we may be able to understand and respect a differing viewpoint while remaining unchanged in our own viewpoint.

Listen with an Open Mind

One of the greatest assets to understanding and empathy is the capacity to listen openly. To actively engage in listening is to be willing to be disturbed, to allow our beliefs to be challenged. Most of us weren't trained to admit what we don't know. Rather, we are encouraged to sound certain and confident.

Sometimes we hesitate to listen for what's different because we don't want to change. We're comfortable with our lives and opinions, and if we were to listen to anyone who raised questions, we might feel compelled to engage in new activities and ways of thinking. But, in striving to understand the world in its complexity, it is helpful to spend more time in a state of uncertainty, though it can be difficult to give up the positions, beliefs, and explanations that lie at the heart of our personal identities. As we allow ourselves to be curious about what others believe, we may acknowledge that their way of interpreting the world might serve us.

Many people tend to stop listening when they hear something they don't like. If you rush to judgment about what you hear, your focus turns to your own programming rather than to the content of the speaker's message. Some people also prejudge a speaker before hearing anything he or she says. If you do not like a person, or if you have preconceived notions about a speaker's ideas or cultural background, you may decide that his or her words have little value before you listen to them. Work to recognize and control your judgments. Being aware of what you tend to judge will help you recognize your blocks and hear important messages and information.

Crucial Conversations

Crucial conversations— conversations that are challenging, frustrating, frightening, or annoying, and, at the same time, could have an impact on the quality of your life

Kerry Patterson et al., in their book *Crucial Conversations*, call conversations that are challenging, frustrating, frightening, or annoying, and, at the same time, could have an impact on the quality of your life, **crucial conversations**. These conversations are usually about tough issues. You may experience physical responses when involved in one of these conversations, such as tightening of the stomach. Look for such clues that you are involved in a crucial conversation.

While it's common to want to back away from such situations, if you know how to master these types of conversations, you can engage in them in ways that benefit all of the participants. Leadership expert Stephen Covey believes that by employing several critical communication skills, it is possible to create a level of "mutual understanding and creative synergy" among people that moves them to agree and act on effective solutions [11]

Make People Feel Safe

People feel safe to share creative ideas or confrontational information when they trust that they won't be attacked or humiliated. When people feel unsafe, they generally either attack defensively or withdraw into silence.[12] A common response is to react in kind, and the communication continues in a downward spiral.

> *He that complies against his will is of his own opinion still.*
>
> **SAMUEL BUTLER**

People who fear the consequences of speaking up generally remain silent. Approximately 98,000 hospital deaths occur each year because of human error. In part, this is because many health-care professionals are afraid to call attention to the errors of their superiors.[13]

Many times, people can receive tough feedback without becoming defensive if they believe that the giver of the feedback is authentically trying to help or support. We can look for the opportunities in such challenging conversations for greater awareness and movement toward our goals.

Ways to create or restore safety include the following:

- Notice when others are withdrawing or attacking.
- Watch the impact you are having on others and how you are feeling in response to others.
- Make others feel respected by recognizing your own weaknesses.
- Consider others' points of view, and look for common interests.

Take Responsibility for Feelings

We all choose our response to the actions and words of others. No one can "make" us feel a certain way; how we feel is always our choice.

In responding to the actions and words of others, it helps to use "I" statements as opposed to "you" statements.

- **"I" statement:** "I feel stressed out and rushed when you give me a deadline for tasks to accomplish without checking with me about my schedule."
- **"You" statement:** "You make me feel stressed out and rushed when you give me a deadline for tasks to accomplish without checking with me about my schedule."

Accept Criticism

Understanding what criticism is and is not can help us avoid getting caught in the downward spiral of communication gone awry. So often we take critiques personally. It may seem that they're not about what we've done, but about us. However, you are not your project or your grade. When criticism is well-intentioned, it does not mean that you failed. It means you can do things to get better. Sometimes, however, people may not mean well. They may have the intention of putting others down. Psychologist Lonnie Barbach describes this person as the "put down" individual: "People who feel insecure and inadequate often get into the right/wrong battle. They try to raise their self-image by being 'right.' One way of proving oneself right is to make the other person wrong. Making someone feel wrong has an alienating effect."[14]

Critically evaluate the criticism you receive. Is it from a source that you respect? Is the criticism itself valid? Is any part of it valid? Can you use this to make changes for the better? If so, then set an intention to do that. If not, then let the criticism go. In the midst of an adversarial conversation, know that you can evaluate the criticism at a later time and that you don't have to respond immediately. Be aware of your physical responses, and remember to focus on the general context of the conversation.

Negotiation

Negotiations occur in many areas of life. We may negotiate a job offer, a relationship, or a treaty among nations. Usually in negotiation, each side takes a position, argues for it, and makes concessions to reach a compromise.

Evaluate What You Want

To negotiate, begin with understanding what you want. Negotiation leads back to our values and our understanding of those values. In the heat of a discussion about an important issue, you may feel intense emotions welling, and you may be tempted to give in or act in an uncharacteristic way. You may feel the need to avoid embarrassment, to win, to be right, or to punish others. As you make an effort to discover your underlying motive, you may conclude that you're pushing harder to win an argument than it merits.

To allow for healthy dialogue to occur in these instances, it is helpful to step away from the interaction and look at your wants in light of the following questions. To avoid this situation, it helps to frame your desires in advance, before you enter into a conversation that is likely to require negotiation. Ask yourself:

- What do I really want for myself?
- What do I really want for others?
- What do I really want for this relationship?

Based on your answers, ask yourself how you would behave if you wanted those outcomes.

Also, evaluate what you don't want to occur for yourself, for others, or for the relationship. Put this evaluation into the following framework:

I want _____ for myself, others, and the relationship AND I don't want _____.

This will give you a foundation for discovering a solution.

Foster Cooperation and Dialogue

Negotiation can be viewed in light of the **typical compromise**, whereby the parties each have their wants and meet as close to the middle as they can get. It can also be seen as a **synergistic compromise**, whereby both parties compromise and achieve the optimum solution for both. (See Figure 6.1.)

Synergistic compromise involves the understanding that our thoughts are interconnected and that, through an intentional dialogue, we can collaborate toward greater understanding and levels of creativity than we could access alone. A group may explore complex issues by involving people with many different points of view. But for dialogue to occur, the participants must agree to share their points of view while suspending their assumptions that their own viewpoints are correct. Participants agree that the possibility exists for an "alternate way" that none of them had previously considered.

Peter Senge, author of *The Fifth Discipline*, says: "We are not trying to win in a dialogue. We all win if we are doing it right."[15] This type of communication is as much about a collective learning process as it about the sharing of information.

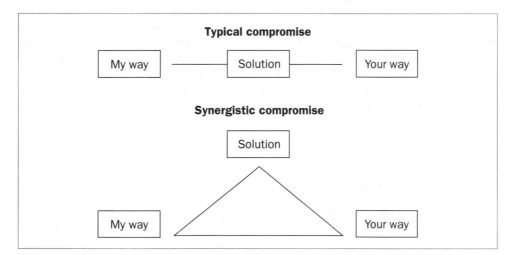

FIGURE 6.1 *Compromise Types*

The basic conditions necessary for dialogue are as follows:

- All participants suspend assumptions. Participants are aware of their programming and opinions and agree to be open to other ways of thinking.
- All participants regard one another as colleagues, peers, or equals. Every participant's input is considered equally.
- There must be a facilitator who makes sure the process is maintained and respected.[16]

Nonviolent Communication

Engaging ourselves as active citizens and agents of social change may involve communicating with others who have viewpoints contrary to our own or who are acting in ways that we find damaging or negative to society. In these situations, it can be a challenge to avoid communicating with aggression, judgment, or withdrawal.

> I don't get angry. I grow a tumor.
>
> **WOODY ALLEN**

We can choose to communicate in a way that provides healing and compassion, rather than further separation and negativity. Martin Luther King Jr., a well-known proponent of nonviolence, said: "Nonviolence is the answer to the crucial political and moral questions of our time; the need for man to overcome oppression and violence without resorting to oppression and violence. Man must evolve for all human conflict a method which rejects revenge, aggression and retaliation. The foundation of such a method is love."[17]

Clinical psychologist Marshall B. Rosenberg, founder and director of educational services for the Center for Nonviolent Communication, developed a methodology called nonviolent communication (or NVC) to provide peaceful alternatives to the violence he was experiencing in the 1960s. He first used NVC in federally funded projects to provide mediation and communication skills training during the 1960s and has continued to use it in initiating worldwide peace programs in war-torn regions.[18]

Rosenberg says: "While we may not consider the way we talk to be violent, our words often lead to hurt and pain, whether for ourselves or others."[19] The NVC method is a guide for transforming how we speak to, and hear, others. It focuses on observing how we are feeling and what needs we are trying to meet, as well as observing the feelings and needs of others.

Team—
a coordinated group of individuals organized to work together to achieve a specific, common goal

EFFECTIVE TEAMS

A **team** is a coordinated group of individuals organized to work together to achieve a specific, common goal. A team can be a community group, part of a business organization, or even a family. The terms *team* and *group* are used interchangeably in this section.

ACTION!

NVC Model

Following are the steps in the NVC model. After reading these, develop a hypothetical conversation between two people using this model.

1. **Observation.**   Observe what others are saying or doing that you like or dislike, without judgment or evaluation. For instance, saying someone is disrespectful is a judgment. But observing that someone didn't call you when they were going to be late is an observation of a behavior.

2. **Feeling.**   State how you feel when you observe this action (for example, happy, frustrated, angry, or afraid). You might say, "I feel hopeless" instead of "I feel like a failure." "Hopeless" is a feeling while "like a failure" is a judgment.

3. **Needs.**   State what personal needs are connected to the feelings you have identified. Use this structure: "I feel _____ (emotion) because I (describe the need or desire)."

4. **Request.**   State what you want from other(s) that would make your life more rewarding. State what you specifically want, as opposed to what you don't want. For example, say, "Would you be willing to drive at the speed limit?" instead of "Would you stop going so fast?"

Sample communication (from one staff member to another):
"When I can't find my scissors or my tape and I find them on your desk, I feel annoyed because I need to know where my things are and not use my time looking for them. Would you be willing to ask me before borrowing my things, or leave me a note as to their whereabouts if I am not around?"

Working in teams offers many advantages. Teams usually make better decisions than individuals working alone because the members' diverse backgrounds, experiences, and resources contribute to the group's ability to generate creative solutions.[20] With more information available, the group is more likely to discuss all sides of an issue and is more likely to arrive at a better solution.[21]

An example of group strength is illustrated in Daniel Goleman's book *Working with Emotional Intelligence*. In the example, students studied and worked in groups during a class, and, for the final exam, each took a portion of the exam individually. After turning in their individual answers, they were given an additional set of questions to answer as a group. Results from hundreds of groups tested showed that 97 percent of the time the group scores were higher than those of the highest-scoring individuals.[22]

Working in groups also presents challenges. Group members may pressure others to conform to the majority opinion. Working with others can involve compromise, negotiation, and handling conflict. Most people do not like conflict, and group members may agree on a bad solution rather than confront potential conflict. Social psychologist Irving Janis has labeled this phenomenon **groupthink**.[23] One individual may also dominate the group, or some group members may rely too much on others to get the job done. Working in a team may be time consuming as well, if the group process is ineffective. With an understanding of the nature of teams, we can help make our teams effective.

Groupthink—
group members agree in order to avoid conflict

Why People Join Groups

One of the primary ways to meet our different needs is to interact with others. Understanding others helps us work with them and communicate with them to accomplish goals.

People also join groups to meet interpersonal needs and goals or because of interpersonal or group attraction. Many theories have been developed over the past several decades to explain human needs and motivation.

No member of a crew is praised for the rugged individuality of his rowing.

RALPH WALDO EMERSON

Hierarchy of needs—
Maslow's view that human needs are prioritized and satisfied in a certain order

Maslow's Hierarchy of Needs

Psychologist and sociologist Abraham Maslow developed his hierarchical approach to motivation in the 1950s. According to Maslow, all people have needs that can be categorized into five sequential levels (see Figure 6.2):

- **Physiological needs**—food, water, sleep, and shelter
- **Safety needs**—security and protection
- **Social needs**—friendship with others, giving and receiving affection, participating in an exchange of ideas and activities
- **Esteem needs**—desire to feel positive about ourselves, recognition, status
- **Self-actualization needs**—desire to develop one's full potential

Maslow's theory suggests that people are motivated to satisfy the lower needs first and then, in order of sequence, each of the higher needs. Clay Alderfer modified Maslow's theory a bit in the 1970s, saying that people could work to satisfy more than one set of needs at a time. Maslow lists the human need for community as third in his hierarchy of needs. We have a profound social need for belonging and acceptance, or being part of a group or family. We are driven to satisfy this need and create the support of community in our lives.

Choice Theory

William Glasser's Choice Theory states that people are driven by four psychological needs: (1) the need to belong, (2) the need for power (or empowerment),

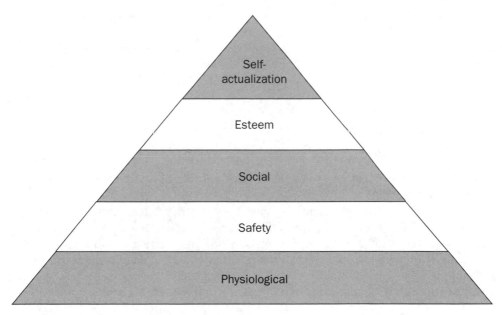

FIGURE 6.2 *Maslow's Hierarchy of Needs* (*Source:* MOTIVATION AND PERSONALITY 3/E by Maslow, © 1997. Adapted by permission of Pearson Education, Inc., Upper Saddle River, NJ.)

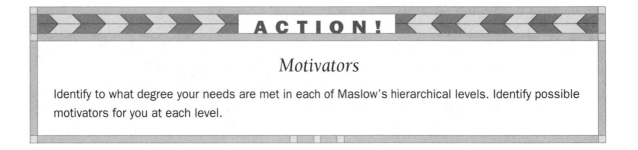

ACTION!

Motivators

Identify to what degree your needs are met in each of Maslow's hierarchical levels. Identify possible motivators for you at each level.

(3) the need for freedom, and (4) the need for fun. According to this theory, people are the most important factors in our lives because interacting with others is the primary way our needs are met. People help us to feel as if we belong and to feel that we are important and capable, that we can make good choices, and that we can have fun in life.

What these and other motivation theories tell us is that different people have different motivators and that we are driven to belong to groups. We are generally attracted to individuals and groups that are similar to us. A danger in forming groups with people too similar to us, however, is that the group may be too homogenous to approach a complex task effectively. Research on classroom groups has found that by a two-to-one margin, students reported that their worst experiences occurred in groups they had chosen themselves and that their best experiences occurred in groups to which the professor had assigned them.[24]

Team Structure and Roles

Teams come in many shapes and sizes, and the team experience will vary depending on the team's structure and the roles and personalities of the individual team members. Teams may be highly structured, in which everyone's role on the team is predetermined and clearly defined, or unstructured, in which roles emerge as the team members begin to interact.

Individuals can play numerous roles as part of a team. Formal, or assigned, roles can include team leader, note-taker, or scheduler. Informal roles develop during group interactions and generally fall into two categories: roles that focus on the accomplishment of tasks, the **task specialist role**, and roles that focus on the social and emotional needs of the group or the team's working relationships, the **socioemotional role**. The most effective teams will have members that fulfill roles in both of these areas and not all in one or the other.[25]

Team members in the *task specialist* role will frequently engage in the following behaviors:

- **Initiater:** proposing solutions and opinions to team members
- **Information seeker:** asking for task-relevant facts
- **Summarizer:** pulling ideas together
- **Energizer:** stimulating a team into action when interest falls

Team members in the *socioemotional role* frequently perform the following functions:

- **Encourager:** praising others; encouraging others' ideas
- **Harmonizer:** reconciles group conflicts; reduces tension
- **Compromiser:** compromises opinions to go along with the group

You will likely play different roles in different groups. No matter what role you play, your participation, as well as the participation of each participant, is valuable and important to the success of the overall team. The value of the team is the combination of talents, knowledge, and insights that each person brings.

Team Development Stages

After a team has been created, the team will go through distinct stages in order to be productive. The stages may last a short time, depending on the team members and task deadline. In the worst case, a team may never move into the final performance stage. Understanding this process will help the team members move more quickly through the stages and face the inevitable challenges that typically arise in group situations. When a team is formed initially, the team members will get to know one another, establish their roles and norms, divide up the work, and understand their task. The following stages generally occur in sequence.[26]

Forming

In the **forming** stage, members break the ice and test one another for friendship opportunities and task orientation. Uncertainty runs high during this stage as members wonder what the ground rules are, what their duties will be, and if they will fit in. Social discussions should be encouraged.

Storming

During the **storming** stage, individual personalities emerge and people become more assertive in clarifying their roles and what is expected of them. Conflict and disagreement may occur, possibly over the team's tasks and goals or individual positions within the team. Several members may jockey for the leadership role. This stage is unavoidable, though if a team stays here for long, it may never achieve its goals. Members should propose ideas, disagree with one another, and work through the uncertainties. During this stage, the members should concentrate on defining the group's goals.

Norming

During the **norming** stage, conflict is resolved. A consensus emerges as to who the leader is and the other members' roles. Members develop a sense of cohesion and belonging. This stage typically lasts a short time.

Performing

During the **performing** stage, the major emphasis is on accomplishing the assigned tasks. Problems will be solved, and most discussion will be based around the goals. Members who have mainly played the socioemotional role will now contribute to the task.

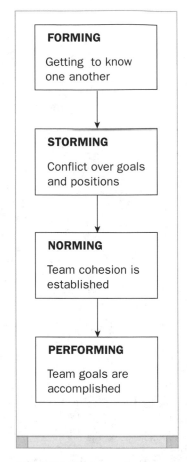

FIGURE 6.3 *Group Stages*

Characteristics of an Effective Team

Effective teams get results and provide satisfaction and meaning to their members. Characteristics of effective teams include the following:

The team has developed well-defined, elevating goals. The goals of effective teams are usually very specific and measurable. They are also larger goals than any individual could accomplish and are considered by the group to be elevating and important.[27]

All for one and one for all!

■

ALEXANDER DUMAS, *THE THREE MUSKETEERS*

Team members have clearly defined roles and responsibilities. Research has shown that people who belong to an effective team usually have a clear sense of their particular role or function in the team as well as of the function of other members.[28]

Team members share leadership. All members of the team are encouraged to take responsibility and give input into decision making and direction of the team. Open exchange occurs among members as equal colleagues or peers.[29]

Team members prioritize collaboration and partnership. The team develops a collective vision and strategies and methods, rather than carrying out directives or acting on preformed opinions. Team members are encouraged to express their own ideas. Mutual inspiration is valued above competition.

Disorder is considered as a source of creativity. Effective teams look for opportunities in fluctuations, chaos, and disturbances, and use these opportunities for growth and learning.[30]

Team members are competent. Team members need to know not only what their assignment is but also how to perform their job.[31] Members need adequate training in teamwork, problem solving, and job skills in addition to being open, straightforward, supportive, action-oriented, and friendly.[32]

The team applies standards of excellence. A team is more likely to achieve its potential if it establishes high standards.

Team members give one another useful feedback. One way team members support one another in developing excellent performance is to give and receive feedback effectively. Studies show that when people are deprived of information regarding their performance, their self-confidence suffers as much as when they are criticized.[33] Constructive feedback, on the other hand, is an effective way to support positive growth.

Giving useful feedback requires using empathy, sensitivity, and self-awareness. Although we may not know what most helps someone else, we can share what works and doesn't work for us.

Some tips for giving and receiving feedback include the following:

Giving Feedback to Others

- Ask if they want feedback before offering any.
- Be mindful of the timing and environment. Avoid emotional situations and giving feedback in public settings.
- Find something positive about their performance, and comment on it.
- Give others a chance to give feedback to themselves.
- Be specific—refer to specific scenarios or situations.
- Suggest how you believe they could be more effective.

Receiving Feedback from Others

- Let others know if the timing or location doesn't work for you.
- Assume the givers have your best interests at heart.
- Be open and nondefensive.
- Ask questions if you are unclear. Strive for understanding.
- Ask how you could have done things differently.

Virtual Teams

Galvanizing support generally requires that we work with people from all over the country and world. Logistics require that we do much of this work virtually.

Using technology in teams, however, does not automatically improve group effectiveness and success. According to Jaclyn Kostner, author of *Bionic eTeamwork*, people have to "use technology to extend their human reach, their human touch and their human capability." Kostner believes that virtual teams cannot reach their full potential until the human side is satisfied.[34]

Martha Haywood suggests using the following four principles to manage virtual team member interaction:

1. Develop standards for availability and acknowledgment.

2. Replace context. Physical, social, and situational context can be lost in virtual communication. Be sure to include more about background, feelings, and opinions, and making sure the background and all related conversations and events on the issues are conveyed to other team members.

3. Use synchronous communication. It helps people feel more connected.

4. Prioritize communication. Agree whether high communication items should be sent via e-mail, fax, mail, phone call, or voice mail, and then use that medium for only high-priority communication items.[35]

Suggestions for e-mail include the following:

- Be specific about what you want from people.
- Send messages only to people who need to be included.
- Use urgent and important tags sparingly.
- Ask for confirmation of receipt of messages.
- If sending a document for comments, note how you would like each participant to annotate a document (underline, bold, color, caps).
- Include the entire message "chain" so all recipients have the context for the message.
- Write expressively to help build relationships.

Suggestions for voice mail include the following:

- State your name and telephone number at the beginning and ending of the message.
- Keep the message short and to the point.

- Be clear about what you need and when.
- State whether the person should respond.
- Think about who will receive it if you are sending a broadcast message.

Suggestions for telephone conferences include the following:

- Limit participation to no more than eight speaking participants.
- Have a clear agenda and purpose.
- Before you speak, state who you are.
- The facilitator should summarize the conversation at the end of the meeting.

Studies suggest that the benefit of video conferencing is not necessarily in the outcome of the immediate conversation but in its contribution to building relationships. Suggestions for video conferences include the following:

- Monitor your gestures and facial expressions.
- Don't interrupt.
- Dress for the camera. Don't wear white; avoid patterns, shiny jewelry, or other fashion accents.
- Become familiar with the technology beforehand.

Principles of Effective Meetings

Meetings can undermine teams if they are not structured well and do not respect the time commitment of the team members. Planning and facilitating effective meetings helps bring out the creativity of team members, achieves a satisfying purpose, and keeps teams motivated. Following is a list of the primary meeting "sins," presented by Roger Mosvick and Robert Nelson in *We've Got to Start Meeting Like This!*:

- Getting off subject
- No goals or agenda
- Too lengthy
- Poor or inadequate preparation
- Inconclusive
- Disorganized
- Ineffective leadership/lack of control
- Irrelevance of information discussed
- Time wasted during meetings
- Starting late
- Individuals dominate/aggrandize discussion

Well-planned meetings help to best use the resources of team members.

- Rambling, redundant, or digressive discussion
- No follow-up actions
- No premeeting orientation
- Canceled or postponed meetings[36]

To make a meeting effective:

- **Determine the meeting goal.** Only meet when a specific purpose requires it, and identify what you would like to have accomplished at the end.
- **Organize the agenda.** Group members need to have the freedom to express ideas. If there is too much structure, it is not a meeting. However, if too little structure exists, minimal attention is given to the time it takes to get the job done. The middle of the meeting should be reserved for the most challenging issues.

Leader	Participants
Before the Meeting	
1. Define the objective.	1. Block the time on your schedule.
2. Select the participants.	2. Confirm your attendance.
3. Make preliminary contact with the participants to confirm availability.	3. Define your role.
4. Schedule a meeting room, and arrange for equipment and refreshments.	4. Determine what the leader needs from you.
5. Prepare the agenda.	5. Suggest other participants.
6. Invite the participants and distribute the agenda.	6. Know the objective.
7. Make a final check of meeting room.	7. Know when and where to meet.
	8. Do any required homework.
During the Meeting	
1. Start promptly.	1. Listen and participate.
2. Follow the agenda.	2. Be open-minded/receptive.
3. Manage the use of time.	3. Stay on the agenda and subject.

(continued)

During the Meeting *(continued)*

4. Limit/control the discussion.	4. Limit or avoid side conversations and distractions.
5. Elicit participation.	5. Ask questions to ensure understanding.
6. Help resolve conflicts.	6. Take notes on your action items.
7. Clarify any action to be taken.	
8. Summarize the results.	

After the Meeting

1. Restore the room and return any equipment.	1. Evaluate the meeting.
2. Evaluate your effectiveness as the meeting leader.	2. Review the memorandum summarizing the discussion.
3. Send out meeting evaluations.	3. Brief others as appropriate.
4. Distribute a memorandum of the discussion.	4. Take any action you agreed to.
5. Take any action you agreed to.	5. Follow up on action items.
6. Follow up on any action items.	

Applications

1 Get in groups of five to seven people, and choose an issue or aspect of your community, or of society as a whole, that is important to you. Your topic should be something that you want more of or that you support (for example, a clean environment, peace, a close-knit community, a good educational system).

- Go around the circle, allowing each person to answer the question "When and how in your life have you experienced _____?" (Decide on the number of minutes each person has; have someone keep time and let the person know when time is up.) It is important that each person speak and be listened to attentively by the group.
- Go around the circle, and have each person answer the question "What in our community/society is undermining _____?" This is an opportunity for each person to think critically about the systems and policies in place that may be unjust or ineffective, as well as what could work better.

- Go around the circle, and have each person respond to the question "What small thing can you do this week to create more _____ in your life?" This helps participants to consider what they can personally do to make a difference.
    Describe how the process of communication worked in the group. Describe the structure and the team roles everyone played.

Using the NVC model in your conversation, discuss a controversial topic with a classmate who has a different viewpoint. Describe how the use of this model affected your conversation.

IDENTIFY EFFECTIVE TEAMS. Look through newspapers from the past few weeks, and identify an example of a group or team that has accomplished some result. Describe the accomplishment and, using the characteristics of effective teams listed in this chapter, describe the group or team.

Participate in a form of virtual communication, and describe the communication. What other types of virtual communication have you used or could you use to communicate more effectively?

Discuss the signals you get when you are in a crucial conversation.

QUIZ

1. Communication:
    A. needs at least two people to participate in order to occur
    B. can be viewed as a system in which a sender and receiver interact
    C. is usually effective only if we have a clear purpose
    D. all of the above

2. Synchronous communication
    A. is a category of virtual communication that takes place at the same time
    B. is a category of virtual communication that takes place at different times
    C. can be a type of nonverbal communication that occurs without awareness
    D. B and C

3. Crucial conversations are:
    A. conversations that provide a lot of information
    B. conversations that occur while we are very busy
    C. challenging and could have an impact on the quality of your life
    D. make people feel safe

4. In negotiation, it helps to:
   A. evaluate what you want
   B. push hard to win
   C. keep your point of view somewhat guarded
   D. keep in mind what you want and do not sway from it

5. Nonviolent communication:
   A. was championed by Ghandi and Martin Luther King Jr.
   B. is usually ineffective in high-stress situations
   C. requires acceptance by all parties in order to be effective
   D. all of the above

6. The group member who proposes solutions is acting in the:
   A. socioemotional role
   B. information seeker role
   C. initiater role
   D. energizer role

7. When sending e-mail, it is important to:
   A. write in a businesslike tone
   B. use urgent tags frequently
   C. be specific about what you want
   D. leave out the rest of the message chain

8. Effective teams:
   A. have well-defined goals
   B. share leadership
   C. consider disorder a source of creativity
   D. all of the above

9. Before a meeting:
   A. the leader should define the objective
   B. the participants should prepare an agenda
   C. the leader should define the roles of the participants
   D. all of the above

10. Groupthink:
    A. is defined as group members who agree in order to avoid conflict
    B. helps when project deadlines are approaching
    C. often leads to better solutions
    D. none of the above

ENDNOTES

1. Quoted in Williamson, Marianne, ed. *IMAGINE: What America Could Be in the 21st Century*. Daybreak, 2000.

2. Salazar, A. J. "Ambiguity and Communication Effects on Small Group Decision Making Performance," *Human Communication Research* 23 (1996): 155–92; L. Hirokawa, D. DeGooyer, and K. Valde. "Using Narratives to Study Task Group Effectiveness," *Small Group Research* 31 (2000): 573–91; Jarboe, S. "Procedures for Enhancing Group Decision Making," in R. Y. Hirokaway and M. S. Poole, eds., *Communication and Group Decision Making*, Thousand Oaks, Calif.: Sage, 1996.

3. Gitlin, Todd. *The Twilight of Common Dreams*. New York: Owl Books, 1995.

4. Quoted in Ornish, Dean. *Love and Survival: The Healing Power of Intimacy*. New York: HarperCollins 1998.

5. Walther, J. B., and Lisa Tidwell. "When Is Mediated Communication not Interpersonal?" In K. Galvin and P. Cooper, *Making Connections*. Los Angeles: Roxbury Press, 1996.

6. Scott, C. R. "Communication Technology and Group Communication." In L. Frey, ed., *The Handbook of Group Communication Theory and Research*, pp. 432–72. Thousand Oaks, Calif.: Sage, 1999.

7. Wheatley, Margaret. *Turning to One Another*. San Francisco: Berrett-Koehler, 2002.

8. Quoted in Williamson, ed., *IMAGINE*.

9. Senge, Peter. *The Fifth Discipline: The Art and Practice of the Learning Organization*. New York: Currency Doubleday, 1990.

10. His Holiness the Dalai Lama and Howard Cutler. *The Art of Happiness*. New York: Riverhead Books, 1998.

11. Quoted in Patterson, Kerry, Joseph Grenny, Ron McMillan, and Al Switzler. *Crucial Conversations*. New York: McGraw-Hill, 2002.

12. Patterson et al., *Crucial Conversations*.

13. Simon, Hermann. "Hidden Champions: Lessons from 500 of the World's Best Unknown Companies." Boston: Harvard Business School Press, 1996.

14. Barbach, Lonnie. *For Each Other*. New York: Anchor Press/Doubleday, 1982.

15. Senge, *The Fifth Discipline*.

16. Senge, *The Fifth Discipline*.

17. Quoted in Larson, Jeanne, and Madge Micheels-Cyrus, eds. *Seeds of Peace*. Philadelphia: New Society Publishers, 1987.

18. Rosenberg, Marshall B. *Nonviolent Communication: A Language of Compassion*. Encinitas, Calif.: PuddleDancer Press, 1999.

19. Rosenberg, *Nonviolent Communication*.

20. Stewart, D. D. "Stereotypes, Negativity Bias, and the Discussion of Unshared Information in Decision-Making Groups," *Small Group Research* 29 (1998): 643–68.

21. Cooke, J., and N. Kernaghan. "Estimating the Difference Between Group Versus Individual Performance on Problem-Solving Tasks," *Group & Organization Studies* 12 (September 1987): 319–42.

22. Goleman, Daniel. *Working with Emotional Intelligence*. New York: Bantam Books, 1998.

23. Janis, Irving L. "Groupthink," *Psychology Today* 5 (November 1971): 43–46, 74–76.

24. Feichtner, Susan Brown, and Elain Actis Davis. "Why Some Groups Fail: A Survey of Students' Experiences with Learning Groups." In Anne Goodsell, Michelle Maher, and Vincent Tinto, *Collaborative Learning: A Sourcebook for Higher Education*, pp. 59–67. University Park, Pa.: National Center on Postsecondary Teaching, Learning and Assessment, 1997.

25. Prince, George. "Recognizing Genuine Teamwork," *Supervisory Management*, April

1989, 25–36; Benne, K. D., and P. Sheats, "Functional Roles of Group Members," *Journal of Social Issues*, 4 (1948): 41–49; and Bales, R. F., *SYMOLOG Case Study Kit*, New York: Free Press, 1980.

26. Jewel, Linda, and H. Joseph Reitz. *Group Effectiveness in Organizations*. Glenview, Ill.: Scott Foresman, 1981.

27. Larson, Carl E., and Frank M. J. La Fasto. *Teamwork: What Must Go Right/What Can Go Wrong*. Thousand Oaks, Calif.: Sage, 1989.

28. Devine, D. J., L. D. Clayton, J. L. Philips, B. B. Dunford, and S. B. Melner. "Teams in Organizations: Prevalence, Characteristics and Effectiveness," *Small Group Research* 30 (1999): 678–711.

29. Kenny, Robert. "Spread Leadership," *YES! Magazine*, Fall 1999, 39.

30. Wheatley, Margaret. *Leadership and the New Science*. San Francisco: Berrett-Koehler, 1994.

31. Devine, D. J., et al., "Teams in Organizations."

32. LaFasto, Frank, and Carl Larson. *When Teams Work Best*. Thousand Oaks, Calif.: Sage, 2001.

33. Goleman, *Working with Emotional Intelligence*.

34. Kostner, Jaclyn. *Bionic eTeamwork*. Chicago; Ill.: Dearborn Trade Publishing, 2001.

35. Haywood, Martha. *Managing Virtual Teams: Practical Techniques for High Technology Project Managers*. Norwood, Mass.: Artech House, 1998.

36. Mosvick, Roger K., and Robert B. Nelson. *We've Got to Start Meeting Like This!* Glenview, Ill.: Scott Foresman, 1987.

Leadership and Change

Never doubt that a small group of thoughtful, committed citizens can change the world; indeed, it's the only thing that ever has. —MARGARET MEAD

Active citizenship is about creating desirable change in our society. Significant accomplishments and changes that occur in this realm are usually the result of extended periods of learning and a diligent pursuit of a vision in the face of adversity. Historical and present-day examples teach us how seemingly impossible changes result from efforts of ordinary people who learn to act despite their initial feelings of resistance. To facilitate change, it helps to know how to best deal with the continual change we face in our lives. Once we know how to master change, we can move beyond the fear of it, create an atmosphere for it, and actively become a leader for it.

People who achieve great things may not be the ones we would naturally label "leaders." However, on closer inspection, they usually possess qualities common to leaders and agents of change. These qualities include having a great dream or vision; an extraordinary ability to remain committed to, and in action toward, that vision; and the ability to mobilize others to action toward the vision. This kind of commitment by common citizens, such as those seen in the abolitionist, women's suffrage, populist, and environmental movements, created significant change for generations to come.

Bill Shore, author of *The Cathedral Within*, defines leadership as "getting people to a place they would not get to on their own."[1] Leaders have the ability to catalyze change within themselves and others; a common denominator of leaders is the acceptance and stewardship of change. Leaders foster change and create an environment where change is the norm.

Perseverance toward a vision of change in our lives or in the world is very difficult for one individual to sustain alone. We benefit from a community of support around us to encourage us. In addition, any transformation we make, whether in our personal lives or in our communities, involves mastering resistance and creating an environment for

OBJECTIVES

After studying this chapter, you should be able to:

- Evaluate the characteristics of change you have experienced

- Identify strategies to use for change depending on problem-solving style

- Recommend how to create a good environment for change

- Discuss systems thinking in relation to change

- Evaluate leadership qualities in current leaders

- Understand positive aspects of chaos regarding change

change. How individuals manage change and develop the leadership to create change in service to their communities is the focus of this chapter.

CHANGE THROUGH SYSTEMS THINKING

Macrosystem—
large institutions and bureaucracies

Bringing about social change often requires that we work with the large institutions and bureaucracies that currently organize and influence our lives. These large organizations, governments, economic institutions, and multinational corporations are often referred to as **macrosystems**. It takes a long time for a macrosystem to become established and entrenched in society. The process of change takes place through a system.

The Individual and the System

Systems thinking is an idea that has grown out of the emergence of quantum theory. All organizations and institutions are groups of people who operate within a system. Because of the innate complexity of systems, our traditional ways of thinking about cause and effect and our relationship to systems are often ineffective. We tend to isolate ourselves as perceivers, or judgers, when we observe systems, without taking into account our inherent participation in the system.

When we try to pick out anything by itself, we find it hitched to everything else in the universe.

JOHN MUIR

Our understanding of an individual's ability to cause change within systems has expanded with the emergence of quantum physics and the ability to measure the interconnectedness of things. A quantum understanding of change is based on the fundamental connection between the agent of change and that which is being acted upon. This understanding came about with the experimental confirmation of Bell's Theorem in 1975, illustrating that one distinct particle could be affected by disturbances to another particle. The implications of this theorem for human systems is that as we change, we simultaneously effect change because we are, in essence, inseparable from others, our surroundings, and our political and social systems. When we view the world as a system, it is easier to see that by working on ourselves, we are also working on the system.

Quantum physicist David Bohm believes that personal transformation is the key to societal transformation.[2] By building self-awareness, continually challenging our guiding beliefs and mental programming, and seeking to understand the beliefs and systems that guide our world, we participate significantly as forces of change to the system.

Parts of the Whole

We may have a tendency to look at problems that are actually symptoms of a greater problem. As Peter Senge, author of *The Fifth Discipline*, says: "We tend to

738 DAYS—ONE AT A TIME

On December 10, 1997, Julia "Butterfly" Hill climbed high into a 1,000-year-old redwood tree she named "Luna" to live on a small platform. Her aim was to prevent the destruction of the tree by making it impossible to destroy the tree without killing her. Julia was one of hundreds of activists working to save the Headwaters Forest through a variety of nonviolent tactics. As the months went by, celebrities with ties to the environmental movement came to visit her, politicians talked with her on her mobile phone, and the world's media camped at the base of the tree to see what was going on and document her life and her mission. In her tree, she knew fear and cold. Lumber company employees harassed her and tried to scare her down. Conservative commentators belittled her action. Meanwhile, timber company officials were negotiating with state and federal departments to come up with a lasting solution to what was increasingly being seen as a crisis.

On December 18, 1999, 738 days after she climbed up the tree, she climbed down. She had struck a deal with Pacific Lumber/Maxxam Corporation to spare Luna and create a three-acre buffer zone; in the process, she brought world awareness to the destruction of redwood forests. Julia recalls:

I think back to my first night preparing to sit in the ancient redwood, Luna. I was so jumpy, I felt like my nerves were about to burst out of my skin. I was excited, scared, nervous, and curious all at the same time. When my hiking mates and I stood at the bottom of the mountain, looking way up to its top where tree-sit awaited, an overwhelming feeling came over me: "I can't do this. This is way too much for me. What was I thinking?" I took a deep breath and said to myself, "One foot at a time, Julia. That is the way to climb a mountain." I share this story because I know that as human beings we all reach points of feeling completely overwhelmed. Too much information. Too much to do. How can I, as one person, make a difference in all this? People often come up to me and say, "Julia, I can't believe what you did. I could never do that." I always feel my face breaking into a grin because you could not have paid me enough money that first night to make me believe that I would be able to go through such an intense experience. If I had seen what was coming, I would have gone screaming in the opposite direction. But you see, luckily for us, life does not show us everything at once. I did not live 738 days in a tree all at once, crammed into one moment; it was one day at a time, one moment at a time. For me, it became an incredible "one breath, one prayer at a time." I know from experiences that when our hearts open, we can find the courage to do things that our minds will always say are too difficult. It all begins with the first step—do the right thing because it is the right thing to do, regardless of the outcome.

I believe we all have our own personal tree to sit in. For me, this means committing to waking up every morning and asking, "What can I do today to make the world a better place?" One breath at a time, one step at a time, we will find we have crossed our own perceived boundaries and limitations. Our lasting legacy is the life we leave behind. *One does make the difference. You are the one.* And you are not alone. Together, as one, we are changing the world.

Adapted from Julia Butterfly Hill, *One Makes the Difference,* San Francisco: HarperSanFrancisco, 2002. Photo by Shaun Walker/ OtterMedia.com focus on snapshots of isolated parts of the system, and wonder why our deepest problems never seem to get solved."[3] Quantum theory tells us that it is not possible for the whole to benefit if any part is compromised. We may realize that it is in our self-interest to improve society, because we are inseparable from that society. Social scientist Wendell Berry states that a good solution "should not enrich one person by the distress or impoverishment of another. In an organism, what is good for one part is good for another."[4]

Using traditional cause-and-effect thinking, we tend to focus on parts of a system or problem. To increase crop production, for instance, it may seem to make sense to use genetically modified organisms. With more crop yield, we can feed more people. Using systems thinking, however, we consider the whole and consider the interconnectedness of all actions and occurrences. For example, if the genetic change to a crop affects the insects who feed on the crop, and thus interrupts the balance of the ecosystem, there may be adverse consequences in addition to a higher crop yield. Through the action of any part, transformative change to the whole may occur.[5] While it may be difficult to anticipate the unpredictable consequences of actions, by using systems thinking we can understand that all of our actions have the ability to influence our communities and society.

Continual Learning

Changing the way we think about ourselves in relationship to complex and changing systems requires that we be constantly learning. To create better systems, we need to be able to think differently about new possibilities.

> People with a high level of personal mastery live in a continual learning mode. They never 'arrive.'
>
> **PETER SENGE**

With the implications of personal transformation to effect societal transformation, our ability to change personally becomes an important asset to leading and managing change. Peter Vaill, author of *Learning as a Way of Being: Strategies for Survival in a World of Permanent White Water*, asserts that constant learning is the foremost requirement of leadership.[6]

Warren Bennis, leadership specialist, says: "The point is not to become a leader. The point is to become yourself, to use yourself completely—all your skills, gifts, and energies—in order to make your vision manifest."[7] As we become more effective human beings, we in turn become more effective citizens serving society with the best that we have to offer. We become more effective leaders through opening ourselves to new information, new ways of thinking, new ways of relating to others, and a basic willingness to be a beginner.

LEADERSHIP QUALITIES

Leadership is the process of influencing others' actions to achieve a mutual goal. Leadership works best not as a function of age, position, job title, or individual characteristic but as a characteristic of a community. This distributed leadership calls on everyone associated to take responsibility and to assume leadership roles in areas in which they are competent and skilled. This view of leadership reaches far beyond including the voices and opinions of others. Nor is it a matter of assigning tasks to people. Implicit in this kind of leadership is the development by a community of a joint mission, shared purpose, and common culture.

> **Leadership—**
> the process of influencing others' actions to achieve a mutual goal

Vision

Having a clear vision of where you are going and why is a basic ingredient of leadership. It is compelling enough to inspire persistence in the face of setback and even failures.

In addition to possessing vision, leaders must be able to speak this vision in a way that motivates others to take action toward it. President John F. Kennedy provided a powerful example of presenting a vision of the future that inspired others to create the possibility of walking on the moon: "When President Kennedy announced his moonwalk vision, there were no solutions to the problems that lay ahead: Congressional approval, appropriation of funds, technological breakthroughs, and the rejuvenation of the National Aeronautics and Space Administration (NASA), which had languished for years in the internecine rivalry of Army versus Navy versus Air Force rocket programs."[8]

Even in the face of these problems and the lack of precedent for such an accomplishment, Kennedy's vision inspired others to create a reality that previously did not exist.

For a vision to inspire others, it must first inspire us. A personally inspiring vision can:

- Express our personal values and goals
- Be one we feel passionately about
- Engage our imagination and creativity
- Motivate us in the face of adversity
- Create value for others

As Kennedy's example illustrates, a vision can be a dream about something that seems unlikely to occur, but if it inspires the passion and commitment of enough others, anything is possible. City Year, a youth civic action program, echoes this idea in its training handbook: "Make all decisions with your ultimate vision in mind, but do not be worried if you cannot answer every question when you are just starting out. If the vision is strong and coherent, the path, to a degree, reveals itself."[9]

Effective Speaking Skills

The **EPIC** format is a useful speaking tool to enroll others in acting on an idea. EPIC consists of four steps: engage, propose, illustrate, and call to action.

Engage

The process begins by drawing someone into a conversation by engaging his interest or curiosity in what you have to say. You may share a startling fact, a statement of a problem, a question, or an acknowledgment of something they are already interested in that relates in some way to what you have to share. Some examples follow:

- "Did you know that fewer than half of those able to vote in our country actually vote?"
- "Would you be willing to listen to an idea I have for a project that I think will fulfill your goals for this course in a creative way?"
- "I know that as a PTA member you are really committed to our kids' education. Can I share with you something that I learned recently?"

Propose

In this step, you state the solution or initiative that you are proposing. It helps to be direct and bold. Simply state what you are proposing without giving background information or justification for it. For example:

- "I am putting together a voter registration table at the next college fair at the local community college. There are 150 students expected, and I'd like to get at least 40 of them to register to vote. I'd love to have your help, if you're interested."
- "I'd like to volunteer at the local homeless shelter during this semester and write a final paper on my suggestions for improvement to their services."
- "Congress is proposing to change the administration of the Head Start program, which serves low-income children and their families with a successful preschool program. The proposed changes will compromise the quality of the program, as well as the funding for it. I would like to put together an action group of teachers and students who would call and write our Members of Congress to oppose these changes."

Illustrate

At this point, it is important to use examples and stories to make your proposal vivid to the listener. Use stories that bring out your passion for your proposal. Check for understanding and interest from the listener as you speak. Ask questions to find out if what you are sharing is interesting to your listener. Try another illustration if the response is not enthusiastic at first. For example:

- "Do you remember the local election last year when we voted on whether or not to approve a recycling facility for the county? I recently found out that that facility passed by only 50 votes. Just think what 40 or 50 additional voters can mean to important issues."

- "A friend of mine who graduated from Jenson University volunteered at a shelter for battered women for a Women's Studies class she was taking. She wrote a paper on her experience that she also submitted to the director of the shelter. The director ended up using some of her suggestions for improvements to the program, such as starting a child care facility that not only brought in income for the center but trained clients of the center for jobs in child care."
- "Last year, a group of citizens in Tucson, Arizona, got their Representative to visit a local Head Start program. He wasn't a supporter of the program initially, but after seeing what a difference it was making in his district, he agreed to support a bill to increase funding for it."

Call to Action

Finally, make one or more powerful requests of your listener. Assume the person could be as committed as you are and just needs to be asked. However, it is important to allow the person to decline your request without pressuring her to accept. For example:

- "Would you consider spending the morning of August 12 encouraging young people to register to vote?"
- "Would you help me find a way to join my passion for solutions to homeless issues with the learning goals you have for this course?"
- "I'd like to work with you to create a citizen action group here in Winetka to see if we can't get our Members of Congress to support quality preschool education through support of Head Start. Would you help me gather a group of five or six people for an initial meeting about this?"

Evaluation and Reflection

Evaluation and reflection are integral parts of leadership. When we allow ourselves time to evaluate our process, consider the lessons we are presented with, and reassess the values that guide our efforts, we help ensure that our efforts overcome any internal or external resistance we encounter.

Change—
to become different, to pass from one phase to another, to undergo transformation and transition

CHARACTERISTICS OF CHANGE

According to *Webster's Dictionary*, **change** is "to become different, to pass from one phase to another, to undergo transformation and transition." The stress or unfamiliarity we experience with rapid change is similar to how we feel when we play a game we have never played before. Understanding the process of change, and anticipating the characteristics that are usually present when change occurs, will help you navigate through it.

Chaos

Peter Vaill describes the state of continual change that we are in as "permanent white water" in which chaos, tumult, and surprise are the norm.

The process of finding solutions to the larger social problems in the world today—such as globalization, war and violent unrest, and environmental challenges—is inherently complex, and change often appears chaotic and unpredictable.

Often stress is experienced in response to the sometimes unpredictable and chaotic nature of the change process. **Stress** refers to any environmental or social demand that creates a state of tension, threat, or disruption. Many people have a strong preference for order, continuity, and predictability in their lives—the more change that is required, the more stress that may be experienced.

Understanding that the natural occurrence of a chaotic process has eventually brought about order and equilibrium in many instances of evolution can help in dealing with chaos. Looking at it in this light, we can find the disorderliness of chaos to be valuable. We can benefit from the growth available through chaos, growth that is unavailable when things are static. We can accept chaos as an opportunity for creativity and for the emergence of new and better ideas and policies. In addition, other stress management techniques, such as meditation, can help us approach chaos more effectively.

Confusion is a word we have invented for an order which is not yet understood.

HENRY MILLER

Stress—
any environmental demand that creates a state of tension or threat

Resistance

Resistance to change takes a high toll in emotional energy and can lead to frustration and defeat. People experience resistance to change in differing levels. Some welcome change, most go along with it, and a few will fiercely avoid it.

Where we fall along this continuum depends on the specific nature of the change and how much uncertainty, fear, clarity, or joy the prospect of change entails. The widely agreed upon formula that applies to change resistance is 30/45/25—that is, 30 percent will welcome a change; the majority, about 45 percent of those affected, will go along quietly, assuming that the nature and need for change is explained; and the rest, the other 25 percent, will battle to defeat change.[10]

Common sources of resistance include the following:

One cannot step into the same river twice.

OLD ARABIC SAYING

Habit. Actions or beliefs that we repeat over time can become ingrained or programmed patterns. People may resist change because they are seeking the path of least resistance, which is maintaining the status quo. Even when a habit has negative effects on our life, we are slow to change because we are accustomed to the behavior.

Fear. We may fear the known consequences of a change. Our fear and apprehension about the possible unknown consequences may produce resistance.

Loss. Some people experience resistance because with most change comes loss. Even when change is for the better, leaving the old behind is still a loss that usually instills some sense of grief.

Overcoming Resistance

Awareness of our core values can help us reduce resistance and remain committed to what is most important. The support and collaboration of others will also help us overcome our resistance, as will dealing openly and honestly with any feelings of fear and loss. When the resistance comes from those around you, the following methods can be used.

Communicate. Resistance often comes from a lack of understanding of others. When something is important enough to us to engage in the change process, we may make the mistake of assuming that others understand why. We have gone through the process of gaining knowledge, formulating opinions, and deciding upon action. However, those around us, even those close to us, may not have gone through that same process. To help diffuse others' possible experience of stress in reaction to our intended change, we can share our knowledge of the benefits of that change. We can do our best to educate others about why we see a need for change and then listen and respond to their ideas and concerns. Trying to see the situation from the viewpoint of others helps in anticipating and managing resistance.

> *We do not describe the world we see, but we see the world we describe.*
>
> **JOE JAWORSKI**

Once you've identified the reason for change, then a strategy and set of goals must be developed and communicated to give people a clear view of the changes needed, the compelling reasons for the change, the strategy for making the changes, and the ultimate goal or end state.

Facilitate and support. As simple as it sounds, asking for help is one of the best ways to overcome the resistance of others and engage their support of your efforts. When we ask for help, we are acknowledging the gifts that others have to offer us, and in turn, we allow others to experience our value of their gifts. And, we almost always need more help and support than we expect.

Involve others. Resistance often increases when others feel left out or excluded from our efforts. Whenever possible, offer others the opportunity to join in your citizenship efforts. Let them know what kind of participation is available to them in the initiatives in which you are involved. It is also helpful to be clear about what kind of commitment you would request from them. Supportive relationships and group interaction build a sense of belonging, cohesiveness, and community, which increase learning.[11]

ACTION!

Thinking About Change

Identify a time when you were resistant to change. What caused the resistance, and what did you learn from the process? What would you do next time you faced resistance or chaos in the change process?

PROBLEM-SOLVING STYLES

Although all people deal with change differently, we experience some things in common depending on our predominant problem-solving style. Understanding your style may help you determine what you need during change. The four basic styles, mentioned earlier in this text, are as follows.

Technician

People with this style are best at finding practical uses for ideas and theories and would rather deal with technical tasks and problems than with social and interpersonal issues.

Change is generally viewed as an interesting puzzle by technicians. They look forward to solving the puzzle as long as the goal seems logical and they have data to support the need for change. They may need time to work through it and gather information, study data, draw conclusions, and review findings before a change is made. They will usually be logical and methodical in reviewing and initiating change plans. When not provided sufficient time and information, technicians are likely to resist change. If they can't justify the change based on logic and data, they will not want to alter familiar routines.

If you are working with technicians to initiate change, supply them with useful information and allow them to contribute to creating logical and methodical steps for initiating a plan. Give them time to study the data and determine how change can best be achieved.

If you are a technician, it helps to analyze and rationalize the change. Actively participate in planning for the change. See it as your duty to create plans that will bring about a new stability. Help establish the new routines. Stay logical and focused rather than dwelling on the past. Expect more changes, and see change as part of an ongoing process.

Diplomat

People with this style are best at viewing concrete situations from many different points of view. The first question diplomats usually ask is "How does everyone feel?" They work best when they know the group, team, or other family members support one another and champion change efforts. They need communication to know that others are comfortable. When changes happen that adversely affect others, they see the change as a crisis.

If you are working with diplomats in a change process, tell them up front how change will affect others. Data, rules, and plans won't matter if people's feelings aren't considered as well.

If you are a diplomat, support others and be sensitive to their feelings. Help provide closure for yourself and others. Look to the new projects you will begin rather than focusing on what you are leaving behind. Initiate celebrations for small successes leading to end results.

Strategist

People with this style are best at understanding a wide range of information and putting it into concise, logical forms. Strategists usually find it more important that a theory have logical soundness than practical value.

Strategists more easily see the big picture associated with change. They need to be involved in defining what needs to change and why. They are visionaries who help others see the future result. They will be highly committed to achieving the goals they have helped plan. When not part of the change process, strategists can resist change and convince others to resist as well. If the plans don't have a clear benefit or fit into the overall vision, strategists won't commit. Feelings, not data, will sway the strategist.

If you work with strategists in change, ask for their opinions and ideas. Allow them to lead brainstorming sessions to generate innovative plans. Give them the opportunity to envision the benefits of end results.

If you are a strategist, constantly search for the growth experiences and new opportunities that will inspire you to accept change. Find ways that you can help lead change and motivate others to see the new vision.

Activist

People with this style enjoy carrying out plans and involving themselves in new and challenging experiences. Their tendency may be to act on "gut" feelings rather than on logical analysis.

Activists may need to know exactly how change will affect them and what they are responsible for during change. They aren't comfortable with "just going with the flow."

During change, if you are working with activists, give them clear targets to achieve. They don't necessarily need the details behind the need for change—they want to be able to take charge and create results.

If you are an activist, look to the new goals rather than past achievements. Look at all the angles, and discover what needs to get done. Be decisive and able to make difficult decisions to help initiate change.

> *Management is doing things right;*
>
> *leadership is doing the right things.*
>
> **PETER DRUCKER**

CREATING THE ENVIRONMENT FOR CHANGE

One of the most distinguishing qualities of agents of change is their ability to remain committed to their goals and values in the face of adversity, which they may encounter either internally, in the form of negative mental and psychological patterns, or externally, as resistance from others. Effectiveness in creating change improves when you create a good environment in which change is likely.

Develop Conviction and Courage

We need courage to make changes. The word *courage* comes from the root *cuer*, which means "heart." The more we come from the heart, or believe in something, the more likely we are to have the courage to manifest it. A greater understanding of personal and societal issues aids us in developing the certainty necessary to act. Certainty, or conviction, can create a sense of urgency to create change. Conviction aids us when courage is necessary.

People own what they create.

MARGARET WHEATLEY

Robert F. Kennedy described this when he said: "Few are willing to brave the disapproval of their fellows, the censure of their colleagues, the wrath of their society. Moral courage is a rarer commodity than bravery in battle or great intelligence. Yet it is the one essential, vital quality for those who seek to change a world that yields most painfully to change."[12]

Develop an Attitude of Learned Optimism

When we accept that change is inevitable, we can choose our attitudes in the face of change and look at it as an opportunity. Deepening our awareness of our attitude allows us to choose behaviors that will empower our leadership and ability to create positive change. Some people have dedicated their lives to social activism, while others can barely find the motivation to make it to the voting booth on election day. People who are active citizens feel that what they are doing makes a difference, while those who are not motivated often feel that their actions are of little consequence.

Martin Seligman began studying optimism and pessimism in 1969. His research of the concept of learned optimism shows that the way people respond to outside threats and problems is determined by their beliefs.[13] People react in different ways to the same set of circumstances based on how they explain their situations to themselves. For example, depressed people have become convinced that the difficulties in their lives are permanent and a result of their personal failings. They believe there is nothing they can do to improve their situation, thus rationalizing or excusing their inaction. When we tell ourselves that social problems are so vast and complex that there is nothing we can do about them, and then excuse ourselves from acting, we are, in effect, socially depressed.

In contrast, optimistic people tell themselves a different story. They consider problems to be temporary and take action to change them. Action breeds confidence and further empowers people to confront new challenges.

Nurture Self-Esteem

Self-esteem is confidence in, and respect for, oneself. Our choice to see ourselves as valuable, capable of making a difference in the world, and worthy of respect is crucial to our ability to lead effective lives. Corrine McLaughlin and Gordon Davidson, authors of *Spiritual Politics: Changing the World from the Inside Out*, relate self-esteem to active citizenship: "Self-esteem builds faith in ourselves and our own innate capacities, and enhances our inclinations toward becoming constructive, life-affirming, responsible, and trustworthy citizens."[14]

Self-esteem— confidence in, and respect for, oneself

People with healthy self-esteem come from backgrounds that nurtured their sense of security, personal identity, belonging, purpose, and competence. Having these factors supported in our present circumstances continues to support our self-esteem, and the absence of them, or support of their negative counterparts, can compromise it. Low self-esteem can make it more difficult to sustain healthy relationships or achieve important goals. Studies show that at any stage of life, self-esteem can be nurtured and result in positive outcomes for individuals, and in turn, society.[15]

When our self-worth is firmly established within us, it doesn't matter what others think or do—they do not diminish our value of ourselves and our activities. In the arena of social change, where we encounter resistance and doubt, as we continue to build self-esteem we become better able to provide leadership toward personal and collective goals. Self-esteem also allows us to be comfortable relating to those of different race, gender, or age, which helps build a more collaborative democracy.

Take Action

Action reinforces empowerment. Planning an action strategy helps guide effective action. When our determination falters, remaining committed to taking the action we have planned can reactivate our enthusiasm.

Robert F. Kennedy spoke to the power of action to inspire hope and create change: "Each time a person stands up for an idea, or acts to improve the lot of others, or strikes out against injustice, [s]he sends forth a tiny ripple of hope, and crossing each other from a million different centers of energy and daring, those ripples build a current that can sweep down the mightiest walls of oppression and resistance."[16]

> *Bear in mind, if you are going to amount to anything, that your success does not depend upon the brilliance and the impetuosity with which you take hold, but upon the ever lasting and sanctified bull doggedness with which you hang on after you have taken hold.*
>
> **DR. A. B. MELDRUM**

Actions in Democratic Movements Through Time

Democratic movements—unlike interest groups, which compete in the political arena to serve their own interests—attempt to put into practice an alternative or reformed understanding of democracy oriented toward some conception of the public good. Such movements often use political action to persuade the broader public of the justness of their cause and the need for reform. As the chart in Figure 7.1 illustrates, many of our most cherished democratic practices in the United States have their origins in the actions of regular citizens who participated in such movements.

Persevere

Perseverance involves commitment, enthusiasm, and drive. It is a resolve that drives us forward and gives us strength when difficulties arise. Remaining clear and committed and in action toward change requires ongoing effort. Just as athletes build up their endurance in order to maintain effort over time, we can develop practices in our lives that support us in maintaining the endurance necessary for change. To persevere, we must have patience. The learning process can be slow and frustrating, with great leaps forward or insights occurring unpredictably.

Engage Others

One of the greatest challenges to remaining committed to change is our own unreliable human nature. This is due to the unpredictable nature of life, our changing personalities and moods, and the great challenge that it is to create social change. Leadership experts advise citizens to network with one another, connect with one another, learn to communicate, and distinguish common goals.[17]

Support Network

By surrounding ourselves with a community of friends and colleagues who remind us of our values and who call forth the best in us, we create an environment in which we can be more sure of following through on our best intentions and dreams.

> *If I am not for myself, who will be for me?*
>
> *And if I am only for myself, what am I?*
>
> RABBI HILLEL

We are often prey to the tendency to discourage ourselves without the support of community. The word *encouragement* means "with courage." Like-minded friends and associates who are committed to our best interests often put us in touch with our courage.

Collective Wisdom

Another benefit of working with others is the greater intellectual capacity of a group compared to that of an individual. Our potential for insight, creativity, and problem solving is greatly enhanced when we join with others toward a common goal. When individuals come together, each with their own combination of talent, experience, and passion, they can augment one another's gifts.

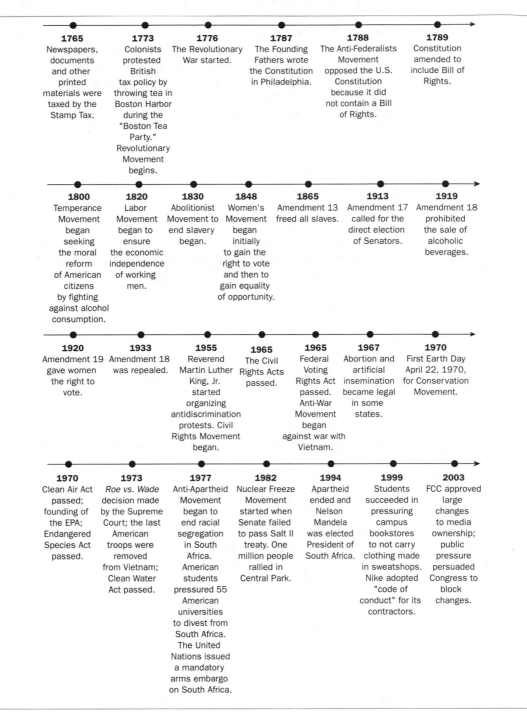

1765
Newspapers, documents and other printed materials were taxed by the Stamp Tax.

1773
Colonists protested British tax policy by throwing tea in Boston Harbor during the "Boston Tea Party." Revolutionary Movement begins.

1776
The Revolutionary War started.

1787
The Founding Fathers wrote the Constitution in Philadelphia.

1788
The Anti-Federalists Movement opposed the U.S. Constitution because it did not contain a Bill of Rights.

1789
Constitution amended to include Bill of Rights.

1800
Temperance Movement began seeking the moral reform of American citizens by fighting against alcohol consumption.

1820
Labor Movement began to ensure the economic independence of working men.

1830
Abolitionist Movement to end slavery began.

1848
Women's Movement began initially to gain the right to vote and then to gain equality of opportunity.

1865
Amendment 13 freed all slaves.

1913
Amendment 17 called for the direct election of Senators.

1919
Amendment 18 prohibited the sale of alcoholic beverages.

1920
Amendment 19 gave women the right to vote.

1933
Amendment 18 was repealed.

1955
Reverend Martin Luther King, Jr. started organizing antidiscrimination protests. Civil Rights Movement began.

1965
The Civil Rights Acts passed.

1965
Federal Voting Rights Act passed. Anti-War Movement began against war with Vietnam.

1967
Abortion and artificial insemination became legal in some states.

1970
First Earth Day April 22, 1970, for Conservation Movement.

1970
Clean Air Act passed; founding of the EPA; Endangered Species Act passed.

1973
Roe vs. Wade decision made by the Supreme Court; the last American troops were removed from Vietnam; Clean Water Act passed.

1977
Anti-Apartheid Movement began to end racial segregation in South Africa. American students pressured 55 American universities to divest from South Africa. The United Nations issued a mandatory arms embargo on South Africa.

1982
Nuclear Freeze Movement started when Senate failed to pass Salt II treaty. One million people rallied in Central Park.

1994
Apartheid ended and Nelson Mandela was elected President of South Africa.

1999
Students succeeded in pressuring campus bookstores to not carry clothing made in sweatshops. Nike adopted "code of conduct" for its contractors.

2003
FCC approved large changes to media ownership; public pressure persuaded Congress to block changes.

FIGURE 7.1 *Timeline of U.S. Social Change Movements (Compiled with assistance from Dr. William Niemi, associate professor of political science, Western State College, Gunnison, CO.)*

More and more businesses are using a collaborative model in their research and design, management, and other organizational processes. The director of a Xerox design facility shares: "Everything is done collaboratively, like everywhere in today's high-tech world. There are no lone geniuses anywhere . . . ideas don't come from a lone head, but from collaboration in a deep sense."[18] Groups working for social profit may use collaboration to enhance their effectiveness as well.

Civic Community

We can also engage with others by involving ourselves in our communities. *Civic community* refers to communities marked by the active participation in public affairs of citizens who remain trusting and respectful even when community difficulties arise.[19] Change efforts are more effective when civic community exists due to the connectedness and support within these communities. Civic community can be fostered by bringing members of diverse factions and ethnic and cultural groups together to participate in collaborative efforts that benefit the community.

Applications

1 Evaluate the leadership qualities of two current leaders.

2 Using a social issue important to you, discuss the implications of systems thinking. What does this mean in terms of your approach to effecting change concerning this issue?

3 What is your predominant problem-solving style? How might you best adapt to change based on this style?

4 Suggest ways that others you know can create a positive environment for change. How does that apply to your life?

QUIZ

1. A macrosystem is a:
   A. system of change
   B. a large institution or bureaucracy
   C. a mathematical equation
   D. a system with one determined leader

2. Systems thinking is an idea that grew out of which of the following theories?
   A. chaos
   B. structure
   C. complexity
   D. quantum

3. Leadership is defined as:
   A. the process of becoming a manager
   B. the process of influencing others to achieve a mutual goal
   C. the process of organizing resources
   D. the process of community involvement

4. EPIC stands for:
   A. encourage, present, include, consult
   B. engage, purpose, illustrate, call to action
   C. entertain, perform, initiate, conclude
   D. escape, pull out, improve, correlate

5. What can chaos best be described as?
   A. a state of continual change that is best to avoid at all costs
   B. a state of continual change that is a natural process providing growth opportunities
   C. an abnormal state
   D. none of the above

6. Resistance commonly stems from all of the following *except:*
   A. habit
   B. fear
   C. loss
   D. communication

7. A technician might deal with change by:
   A. taking time to gather information and study it
   B. jumping into it
   C. communicating with others
   D. looking at the big picture

8. To create an environment for change, it helps to:
   A. nurture self-esteem
   B. take action
   C. use a support network
   D. all of the above

9. ☐ True or False: Optimists generally experience only positive events in their lives.

10. ☐ True or False: Some people experience little resistance to change.

ENDNOTES

1. Shore, Bill. *The Cathedral Within*. New York: Random House, 1999.

2. The Round Table Gathering, audiotapes. American Leadership Forum, Stanford, 1993.

3. Senge, Peter. *The Fifth Discipline*. New York: Currency Doubleday, 1994.

4. Berry, Wendell. "Solving for Pattern." In *The Gift of Good Land: Further Essays Cultural and Agricultural*. San Francisco: North Point, 1981.

5. Wheatley, Margaret. *Leadership and the New Science*. San Francisco: Berrett-Koehler, 1992.

6. Vaill, Peter. *Learning as a Way of Being: Strategies for Survival in a World of Permanent White Water*. San Francisco: Jossey-Bass, 1996.

7. Bennis, Warren. *On Becoming a Leader*. New York: Addison-Wesley, 1989.

8. Pascale, Richard T., Mark Millemann, and Linda Gioja. *Surfing the Edge of Chaos*. New York: Random House, 2000.

9. Shore, *The Cathedral Within*.

10. *Ardell Wellness Report* 43:1 (Summer 1996).

11. Cohen, E. G. *Talking and Working Together: Status, Interaction and Learning*. In *The Social Context of Instruction*, edited by P. L Peterson, L. R. Wilkinson, and M. Hallihan. New York: Academic Press, 1984.

12. Quoted in McLaughlin, Corrine, and Gordon Davidson. *Spiritual Politics: Changing the World from the Inside Out*. New York: Ballantine Books, 1994.

13. Seligman, Martin. *Learned Optimism: How to Change Your Mind and Your Life*. New York: Pocket Books, 1998.

14. McLaughlin and Davidson, *Spiritual Politics*.

15. McLaughlin and Davidson, *Spiritual Politics*.

16. Quoted in McLaughlin and Davidson, *Spiritual Politics*.

17. Shore, *The Cathedral Within*.

18. Quoted in Goleman, Daniel. *Working with Emotional Intelligence*. New York: Bantam Books, 1998.

19. Chrislip, David, and Carl Larson. *Collaborative Leadership*. San Francisco: Jossey-Bass, 1994.

American Democracy and Government Structure

We aren't passengers on spaceship Earth; we're the crew. We aren't residents on this planet; we're citizens. The difference in both cases is responsibility. —RUSTY SCHWEICKART, APOLLO ASTRONAUT

D emocracy comes from the Greek roots *demos*, or "of the people," and *kratia*, or "government." At its most fundamental level, democracy requires the participation of the people. It is our responsibility to "get in the driver's seat" of our democracy and use it as the tool it was intended to be to effect change and improve the quality of life in our country and our world.

With an understanding of the basic principles upon which our democracy stands comes the power needed to engage in the process. By knowing the rules of the game, we can use them to create and maintain the "life, liberty and pursuit of happiness" that our Constitution affirms for all citizens. When we know the rules, we can act and call "foul" when they are broken. By working through our democratic system, we have the ability to organize and create the society we want.

James Grant, former executive director of UNICEF, says: "Each of the great social achievements of recent decades has come about not because of government proclamations, but because people organized, made demands and made it good politics for governments to respond. It is the political will of the people that makes and sustains the political will of governments."[1]

Speaking of citizen participation when accepting the 2003 America's Future Lifetime Leadership Award, Bill Moyers had this to say:

Ideas have power . . . But ideas need legs. The eight-hour day, the minimum wage, the conservation of natural resources and the protection of our air, water, and land, women's rights and civil rights, free trade unions, Social Security and a civil service based on merit—all these were launched as citizen's movements and won the endorsement of the political class only after long struggles and in the face of bitter opposition and sneering attacks. It's just a fact: Democracy doesn't work

OBJECTIVES

After studying this chapter, you should be able to:

- Differentiate the purposes of the founding documents

- Discuss how the U.S. government maintains separation of powers

- Determine how the electoral college functions

- Evaluate the importance of primary elections

- Know the process a recent bill went through to become a law

- Compare advocacy and lobbying

- Research and contact Members of Congress

175

without citizen activism and participation, starting at the community. Trickle down politics doesn't work much better than trickle down economics. It's also a fact that civilization happens because we don't leave things to other people. What's right and good doesn't come naturally. You have to stand up and fight for it—as if the cause depends on you, because it does. Allow yourself that conceit—believe that the flame of democracy will never go out as long as there's one candle in your hand.[2]

The tools presented in this chapter can help you understand the rules of democracy and use them to bring about your desired change. In this chapter, we will review the philosophy of democracy as stated in the founding documents of our government, the structure of our government, and the process for powerfully participating in advocacy and lobbying.

FOUNDING DOCUMENTS

The Declaration of Independence

Declaration of Independence—the formal declaration of the separation and freedom of the 13 American colonies from England, written mainly by Thomas Jefferson

On July 4, 1776, in Philadelphia, Pennsylvania, the Second Continental Congress approved the **Declaration of Independence.** It was the formal declaration of the separation and freedom of the 13 American colonies from England and was written almost entirely by Thomas Jefferson, who was considered the most eloquent writer among the drafting committee. The other committee members were John Adams, Benjamin Franklin, Roger Sherman, and Robert B. Livingston.

Jefferson based the Declaration and the right of the colonies to revolt on the theory of English philosopher John Locke. Locke's theory of man's "natural rights" included property, life, and liberty. Since the government of King George III denied the colonists these natural rights, Jefferson held that it was their duty to gain the rights for themselves. Jefferson substituted the pursuit of "happiness" for "property" as an inalienable right and maintained that happiness was the result of civic responsibility and participation.

The original draft included a passionate criticism of the slave trade. However, since South Carolina and Georgia wanted to keep importing slaves, the Continental Congress decided to strike that passage from the document.[3]

The Constitution

Articles of Confederation—the first organizing documents that governed the loose union of separate states

The first organizing documents that governed the loose union of separate states were called the **Articles of Confederation.** Each of the states was represented in a Congress. As the war with Britain drew to a close, it became clear that this structure was too weak to make the states obey congressional mandates and deal with the debt and foreign policy issues of the new emerging nation. The states were on the brink of economic disaster as bankrupt farms were seized and angry farmers began to revolt.

At first, it looked unlikely that enough of the state delegates would agree to gather and address the need for a new central government. Even George Washington delayed accepting his invitation to join the delegation, fearing that it was doomed to failure. Upon his arrival, General Washington was unanimously elected to preside over the Constitutional Convention. In 1788, Washington would be elected the first president of the United States.

Throughout the summer of 1787, delegates to the Continental Congress drafted the framework of the United States government called the **Constitution.** It was a monumental effort of compromise and collaborative statesmanship. Some of the major issues they struggled with were how much power to allocate to the central government, how many representatives from each state should be in the Congress, and whether these representatives should be elected directly by the people or by state legislators.[4]

Constitution— framework of the U.S. government

The Bill of Rights

As the states debated the adoption of the Constitution, opponents expressed a desire for stricter clarification of the rights of the people and additional regulations to prevent the abuse of the central government's powers. The abuse of civil rights by the British was a powerful reminder of the need to carefully regulate governmental power. The independently governed states were hesitant to compromise their liberty, and their ratification of the Constitution was dependent on having a bill of rights.

In September 1789, the First Congress of the United States proposed 12 amendments to the Constitution, which addressed the states' most pressing concerns. Ten of the 12 were ratified by three-fourths of the state legislatures, and these 10 became known as the **Bill of Rights.**[5]

One of the amendments not adopted would have banned commercial monopolies and made it illegal for corporations to own other corporations. This amendment grew, in part, out of the colonists' experience of oppression by England's largest transnational corporation, the East India Company. Because it received special subsidies and exemption from regulations from the British government, the East India Company controlled nearly all commerce to and from North America by the 1760s. Because of its monopoly on the tea sold in America, it wiped out small businesses and tea wholesalers in America. The Boston Tea Party of 1773 was a citizen protest against the actions of the East India Company. The corporations fought against this amendment, and Jefferson and others predicted that corporations would use their power to influence elections and legislation that favored their ability to amass wealth and resources.

Bill of Rights— ten amendments to the Constitution proposed by the First Congress of the United States and ratified by three-fourths of the state legislatures

SEPARATION OF POWERS

One of the priorities of the framers of the Constitution in designing our government framework was preventing consolidation of power in the hands of a ruling elite. They designed a level of inefficiency into the governing process to intentionally keep any branch of government from becoming too powerful. This system, also known as **checks and balances,** requires that each branch of government be accountable to the others. The Constitution provides for three branches of government:

- Legislative
- Judicial
- Executive

The **Legislative branch** is composed of the House of Representatives and Senate (together known as the **Congress**) as described in Article 1 of the Constitution. The **Judicial branch** is composed of the federal courts and the Supreme Court, as described in Article 3. The **Executive branch** is composed of the president, the vice-president, and 15 federal departments.

By law, drawn from Article 2, section 2 of the Constitution, the Presidential Cabinet includes the vice-president and the heads of the 15 executive departments. The Cabinet members advise on any subject related to the duties of their respective departments, which include Agriculture, Commerce, Defense, Education, Energy, Health and Human Services, Housing and Urban Development, Interior, Labor, State, Transportation, Treasury, Veterans Affairs, Attorney General, and Homeland Security. The president is also able to appoint others to the Cabinet, as did President George W. Bush when he accorded Cabinet-level rank to the administrator of the Environmental Protection Agency, the director of the Office of Management and Budget, the director of the National Drug Control Policy, and the U. S. trade representative.

The recent addition of the Department of Homeland Security to the Executive branch was the largest change to government structure since the addition of the Department of Defense 50 years prior. The new department was established on November 25, 2002, and officially began operation on January 24, 2003, with the intention of consolidating U.S. Executive branch organizations related to homeland security into a single cabinet agency by 2004. The new department assumes a number of government functions previously held by other departments. This department is organized into four divisions and incorporates many existing federal functions:

1. **Border and Transportation Security**
   United States Customs Service (from Deparment of Treasury)
   Immigration and Naturalization Service (from Department of Justice)
   Border Patrol (from Department of Justice)
   Animal and Plant Health Inspection Service (from Department of Agriculture)
   Transportation Security Administration (from Department of Transportation)
   Federal Protective Service (General Services Administration)
   U.S. Coast Guard (from Department of Transportation)

Checks and balances— the system designed to keep any branch of government from becoming too powerful

Legislative branch (Congress)— members of the House of Representatives and the Senate

Judicial branch— the federal courts and the Supreme Court

Executive branch— the President, Vice-President, and the 15 federal departments

The chief magistrate derives all his authority from the people.

ABRAHAM LINCOLN

2. **Emergency Preparedness and Response**
   Federal Emergency Management Agency (FEMA)

3. **Chemical, Biological, Radiological, and Nuclear Countermeasures**
   Lawrence Livermore National Laboratory (from Department of Energy)
   Plum Island Animal Disease Center (from Department of Agriculture)

4. **Information Analysis and Infrastructure Protection**
   National Infrastructure Simulation and Analysis Center (from Department of Energy)
   Critical Infrastructure Assurance Office (from Department of Commerce)
   National Infrastructure Protection Center (from Federal Bureau of Investigation)
   Federal Computer Incident Response Center (from General Services Administration)
   National Communications System (from Department of Defense)

Each of the government branches—Legislative, Executive, and Judicial— has powers endowed to it and checks installed to safeguard against abuse of those powers.

Legislative Branch

Powers
- Passes all federal laws
- Establishes all lower federal courts
- Can override a presidential veto
- Can impeach the president

Checks to Legislative Branch Power
- Both the House and the Senate must agree on legislation, preventing consolidation of power in either house of Congress.
- The Executive branch can veto any bill and call Congress into session.
- The Judicial branch can declare laws unconstitutional.

Executive Branch

Powers
- Has veto power over all bills
- Appoints judges, department secretaries, and other officials
- Makes treaties
- Ensures laws are carried out
- Is Commander-in-Chief of the military
- Issues pardons

Checks to Executive Branch Power

- The Legislative branch can override vetoes.
- Legislative can refuse to confirm appointments.
- Legislative can reject treaties.
- Legislative can declare war.
- Legislative can impeach the president.
- The Judicial branch can declare Executive acts unconstitutional.

Judicial Branch

Powers

- Can try federal cases and interpret constitutional law in those cases
- Can declare any law or Executive act unconstitutional

Checks to Judicial Branch Power

- Members are appointed by the Executive.
- Legislative can impeach judges and approves Executive appointments.
- Legislative can propose amendments to overturn judicial decisions.

VOTING AND THE ELECTORAL PROCESS

Although many Americans may believe voting to be the most active way that people express themselves as citizens, only 51.3 percent of Americans of voting age voted in the 2000 presidential election.[6] The percentage is usually lower for state and local elections. The 2000 presidential election was an example of the impact voting can have. The leadership of our country, and its vast influence on the world, came down to a few hundred controversial votes in the state of Florida.

Voting Resources

James Madison, framer of the Constitution and fourth president of the United States, said: "A popular government, without popular information, or the means of acquiring it, is but a prologue to a farce or a tragedy . . . a people who mean to be their own governors must arm themselves with the power which knowledge gives."[7]

The absence of an accessible, reliable, and unbiased source of information about candidates and issues is a factor that makes voting decisions frustrating and time-consuming. Project Vote Smart was started in 1992 with the purpose of compiling a complete database of political data, which they make available to the public for free. It includes candidates for the presidency, the U.S. Congress, governorships, and state legislatures and enables voters to determine how they stand on the issues. The following information is provided by Project Vote Smart:

- Biographies of elected officials and candidates for office
- Voting records and positions on issues

The Impact of Voting

In some cases, just a few votes have made a significant impact on policy in our country. Following are some historical and recent examples of how a few votes—in some cases, only one—have made a difference.

- In 1776, one vote gave America the English language instead of German.
- In 1800, President Jefferson beat Aaron Burr by one vote in the House following an electoral tie.
- One vote brought Texas and California into the Union.
- A single vote saved President Andrew Johnson from an impeachment conviction.
- One vote gave Rutherford Hayes the presidency of the United States.
- One vote gave women the right to vote.
- John F. Kennedy's margin of victory over Richard Nixon in 1960 was less than one vote per precinct.
- In 1977, Vermont State Representative Sydney Nixon was seated as an apparent one-vote winner, 570 to 569. Mr. Nixon resigned when the State House determined, after a recount, that he had lost to Robert Emond, 572 to 571.
- In 1989, a Lansing, Michigan, School District millage proposition failed when the final recount produced a tie vote. The result meant that the school district had to reduce its budget by $2.5 million.
- In 1994, Republican Randall Luthi and Independent Larry Call tied for the seat in the Wyoming House of Representatives from the Jackson Hole area. A recount produced the same result. Mr. Luthi was finally declared the winner when a Ping Pong ball bearing his name was pulled from a hat.
- In 1996, Loretta Sanchez was elected to Congress from California by a margin of less than four votes per precinct.
- In 1997, South Dakota Democrat John McIntyre led Republican Hal Wick by four votes for the second seat in Legislative District 12 on election night. A subsequent recount showed Wick the winner by one vote. The State Supreme Court, however, ruled that one ballot counted for Wick was invalid due to an overvote. After hearing argument from both sides, the State Legislature voted to seat Wick.
- In 1998, Donald Sherwood was elected to the House of Representatives from Pennsylvania by a margin of less than one vote per precinct.
- In 1999, Leslie Byrne was elected to the Virginia Senate by a margin of less than one vote per precinct.

A C T I O N !

Information Exercise

Find information about two national candidates or potential candidates.

- Financial campaign contributors
- Texts of speeches
- Briefings on important issues
- Sources for additional information
- Contact information

Richard Kimball, president of Project Vote Smart, has said that "the typically irresponsible use of mass communication by candidates and political campaign practitioners has resulted in an unprecedented degree of misinformation, disinformation, distortion, confusion and emotional, but empty, imagery at all levels."[8]

Nonpartisan information— information that is impartial to political parties and candidates

In the search for unbiased information, it is important to find **nonpartisan information,** information that is impartial to political parties and candidates. Project Vote Smart, a nonprofit agency, distributes nonpartisan information about candidates and issues.

Bruce Ackerman, a professor at Yale University, and James Fishkin of the University of Texas created the idea of "Deliberation Day" as a way to arm citizens with the power to make informed voting decisions. It would be a national holiday, held one week before major national elections. Voters would gather in day-long local meetings to discuss and share information about issues and candidates. All other work, except for essential services, would be prohibited on that day.

The idea grew out of research on groups who participated in the deliberative process. Polls showed that when participants were better informed, their opinions changed on issues. Ackerman and Fishkin write: "Deliberation Day aims to remind voters that voting is not an occasion for expressing consumer-like preferences, but a crucial moment in which they are confiding ultimate coercive power to representatives who will be speaking for them on matters that may determine the fate of billions of their fellow inhabitants of the planet Earth."[9]

> *The rich have the right to buy more cars than anyone else, more homes, vacations, gadgets and gizmos, but they do not have the right to buy more democracy than anyone else.*
>
> **BILL MOYERS**

Campaign Finance

Understanding the way candidates fund their campaigns is an important part of understanding our current electoral process. The amount of money candidates now spend at the national, state, and local levels has risen to its highest levels yet. Congressional candidates and the national Democratic and Republican parties spent more than $1.3 billion in the 1998 election, which, to give perspective, is the amount of money that UNICEF estimates would provide basic health and nutrition to all the world's poor. In 1998, the average winner of a House seat spent $775,000, and the average Senate seat winner spent more than $5 million.

This scenario requires that those who seek elected offices spend as much or more time on fund-raising than on policy making. And, once elected, candidates who accepted huge contributions find themselves beholden to the interests of those donors. Jim Schultz, author of *The Democracy Owner's Manual*, describes the process this way:

> There should be little debate about the intentions of all this campaign giving. Wealthy special interests, from Microsoft to the alcohol industry, pour millions into candidate and party coffers. They do so not to support democracy, and often not even with the direct aim of helping specific candidates, but to buy access and friendship from whoever wins. The biggest givers cover their bets with huge donations to both sides. A 1999 Common Cause study identified more than three dozen major corporations that had given $50,000 or more to both the Democratic and Republican national parties; among them were AT&T ($832,400), American Airlines ($348,056), Microsoft ($252,100), and Anheuser-Busch ($231,450). There should also be little debate about the effect of such giving—public policy made under the influence of those who can afford to pay for it.[10]

It is this kind of unfair influence of policy making that the framers of the Constitution and the Bill of Rights feared but were unsuccessful in preventing through the governmental structure they created. As our national economy evolved from the predominance of small business to that of big corporations, these corporate interests used more of their resources to gain influence in the political process. As Frank Norris wrote of the railroads in his 1901 epic, *The Octopus*, "They own the ballot box . . . they own us."[11]

Efforts to reform campaign financing include:

- Public disclosure
- Contribution limits
- Limits on campaign spending
- Public funding of campaigns

After the Watergate scandal during the Nixon presidency, it became law to disclose the contributions made to presidential and congressional candidates. This information is available through the Federal Elections Commission (FEC).

In 1996, Maine voters approved a "Clean Money Campaign Reform" initiative, which made full public financing available to candidates who accepted no special-interest contributions and agreed to campaign spending limits. Similar legislation has been adopted in several other states, including Massachusetts, Vermont, and Arizona. A 1996 Gallup Poll reported that 64 percent of voters support a system in which the "federal government provides a fixed amount of money for the election campaigns of candidates for congress and all private contributions [are] prohibited."[12]

The Electoral College

The president and vice-president are not elected by the popular vote of citizens; they are elected by members of the Electoral College. Each state has the same number of Electoral College electors as they do members in Congress, with a minimum number of 3 electors. The national total is 538 electors. A majority of 270 electoral college votes is needed to elect the president and vice-president.

The *U.S. Congressional Handbook* reports: "Though laws vary from state to state, the state parties typically choose electors. Electors in some states cast their ballot based on the popular vote of the state, and others cast their vote based on the party candidate. However, electors rarely ignore the popular vote."[13] Members of the Electoral College gather in December following the November presidential election to cast their votes.

Primary Elections

Primary elections are a "unique U.S. institution born in the era of political reform at the beginning of the 20th century," according to *Encyclopedia Americana*, and they are becoming increasingly important in American politics.[14] The general election is preceded, in many states, by primary elections, in which voters choose the candidates for local, state, or federal elections. According to Peter Renstrom and Chester Rogers, authors of *Electoral Politics Dictionary*, the growth of primaries in U.S. politics during the 20th century is rooted "in concerns that conventions were wholly controlled by the urban political machines."[15]

Through primaries, candidates for office can secure their party's nomination for U.S. Representative or Senator, or for state or local office, without the approval of party officials. The result has been a shift of power toward the voter and away from party officials, thus weakening the power of political parties.[16]

Most states now hold primary elections to choose party nominees, according to *Congressional Quarterly*'s "National Party Conventions." In 1912, 13 states held primaries, and they have since become more important, with more than 40 of the 50 states holding them.

Critics of the primary process believe that the elections cost time and money that could be used in securing a win in the general election. They also believe that voters are not always knowledgeable enough to choose competent candidates and that the quality of leadership has deteriorated since the power of political party organizations has declined.

MEMBERS OF CONGRESS

Members of Congress (MoC) consist of members of the House of Representatives, or representatives, and members of the Senate, or senators. Representatives are commonly referred to as congressmen, congresswomen, or congresspeople. Senators are also technically congresspersons, though they are commonly referred to as senators.

Each state has a number of representatives proportionate to the population of that state. For instance, in 2002 California had 53 representatives while Rhode Island had 2. Representatives serve a two-year term and are elected every second November by the people in a direct election. Representatives must be 25 years or older, must have been U.S. citizens for seven years, and must live in the district they represent. The 2003 representative salary was $154,700.

Each state has two senators regardless of the state's population. Senators serve for six years. Every second November, one-third of the Senate may be reelected in a direct election by the people, leaving an experienced two-thirds of the senators to continue to serve. Senators must be age 30 or older, must have been a U.S. citizen for nine years, and must live in the state they represent. The 2003 senator salary was also $154,700.

Representatives and senators split their time between their states or districts and Washington, D.C. Some maintain homes or apartments in Washington in addition to their primary homes, and some sleep on couches in their offices while in D.C. They often put in 10- to 12-hour days.

MoCs' Office Staff

Representatives and senators maintain offices with separate staff in Washington, D.C., as well as multiple offices throughout their home districts or states. Local offices may have fewer staff members, but the D.C. offices usually include the following:

- **Chief of staff**—Oversees operation of all aspects of a member's office
- **Legislative director**—Oversees legislative staff; keeps member informed about legislative issues and priorities; works to help achieve the member's specific legislative goals
- **Legislative assistant**—Focuses on specific issues, such as defense, foreign affairs, or education, and is the member's main source of information and guidance on those issues; meets with constituents; experienced in their issue focus and the workings of Capitol Hill
- **Legislative correspondent**—Focuses on specific issues and mainly researches and drafts responses to constituents; more likely a junior member of the staff
- **Scheduler**—Creates a schedule for the member that includes committee needs, floor votes and hearings, time with staff, appointments with constituents, and time in the state or district; makes travel arrangements
- **Press secretary/communications director**—Communicates the member's views to the media and to constituents

Committees

All representatives and senators belong to committees that generate laws and policy for specific categories of issues. Committees cover wide-ranging issues, from

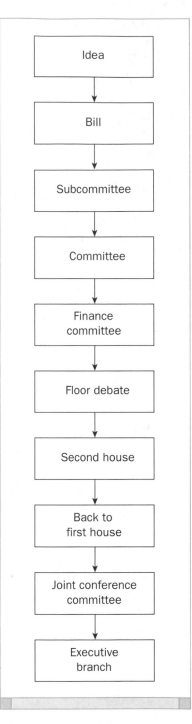

FIGURE 8.1 *How a Bill Becomes a Law*

agriculture to youth violence to international trade. Members have significant influence over the policies concerning the issues of their committees.

Members usually seek membership on committees related to their personal interests and background and to issues that are particularly relevant to their districts or states. Some members will seek out membership on powerful committees, such as appropriations committees, which control the flow of money to programs authorized by other committees. Other powerful committees are the House Ways and Means and the Senate Finance Committees, which consider tax legislation. The respective House and Senate Budget committees establish national priorities for our federal tax dollars.

HOW A BILL BECOMES LAW

Understanding How Bills Get Started

Policy, legislation, and laws all start as ideas, and these ideas can come from any source. For instance, lawmakers may get ideas for laws from citizens, nonprofit groups, media sources, lobby groups, or community groups. Anyone is free to suggest an idea for a bill to an elected official. However, for an idea to become law, it must eventually be strongly supported by a Member of Congress who can strategically steward it through the legislative process.

The process (see Figure 8.1) begins with an idea being structured into the form of a bill, in legal language. The bill can be introduced in either the House or the Senate. It is given a number corresponding to the chamber in which it is introduced (HR-xxxx for the House and S-xxxx for the Senate) and is assigned to the appropriate committee, where the chairperson of that committee decides if the bill needs to be referred to a more specialized subcommittee.

Bills must be "sponsored" by a Member of Congress. Each bill has an initial sponsor or sponsors, who introduce the bill. Bills also gather cosponsors who lend their active support to the bill, which gives the bill more clout throughout the legislative process.

Understanding the Committee Process

Committees are where bills are looked at most carefully. Staff for Members of Congress who specialize in the area that the bill addresses will write analyses of the proposed policy.

Hearings are held, and expert witnesses are often called upon to offer the pros and cons of the proposed policy. Any concerned persons may offer viewpoints or information to the committee during this process. Hearings are usually open to the public.

Most bills don't receive enough support to make it past this committee or subcommittee "markup" stage. The *U.S. Congressional Handbook* reports that, on average, 20,000 bills are introduced during each two-year term of Congress. Of those 20,000, less than 5 percent become law.[17]

Understanding the Typical Legislative Process

If a bill passes, or receives a majority vote of the chamber within which it was originally introduced, it then goes to the other chamber, where the whole process must be repeated—from committee markups to a vote on the floor.

When a bill reaches the floor of the House or Senate for a vote, it may be debated and lobbied for by Members of Congress. Advocates can influence this process by meeting with a member to brief him or her on important aspects of the bill. They may even prepare speaking points or a written speech for the member to deliver before the other members on the floor.

If a bill passes both the House and the Senate, it is then addressed by a conference committee. This committee includes conferees from both the House and the Senate, who are chosen to negotiate and compromise, if necessary, on any differences between the House version and the Senate version of the bill. The committee creates a conference report, which is then voted on by the House and Senate.

At this point, the bill is sent to the White House for the president's signature or veto. If the president vetoes the bill, it can still become law with a two-thirds roll call vote of both the House and the Senate.

> If there is no struggle, there is no progress. Those who profess to favor freedom and yet deprecate agitation are people who want crops without plowing up the ground . . . That struggle might be a moral one; it might be a physical one; it might be both moral and physical, but it must be a struggle. Power concedes nothing without a demand. It never did and never will. People might not get all that they work for in this world, but they must certainly work for all they get.
>
> **FREDERICK DOUGLASS**

ADVOCACY AND LOBBYING

Advocacy and lobbying involve expressing our priorities and values to our government to help create policies and systems that benefit our lives and the common good. When confronted with problems and need in our communities, it is often tempting to address the need or problem without considering the policy or system that may be creating the problem.

For instance, we may volunteer in a soup kitchen to feed the hungry, or volunteer to tutor a student with reading problems. However, to make a larger difference in the issue of hungry Americans, we may need to look at the policies creating un-employment or further economic hardship for low-income Americans. To power-fully address educational problems, we may need to consider the policies that continue to cut funding for early-childhood educational programs and for public education.

When we act as citizens to influence the allocation and priority of our nation's budget and resources, we are able to benefit the lives of many more people than we could ever affect personally. Dr. Jean Mayer, former president of Tufts University, described the power of citizenship this way:

> I see that the efforts of people as citizens are more effective than their efforts as in-dividuals. This is an idea that we in the twentieth century have not yet come to terms with: What any of us can do, good or bad, as individuals, is dramatically en-hanced when we are acting collectively as citizens.
>
> Obviously we can do things as individuals—if you see somebody hungry, you can feed him—but the problem would not have happened in the first place if we had done our job as citizens.[18]

Both advocacy and lobbying are activities available to all citizens and are rights that are protected under the First Amendment, guaranteeing that our government not limit our "right to peaceably assemble, and to petition the government for a redress of grievances." To "petition the government for a redress of grievances" means to solicit or make a formal request that the government act to correct a cause of suffering or wrongdoing.

Advocacy

Advocacy—
publicly supporting a cause you believe in; may involve a wide variety of public actions

Advocacy is publicly supporting a cause you believe in and can involve a wide va-riety of public actions. Advocacy may or may not include lobbying. Advocacy in-cludes the following:

- Marches and demonstrations
- Sit-ins
- Boycotts and strikes
- Pickets
- Public speeches
- Concerts that benefit and/or educate about causes
- Community forums to educate about causes
- Letters to the newspaper or other publications

Lobbying

Lobbying—
activities aimed at influencing public officials to act on specific legislation

Lobbying includes activities aimed at influencing public officials to act on specific legislation. Lobbying always involves advocacy, but advocacy does not necessarily include lobbying. Lobbying includes the following:

- Letters, calls, and visits to elected officials
- Media work
- Protests
- Working directly with elected officials to influence legislation
- Suggesting legislation
- Formally registering your support or opposition to proposed laws
- Testifying in committees

> As citizens, we have every right to raise [a commotion] when we see injustice done, or the public interest betrayed, or the public process corrupted.
>
> **JOHN W. GARDNER, FORMER SECRETARY OF HEALTH, EDUCATION AND WELFARE**

History has shown that when the people create a critical mass of public will for change, then political will follows. Both require perseverance and strategic action toward specific objectives. For example, the civil rights movement included all the forms of advocacy listed above. Eventually, advocacy led to lobbying to specifically pass the Civil Rights Act of 1964, as well as other equal rights laws.

Independent Sector, founded in 1980, is a collection of charitable, educational, religious, health, and social welfare organizations whose mission is "to promote, strengthen, and advance the nonprofit and philanthropic community to foster private initiative for the public good." Bob Smucker, a veteran lobbyist with Independent Sector, says the following about advocacy and lobbying:

> This kind of citizen action has been carried out repeatedly over the years by citizen groups working for the protections of women's rights, child labor laws, stricter laws against drunk driving and smoking, requirements for safe drinking water and clean air, disabled persons' rights, and many more. All initially combined a broad spectrum of non-lobbying advocacy activities, with lobbying employed somewhat later to achieve the needed change in public policy.[19]

Clarifying Objectives

The nature of social problems is complex. They reflect differing interests that must be weighed and slow-moving bureaucracies and entrenched systems and beliefs must be dealt with. In developing objectives for engaging with social problems, it helps most to have long-term objectives that are exciting enough to keep you motivated over the long haul, and short-term objectives that are clear, specific, and attainable. When the long-term, ideal goal is the only focus, it is easy to become overwhelmed or discouraged by what it will take to achieve it. Short-term objectives give us the feeling of movement toward a greater end.

There are many kinds of objectives that an advocacy campaign might choose. As more information is gathered,

> I long to accomplish a great and noble task, but it is my chief duty to accomplish humble tasks as though they were great and noble. The world is moved along, not only by the mighty shoves of its heroes, but also by the aggregate of the tiny pushes of each honest worker.
>
> **HELEN KELLER**

M A K I N G   I T   H A P P E N

PORTRAIT OF A BILL

TIMELINE

January 1984—Twenty-six-year-old Ron Fischman receives education and training in grassroots advocacy. Ron hears about legislation that RESULTS, a nonprofit group, has drafted for a bill to make money available in the foreign aid budget for small loans to very poor people for self-employment. This process, called microcredit or microenterprise, makes it possible for poor people to buy necessary tools (for example, a cow to sell milk, a sewing machine, repair tools) to generate income, instead of renting these resources at exorbitant rates that keep them indebted. Ron becomes so enthusiastic about this legislation that he makes a commitment to convince his congressman, Ed Feighan, to introduce the bill. Ron has no relationship with Congressman Feighan and no experience in advocacy or lobbying. Ron decides to volunteer in Feighan's reelection campaign, create an opportunity to get close to the congressman and ask him to introduce the legislation. Ron recalls that election day was frigid, with freezing rain falling and wind whipping: "My rediscovered sense of mission in my citizenship was affirmed by each soggy, shivering voter."

November 1984—At the postelection party, Ron intercepts Feighan as he is walking to the podium to give his acceptance speech and asks when he can talk to the congressman about a bill he is excited about. The congressman tells him to talk to a member of his staff to get something started. Ron is elated.

January 1987—After two years of Ron's educating Feighan and his staff about microcredit and building a relationship with George Stephanopoulos, Feighan's chief of staff (who would later become senior aide to President Clinton), Feighan agrees to introduce the Self-Sufficiency for the Poor Act in the House.

March 1987—The bill gains support after successful hearings before the House Foreign Affairs Subcommittee on International Economic Policy and Trade.

April 1987—After being amended within the House Foreign Affairs Committee, the microenterprise legislation passes the House. Senator DeConcini (D-AZ) introduces the bill in the Senate. RESULTS volunteers mobilize to gather Republican cosponsors. After more than two years of effort, Denver RESULTS volunteers get a meeting with conservative Republican Senator William Armstrong and get him to cosponsor the bill. Fifty-two other cosponsors are gathered.

May 1987—The Agency for International Development delivers a letter to each member of the U.S. Senate stating opposition to Senator DeConcini's bill.

July 1987—RESULTS organizes a conference call for 28 national journalists, who hear the testimony of microenterprise expert Dr. Muhammad Yunus from Bangladesh. The call generates national positive media attention for the microenterprise legislation.

(continued)

(continued)

September 1987—eight of 13 Senate Foreign Operations Subcommittee members sign a letter to Senator Robert Kasten and Senator Daniel Inouye urging inclusion of the microenterprise provision in their appropriations bill (the bill that makes money available for the programs designated by the legislation). RESULTS volunteers generate 100 editorials around the country and hundreds of letters to the editor in support of the legislation.

October 1987—Legislation passes that makes $50 million available through the Foreign Aid budget for microenterprise loans to the poor.

and more concerns and needs are distinguished, our goals and strategies may shift. But in order to decide on a place to begin, we must have objectives in mind. Before deciding on the right ones, it is worth considering all of them. Some groups or individuals pick initial objectives where the main goal is to lay the foundation of public awareness and support for a larger campaign or objective. Ultimately, advocacy takes aim at some specific change that advances a cause forward. Lobbying focuses on changing government policy in order to change the systems that are creating a social problem.

Advocating for change to many social problems may include working within a political climate where swift change is unlikely. In these situations, your objective may be simply to demonstrate opposition. In the early days of the war in Vietnam, thousands protested even though the United States was unlikely to withdraw. Again, democracy was founded on the principle of citizen engagement. An objective of advocacy is to remind the public and those in power that a dissenting view exists and to keep the debate alive so that the politics of the issue represent the views of the citizens—not just those in power.

An advocacy or lobbying objective needs to be clear and compelling. It must be able to attract the interest of the

Citizens convene at a rally and press conference at the U.S. Capitol.

media and the public, who are busy with other priorities, and motivate their active involvement. However, the objective should also be small enough to achieve something of value within a reasonable amount of time. It will often be a small win that generates momentum toward a larger win. Campaigns that start with huge expectations and don't meet those fairly rapidly will likely lose their participants to other efforts that seem more productive.

Short-term objectives can lay the groundwork for creating a political climate that is part of a long-term strategy. Advocacy campaigns do this by creating public education and awareness of larger issues, by building coalitions of support among individuals and groups, and by building relationships with key leaders and decision makers.

Values Check

After clarifying potential objectives, weigh these objectives and strategies against your values. If they are in opposition in any way, you will experience internal conflict as you proceed. If they are complementary, you will experience added energy as you proceed. Daniel Goleman, author of *Working with Emotional Intelligence*, says: "Choices made in keeping with this inner rudder . . . are energizing. They not only feel right but maximize the attention and energy available for pursuing them."[20]

Working with Members of Congress

The mission of advocacy and lobbying is to influence the actions and decisions of policy makers. Citizens gain a significant advantage in this mission by developing long-term relationships with their MoCs.

The following steps may help in the process of creating a relationship with a MoC and determining if, and how, he or she may provide leadership on issues you care about. This process may be adjusted to apply to any elected official, member of the media, or person of influence with whom you would like to develop a relationship in order to reach civic goals.

Step One: Do Your Homework

Get to know your MoC—his personal background and what he cares about. This may help you determine whether he has an existing interest in issues that are important to you or in a specific objective you have.

- Go to his Web site (www.house.gov for representatives and www.senate.gov for senators).
- Look at his voting record on issues you care about (www.vote-smart.org).
- Research past articles about him in your local newspapers. Make a note of his friends and supporters.
- Find out what committees and/or subcommittees he is on.
- Make a contact list for yourself with phone and fax numbers of the MoC's local office and Washington, D.C., office. As you gather the names of key staff members in each office, add them to this contact list.

Step Two: Start a Relationship

As with any relationship, first impressions are important. Doing your homework on the MoC will show that you are professional and serious about your efforts. Be patient and persistent. It may take time to gain the respect and trust of your MoC and her staff, but if you are able to establish a connection, it will be your most valuable asset in creating the social change you seek.

- Find out which staff member handles the issue you are working on or are most interested in. If he is in the local office, ask to meet with him or invite him to lunch. If he is in the D.C. office, schedule a phone meeting to get to know him. When you meet, ask him what issues most interest him. Ask what the MoC is most interested in. Ask which colleagues in Congress the MoC respects and works closely with.

> *It may well be that the greatest tragedy of this period of social transition is not the glaring noisiness of the so-called bad people, but the appalling silence of the so-called good people.*
>
> **MARTIN LUTHER KING JR.**

- Call the local office to find out the MoC's schedule of town hall meetings and other public appearances. Go to one, and make a point to introduce yourself to the MoC. Be respectful and acknowledge the MoC for something she has supported or just for taking the time to meet with constituents.
- Work on the MoC's campaign.
- Always send a thank-you note after a meeting with a staff member or MoC. If you meet with a staff member, send a thank-you to the MoC acknowledging the staff member for his time and attention, and copy the staff member. This will win you the gratitude of the staff member.

Step Three: Become a Valuable Resource

MoCs and their staff are generally busy and under stress. They are under constant pressure to understand the large number of issues they must make decisions about. If you can establish yourself as a credible and helpful source of information and support on an issue, you will be seen as an asset to your MoC and her staff.

- Set up meetings for them with experts on your issues.
- Set up meetings for them with people in your community who benefit from the programs or policy you are working on (the stakeholders).
- Show them informational videos.
- Send them information and articles from newspapers and other publications on your specific issue.
- Provide them with speaking points for committee discussions, public speeches, or floor debates on your issue.
- Remind them of specific actions they can take to support the legislation that affects your issue.

Step Four: Encourage Their Leadership

Even if your MoC has an interest in the issue you are working on, she may still require encouragement and persistent, specific support in order to take a leadership role on the issue.

It helps to be clear and direct in your requests of your MoC. Help her to see how the actions you are requesting help her to satisfy her own goals and interests, and how the outcomes will benefit her constituents.

Concerned citizens meet with their Member of Congress, Henry Waxman (D-CA), middle, and his legislative assistant, Patricia Delgado, far right.

- Schedule a face-to-face meeting with your MoC when she will be in your district. Have a specific strategy for action to propose to her (see the tips for meetings with a Member of Congress later in this chapter).
- Ask her to cosponsor the legislation that interests you.
- Ask her to speak or write to the committee chair handling the legislation that interests you.
- Arrange a local press conference and ask her to speak along with local experts and stakeholders on the issue or legislation.
- Arrange for her to write an op-ed article on the issue for your local paper (offer to write a draft for her).

Step Five: Acknowledge and Appreciate Them

Like anyone else, your Member of Congress wants to be appreciated for his or her efforts. And since MoCs usually seek reelection, they are very interested in how they are written about and talked about by their constituents. Publicly thanking your MoC for positive actions he or she takes on your issues can make a significant difference in gaining their respect and partnership.

- Write letters to the editor of your newspaper praising your MoC for positive actions on your issues.
- Have community leaders write thank-you notes to him.
- Write personal thank-you notes to him.
- Have friends and associates call his office to voice appreciation for his actions.
- Thank him at community forums and town hall appearances.
- Send him stories of constituents who have benefited from the legislation he has supported.

Letters and Calls

A common misperception exists among citizens that their comments don't make any difference to their representatives in government. Some people may feel that if they were to call or write to their Member of Congress, that their message would be lost among a flood of competing requests and communications about an issue. However, it is estimated that fewer than 10 percent of voters will ever write to elected officials.[21] And if fewer than 50 percent of citizens vote, only a minute portion of citizens are communicating with their government representatives.

Hearing from constituents does make a difference with policy makers. Marc Caplan, author of *A Citizen's Guide to Lobbying*, says: "Legislators hear nothing from their constituents on the vast majority of bills. When they do get a few letters or telephone calls, they take notice. Sometimes a handful of calls can change a vote. On a controversial issue, much more is needed."[22]

Meetings with MoCs and Staff

Meetings in person with MoCs and their staff are great opportunities to build relationships and further your ability to work together toward positive social goals.

Scheduling a meeting with a staff member, either in Washington, D.C., or in the local district, is quite easily accomplished with a call to either office. Scheduling a face-to-face meeting with a representative or senator may take extended persistence, however. Building rapport with the MoC's scheduler is important. You may also need to connect with a community leader, colleague, or friend of the MoC who can use her influence on your behalf to champion your cause and help you get a meeting.

Tips for successful meetings include the following:

- Prepare and practice what you will say. Be able to give the necessary background and requests in a short period of time.
- Have a goal for the meeting. Know what you are trying to accomplish.
- Acknowledge the legislator or staff member for actions he has taken. Be respectful and courteous.
- If you are meeting with the legislator, have the staff member who covers your issue in the room as well. This is an opportunity to educate and inspire both of them.
- Make requests that are clear and specific. Let the legislator know how valuable his leadership is to this issue. Leave written copies of background information and your requests.

Working with the Media

Strategic media work is important to successful advocacy and lobbying campaigns. It is a very powerful tool for influencing the priorities of both the public and elected officials. In *Media, The Second God*, author Tony Schwartz writes: "God-like, the media can change the course of a war, bring down a President or a King, elevate the lowly and humiliate the proud, by directing the attention of millions on the same event and in the same manner."[23]

Newspapers, radio, television, and the Internet are all forms of media. When deciding which medium(s) to work with, you will want to consider the audience you are trying to reach, what you can afford (if there is a cost), and how much control you will have over the message you are trying to share.

Getting media coverage of your viewpoint on an issue is a very effective way to influence Members of Congress and other elected officials. Public officials are very sensitive to how they appear to their constituents, and they know that their constituents watch how they respond to messages in the media. News stories, letters to the editor, editorials, press conferences, and radio talk shows are all ways that you can send messages to your elected officials, and to the public at the same time. A **press conference** is any event to which you invite the press that is designed to publicize and educate about an issue. A press conference may be a simple event, such as a community forum where experts speak about an issue. It may also be a large event that includes celebrities or other creative media draws. A press conference must have some element that attracts the media.

To put on a press conference it is best to work with others. Asking other community groups to "sponsor," or lend their name as supporting groups, to the event is effective. A news advisory, or press release, should be sent to the media beforehand and then followed up by calls to ensure that reporters know about and cover the event.

Press conference— an event to which the press is invited that is designed to publicize and educate about an issue

Grassroots Organizing

The organized and persistent demands of the people have brought about the major social shifts in our country. From the founding of our democracy to the movement to stop the use of sweatshops, we see the examples of the power of public will to create political outcomes that benefit society as a whole. Jim Schultz, author of *The Democracy Owner's Manual*, calls organizing "the foundation of public activism." The late senator Paul Wellstone said: "It is the people at the grassroots level who fight for the changes that are important to all of us."[24]

Organizing citizen support and action for a cause will create a positive outcome to the extent that the strategy and objectives chosen are sound. Since you are asking others to use a precious commodity—their time—you will serve them best if you ask them to use their time toward a specific, positive goal. Spending time to develop sound action strategies and objectives is the first step in successful grassroots organizing.

Working with a Support Network

"There are several reasons why it is worth taking the time to organize a citizen action group," writes Mark Green and others in *Who Runs Congress?* "A group can commit more energy and resources than even the most dedicated individual. A group is more likely to have resources and endurance to carry a seemingly interminable project through to completion."[25]

Because social change involves committing ourselves to causes that we are highly passionate about, it can be emotionally, intellectually, and physically challenging. Working together with others allows us to share the highs and lows and to give and receive the support necessary to sustain action toward our goals. The saying "The whole is greater than the sum of its parts" is relevant in that the combined power of a group of people working toward a goal is greater than the power of those people each working separately toward the same goal.

Enrolling Others

Effective organizing necessarily involves recruiting others. Recruiting and working successfully with others require strong people skills; if you don't have much experience working with others, this is an excellent opportunity to develop those skills.

An obvious place to look for potential partners is in organizations to which stakeholders in your issue belong. You may want to brainstorm all the groups and organizations that have an interest in or are affected by your cause. Make a note of any personal connections you or people you know have to any of these groups or organizations.

To enroll others in your project, you need to develop a clear message. Your message should clearly communicate your objectives and how the individual and the community will benefit from these objectives.

Working on a Political Campaign

Working on a political campaign at the local level can have a big impact, whether you are working for local, state, or national elections. Hillary Clinton, in her book, *Living History*, says that she gained a lot of knowledge when she acted as field coordinator for the state of Indiana during the failed 1976 Jimmy Carter campaign.[26]

Local candidates—in contrast to state and national candidates—generally have a smaller pool of supporters, and their campaigns can use a lot of people with a variety of skills. To work on a political campaign, ask the candidate what you can do. Typical categories of campaign functions are listed below. If you do not see something that interests you here, consider what you would like to do and approach the candidate with your offer.

- **Fund-raising**
  Attending fund-raisers and gatherings
  Finding major donors
- **Advertising**
  Designing television and radio ads
  Helping to find sign locations for candidates
  Passing out literature, signs, and bumper stickers
  Answering phones
- **Researching**
  Determining which groups to target
  Determining the message
  Drafting a questionnaire
  Interpreting results of a survey
  Developing plans based on survey results
  Developing call lists and databases

- **Online campaigning**

  Compiling mass e-mail lists

  Designing Web sites

  Developing graphics

- **Contacting voters**

  Using direct mail

  Going door to door

  Hosting coffees or gatherings to introduce a candidate

  Working for or at a special event

  Getting newcomers in your neighborhood registered to vote

  Calling voters

  Administering surveys

Consider running for office, as well, if this interests you. It helps to learn about your district, gather past election results, and thoroughly read the newspapers before embarking on a campaign. Consider going to community meetings and talking to others (especially community leaders), meeting the press, and practicing speaking about important issues.

CREATING SUSTAINABLE CITIZENSHIP

If we are to make citizenship an integral practice in our lives, we must make sure our practice is sustainable. A common tendency of social activists is to overcommit themselves to a project or cause and exhaust their energy and motivation. While passion is key to maintaining commitment to a goal, obsession is unhealthy and unsustainable. This pattern is something to watch for in both ourselves and others, in our civic participation as well as the rest of our activities.

Personal well-being and health are important priorities for a balanced life in general, and certainly for maintaining a role as an effective citizen. While doing all that it takes to see a project through to completion requires much effort and discipline, it also requires that you make time for the activities, relationships, and self-care that keep you whole and healthy. If you sustain yourself and others with whom you are working and avoid burnout, you will stand a good chance of reaching your civic goals and will be more effective in all other areas of your life.

As you build skills that allow you to contribute powerfully to the governing of the country, you become a great asset to society. Your participation is vital and valuable. Continuing to develop the craft of citizenship includes continuing to create balance, health, and awareness in all areas of your life. As you contribute your thoughtfulness, vision, and vitality to society, may you receive those gifts many times over in return.

Applications

Choose a social problem in your community that interests you (for example, homelessness, an environmental issue, a racial/ethnic issue, an educational issue). Call congressional aides in one of your senator's offices and one of your representative's offices, and ask them what current federal legislation exists that is addressing this issue in your community. Record how the Member of Congress stands on this legislation. Write a short essay assessing the stands of the Members of Congress and how you feel about this legislation. Does the policy address the problem in a way that will bring change in a positive, sustainable manner? Do you agree or disagree with your Members of Congress? Why?

1

Call your county clerk and ask how you vote in the primaries and why it is important. Report on what the clerk says.

2

Call a staff member for your state legislator. Ask which bills the legislator has cosponsored in the past year.

3

QUIZ

1. The word *democracy* comes from the Greek roots *demos* and *kratia*, meaning:
   A. demonstrations and people
   B. people and government
   C. government and voting
   D. people and freedom

2. The first organizing documents that governed the loose union of separate states was:
   A. the Bill of Rights
   B. the Articles of Confederation
   C. the Articles of the Union
   D. the Declaration of Independence

3. The Boston Tea Party, a citizen protest against the actions of the East India Company, was the inspiration of an unadopted amendment that would have banned commercial monopolies and made it illegal for corporations to own other corporations. How many original amendments to the Constitution were proposed in 1789?
   A. 10
   B. 15
   C. 12
   D. 7

4. The system known as checks and balances:
   A. keeps any branch of government from becoming too powerful
   B. is the framework of the U. S. government
   C. is used in federal financial record-keeping
   D. none of the above

5. The Constitution provides for these three branches of government:
   A. Legislative, Congressional, Executive
   B. Executive, Judicial, Legislative
   C. Judicial, Presidential, Congressional
   D. Executive, Judicial, Constitutional

6. Voting is one of the most active ways citizens can participate in the political process. What percentage of Americans voted in the 2000 presidential election?
   A. 72.3 percent   C. 79.8 percent
   B. 51.3 percent   D. 21.6 percent

7. What is the Electoral College?
   A. an entity in which the majority of its members elect the president and vice-president
   B. an institution of higher learning
   C. an entity in which the members rarely ignore the popular vote
   D. both A and C

8. In order for a bill to become a law, the process has to start with:
   A. a floor debate
   B. the joint conference committee
   C. the finance committee
   D. an idea

9. Lobbying is:
   A. any attempt to influence specific legislation
   B. writing letters to newspapers or other publications
   C. publicly supporting a cause you believe in
   D. strategically moving a bill through the legislative process

10. Which of the following would *not* be involved in the process of creating a relationship with a Member of Congress?
    A. becoming a valuable resource
    B. encouraging the MoC's leadership
    C. finding secure funding sources
    D. getting to know the MoC's personal background and what he cares about

ENDNOTES

1. Harris, Sam, and Valerie Harper. *Reclaiming Our Democracy: Healing the Break Between People and Government*. Philadelphia: Camino Books, 1994.

2. Moyers, Bill. "This is Your Story—The Progressive Story of America. Pass It On." America's Future Lifetime Leadership. Washington D.C., June 4, 2003. www.CommonDreams.org.

3. U.S. National Archives and Record Administration. "The Declaration of Independence: A History." www.archives.gov/exhibit_hall/charters_of_freedom/declaration/declaration_history.html.

4. U.S. National Archives and Record Administration. "The Constitution of the United States." www.archives.gov/exhibit_hall/charters_of_freedom/constitution/constitution.html.

5. U.S. National Archives and Record Administration. "The Bill of Rights." www.archives.gov/exhibit_hall/charters_of_freedom/bill_of_rights/bill_of_rights.html.

6. Federal Election Commission. *Voter Registration and Turnout*. July 12, 2003. www.fec.gov/pages/2000turnout/reg&to00.htm.

7. "Voter's Self-Defense Manual." Project Vote Smart, 2002. www.vote-smart.org/ program_publications.php.

8. Ibid.

9. McConnell, Carolyn. "Deliberation Day," *YES Magazine*, Winter 2003, 24: 41.

10. Schultz, Jim. *The Democracy Owner's Manual: A Practical Guide to Changing the World*. New Brunswick, NJ: Rutgers University Press, 2002.

11. Ibid.

12. Center for Responsive Politics. "A Brief History of Money in Politics—The States: 'Laboratories of Reform.'" Washington, D.C., 1999.

13. *United States Congressional Handbook*. Washington D.C: Votenet Solutions, 2001.

14. Pitts, David. "Primaries Unique to American Democracy." www.usembassy.de/usa/etexts/gov/primaries.htm.

15. Renstrom, Peter, and Chester Rogers. *Electoral Politics Dictionary*. ABC-CLIO, 1989.

16. Pitts, David. "Primaries Unique to American Democracy." www.usembassy.de/usa/etexts/gov/primaries.htm.

17. *United States Congressional Handbook*. Washington D.C: Votenet Solutions, 2001.

18. Harris, Sam. *Reclaiming Our Democracy*. Philadelphia: Camino Books, 1994.

19. Halperin, Samuel. "A Guide for the Powerless—and Those Who Don't Know Their Own Power; A Primer on the American Political Process." Washington, D.C.: American Youth Policy Forum, 2001.

20. Goleman, Daniel. *Working With Emotional Intelligence*. New York: Bantam Books, 1998.

21. Williamson, Marianne. *The Healing of America*. New York: Simon & Schuster, 1997.

22. Caplan, Marc. *A Citizen's Guide to Lobbying*. New York: Dembner Books, 1983.

23. Schwartz, Tony. *Media, The Second God*. New York: Anchor Press/Doubleday, 1983.

24. Isaac, Katherine. *Practicing Democracy: A Guide to Student Action*. New York: St. Martin's Press, 1995.

25. Green, Mark, with Michael Waldman, Michael Calabrese, Lynn Darling, Bruce Rosenthal, James M. Fallows, and David R. Zwick. *Who Runs Congress?*, 4th ed. New York: Dell, 1984.

26. Clinton, Hillary. *Living History*. New York: Simon & Schuster, 2003.

References

"2001 Advocacy Manual." Prepared for the National Peace Corps Association by Results Educational Fund, 2001.

Allen, David. *Getting Things Done: The Art of Stress-Free Productivity*. New York: Penguin USA, 2003.

Ardell Wellness Report, 43:1 (Summer 1996).

Asselin, Marlene. "Comprehension Instruction: Directions from Research," *Teacher Librarian* 29 (April 2002): 55+.

Baldwin, J. M., ed. "Reflection," in *Dictionary of Philosophy and Psychology*. Gloucester, Mass.: Peter Smith, 1960.

Bales, R. F., *SYMLOG Case Study Kit*. New York: Free Press, 1980.

Barbach, Lonnie. *For Each Other*. New York: Anchor Press/Doubleday, 1982.

Benne K. D., and P. Sheats, "Functional Roles of Group Members," *Journal of Social Issues* 4 (1948): 41–49.

Bennis, Warren. *On Becoming a Leader*. New York: Addison-Wesley, 1989.

Berry, Wendell. "Solving for Pattern," in *The Gift of Good Land: Further Essays Cultural and Agricultural*. San Francisco: North Point, 1981.

Beyer, B. *Critical Thinking*. Indianapolis, Ind.: Phi Delta Kappa Educational Foundation, 1995.

Brockovich, Erin. *Take It from Me: Life's a Struggle But You Can Win*. New York: McGraw-Hill, 2002.

Bronson, Po. *What Should I Do with My Life? The True Story of People Who Answered the Ultimate Question*. New York: Simon & Schuster, 2003.

Cameron, Julie. *The Artist's Way*. New York: Jeremy P. Tarcher/Putnam, 1992.

Caplan, Marc. *A Citizen's Guide to Lobbying*. New York: Dembner Books, 1983.

Center for Responsive Politics. "A Brief History of Money in Politics—The States: 'Laboratories of Reform.'" Washington, D.C.: 1999.

Chodron, Pema. *When Things Fall Apart: Heart Advice for Difficult Times*. Boston: Shambhala Publications, 1997.

Chrislip, David, and Carl Larson. *Collaborative Leadership*. San Francisco: Jossey-Bass, 1994.

Clinton, Hillary. *Living History*. New York: Simon & Schuster, 2003.

Cohen, E. G. *Talking and Working Together: Status, Interaction and Learning*. In *The Social Context of Instruction*, edited by P. L. Peterson, L. R. Wilkinson, and M. Hallihan. New York: Academic Press, 1984.

Cooke, J., and N. Kernaghan. "Estimating the Difference Between Group Versus Individual Performance on Problem-Solving Tasks," *Group & Organization Studies* 12 (September 1987): 319–42.

Coon, Dennis. *Introduction to Psychology: Exploration and Application*, 6th ed. Eagan, Minn.: West Publishing, 1992.

Covey, Stephen. *Seven Habits of Highly Effective People*. New York: Fireside/Simon & Schuster 1989.

Daley-Harris, Sam, and Valerie Harper. *Reclaiming Our Democracy: Healing the Break Between People and Government*. Philadelphia: Camino Books, 1994.

Davis, Flora. *Living Alive!* Garden City, N.Y.: Doubleday, 1980.

Devine, D. J., L. D. Clayton, J. L. Philips, B. B. Dunford, and S. B. Melner. "Teams in Organizations: Prevalence, Characteristics and Effectiveness," *Small Group Research* 30 (1999): 678–711.

Dewey, J. *Experience and Education*. New York: Collier Books, 1993.

Drucker, Peter. "Toward the New Organization," *Leader to Leader* 3(1997): 6–8.

Du Boulay, Doreen. "Argument in Reading: What Does It Involve and How Can Students Become Better Critical Readers?" *Teaching in Higher Education* 4 (April 1999): 147.

Ennis, R. H. "A Taxonomy of Critical Thinking Dispositions and Abilities." In J. B. Baron and R. J. Sternberg (eds.), *Teaching Thinking Skills: Theory and Practice*. New York: W. H. Freeman, 1987.

Federal Election Commission. "Voter Registration and Turnout," July 12, 2003, www.fec.gov/pages/2000turnout/reg&to00.htm.

Feichtner, Susan Brown, and Elain Actis Davis. "Why Some Groups Fail: A Survey of Students' Experiences with Learning Groups." In Anne Goodsell, Michelle Maher, and Vincent Tinto, *Collaborative Learning: A Sourcebook for Higher Education*, pp. 59–67. University Park, Pa.: National Center on Postsecondary Teaching, Learning and Assessment, 1997.

Frankl, Viktor. *Man's Search for Meaning*, rev. ed. Washington Square Press, 1997.

Garces, E., D. Thomas, and J. Currie. "Longer-term Effects of Head Start," *American Economic Review* 92 (2002).

Gitlin, Todd. *The Twilight of Common Dreams*. New York: Owl Books, 1995.

Goleman, Daniel. *Working with Emotional Intelligence*. New York: Bantam Books, 1998.

Green, Mark, with Michael Waldman, Michael Calabrese, Lynn Darling, Bruce Rosenthal, James M. Fallows, and David R. Zwick. *Who Runs Congress?* 4th ed. New York: Dell, 1984.

Greenleaf, Robert. *Servant Leadership*. New York: Paulist Press, 1991.

Hall, Edward T. *The Dance of Life: The Other Dimension of Time*. Garden City, N.Y.: Anchor Press/Doubleday, 1983.

Halperin, Samuel. *A Guide for the Powerless—and Those Who Don't Know Their Own Power; A Primer on the American Political Process*. Washington, D.C.: American Youth Policy Forum, 2001.

Haywood, Martha. *Managing Virtual Teams: Practical Techniques for High Technology Project Managers*. Norwood, Mass.: Artech House, 1998.

His Holiness the Dalai Lama and Howard Cutler. *The Art of Happiness*. New York: Riverhead Books, 1998.

Hirokawa, D. DeGooyer, and K. Valde. "Using Narratives to Study Task Group Effectiveness," *Small Group Research* 31 (2000): 573–91.

Isaac, Katherine. *Practicing Democracy: A Guide to Student Action*. New York: St. Martin's Press, 1995.

Janis, Irving L. "Groupthink," *Psychology Today* 5 (November 1971): 43–46, 74–76.

Jarboe, S. "Procedures for Enhancing Group Decision Making," in R. Y. Hirokaway and M. S. Poole, eds., *Communication and Group Decision Making*. Thousand Oaks, Calif.: Sage, 1996.

Jaworski, Joseph, and Betty Sue Flowers, eds. *Synchronicity: The Inner Path of Leadership*. San Francisco: Berrett-Koehler, 1998.

Jewel, Linda, and H. Joseph Reitz. *Group Effectiveness in Organizations*. Glenview, Ill.: Scott Foresman, 1981.

Kenny, Robert. "Spread Leadership," *YES! Magazine*, Fall 1999, 39.

Kick, Russ, ed. *Everything You Know Is Wrong*. New York: The Disinformation Company, 2002.

Kolb, David. "Learning Style Inventory." Boston: McBer & Company, 1985.

Kostner, Jaclyn. *Bionic eTeamwork*. Chicago, Ill.: Dearborn Trade Publishing, 2001.

Krugman, Paul. "Standard Operating Procedure," *New York Times*, June 3, 2003.

Kurtz, Howard. "Bush Cousin Made Florida Vote Call for Fox News," *Washington Post*, November 14, 2000.

LaFasto, Frank, and Carl Larson. *When Teams Work Best*. Thousand Oaks, Calif.: Sage, 2001.

Lambert, Craig. *Mind over Water: Lessons on Life from the Art of Rowing*. New York: Mariner Books, 1999.

Larson, Carl E., and Frank M. J. La Fasto. *Teamwork: What Must Go Right/What Can Go Wrong.* Thousand Oaks, Calif: Sage, 1989.

Larson, Jeanne, and Madge Micheels-Cyrus, eds. *Seeds of Peace.* Philadelphia: New Society Publishers, 1987.

Lesser, Elizabeth. *The New American Spirituality.* New York: Random House, 1999.

Loeb, Marshall, and Alicia Ferrari. Newsletter, April 29, 2003, http://www.CBS.MarketWatch.com.

Loeb, Paul Rogat. *Soul of a Citizen.* New York: St. Martin's Griffin, 1999.

Loehr, Jim, and Tony Schwartz. *The Power of Full Engagement.* New York: Free Press, 2003.

Manzo, A., U. Manzo, A. Barnhill, and M. Thomas. "Proficient Reader Subtypes: Implications for Literacy Theory, Assessment and Practice," *Reading Psychology* 21 (2000): 217–232.

Margulies, J. "Grading the States," *School of Library Journal* 14 (October 2001): 16.

McConnell, Carolyn. "Deliberation Day," *YES Magazine* 24 (Winter 2003): 41.

McLaughlin, Corrine, and Gordon Davidson. *Spiritual Politics: Changing the World from the Inside Out.* New York: Ballantine Books, 1994.

McMullen, Lynn. Results International Conference, Washington, D.C., 1999.

Mitchell, Peter R., and John Schoeffel, eds. *Understanding Power: The Indispensable Chomsky.* New York: The New Press, 2002.

Mosvick, Roger K., and Robert B. Nelson. *We've Got to Start Meeting Like This!* Glenview, Ill.: Scott Foresman, 1987.

Moyers, Bill. "This is Your Story—The Progressive Story of America. Pass It On." Speech given at America's Future Lifetime Leadership ceremony, June 4, 2003, Washington, D.C., http://www.CommonDreams.org.

Nagy, W. E., and R. C. Anderson. "How Many Words Are There in Printed School English?" *Reading Research Quarterly.* In Diane Bryant, Nicole Ugel, Sylvia Thompson, and Allison Hamff, "Instructional Strategies for Content-area Reading Instruction, " *Intervention in School & Clinic* 34:5 (May 1999).

Orman, Suze. *The Laws of Money, The Lessons of Life: Keep What You Have and Create What You Deserve.* New York: Free Press, 2003.

Ornish, Dean. *Love and Survival: The Healing Power of Intimacy.* New York: HarperCollins, 1998.

Palmer, Parker. "The Heart of Knowing." *Shambala Sun*, September 1997.

Pascale, Richard T., Mark Millemann, and Linda Gioja. *Surfing the Edge of Chaos.* New York: Random House, 2000.

Patterson, Kerry, Joseph Grenny, Ron McMillan, and Al Switzler. *Crucial Conversations.* New York: McGraw-Hill, 2002.

Pitts, David. "Primaries Unique to American Democracy." www.usembassy.de/usa/etexts/gov/primaries.htm.

Prince, George. "Recognizing Genuine Teamwork," *Supervisory Management*, April 1989, 25–36.

Putnam, Robert. "Bowling Alone," *Journal of Democracy*, January 1995.

Remen, Rachel Naomi. *My Grandfather's Blessings: Stories of Strength, Refuge, and Belonging.* New York: Riverhead Books, 2001.

Renstrom, Peter, and Chester Rogers. *Electoral Politics Dictionary.* ABC-CLIO, 1989.

Rhoder, Carol. "Mindful Reading: Strategy Training That Facilitates Transfer," *Journal of Adolescent & Adult Literacy* 45:6 (March 2002): 498 +.

Rosenberg, Marshall B. *Nonviolent Communication: A Language of Compassion.* Encinitas, Calif.: PuddleDancer Press, 1999.

The Round Table Gathering, audiotapes.

Rosenblatt, L. *The Reader, the Text, the Poem: The Transactional Theory of the Literacy Work.* Carbondale, Ill.: Southern Illinois University Press, 1978.

Ryan, Richard M., and Edward L. Deci. "Self Determination Theory and the Facilitation of Intrinsic Motivation, Social Development, and Well-Being," *American Psychologist* 55:1 (January 2000): 68–78.

Salazar, A. J. "Ambiguity and Communication Effects on Small Group Decision Making Performance," *Human Communication Research* 23 (1996): 155–92.

Schultz, Jim. *The Democracy Owner's Manual: A Practical Guide to Changing the World.* New Brunowick, NJ: Rutgers University Press, 2002.

Schwartz, Tony. *Media, The Second God*. New York: Anchor Press/Doubleday, 1983.

Scott, C. R. "Communication Technology and Group Communication." In L. Frey, ed., *The Handbook of Group Communication Theory and Research*, pp. 432–72. Thousand Oaks, Calif.: Sage, 1999.

Seligman, Martin. *Learned Optimism: How to Change Your Mind and Your Life*. New York: Pocket Books, 1998.

Senge, Peter. *The Fifth Discipline: The Art and Practice of the Learning Organization*. New York: Currency Doubleday, 1990.

Sherfield, Robert, Rhonda Montgomery, and Patricia Moody. *Cornerstone*. Upper Saddle River, NJ: Prentice Hall, 2005.

Shore, Bill. *The Cathedral Within*. New York: Random House, 1999.

Simon, Hermann. "Hidden Champions: Lessons from 500 of the World's Best Unknown Companies." Boston: Harvard Business School Press, 1996.

Snider, V. E. "Reading Comprehension Performance of Adolescents with Learning Disabilities," *Learning Disability Quarterly* 12 (1989) 87–96, 1989.

Stewart, D. D. "Stereotypes, Negativity Bias, and the Discussion of Unshared Information in Decision-Making Groups," *Small Group Research* 29 (1998): 643–68.

United States Congressional Handbook. Washington, D.C: Votenet Solutions, 2001.

U.S. National Archives and Record Administration. "The Bill of Rights." www.archives.gov/exhibit_hall/charters_of_freedom/bill_of_rights/bill_of_rights.html.

U.S. National Archives and Record Administration. "The Constitution of the United States." www.archives.gov/exhibit_hall/charters_of_freedom/constitution/constitution.html.

U.S. National Archives and Record Administration. "The Declaration of Independence: A History."
www.archives.gov/exhibit_hall/charters_of_freedom/declaration/declaration_history.html.

Vaill, Peter. *Learning as a Way of Being: Strategies for Survival in a World of Permanent White Water*. San Francisco: Jossey-Bass, 1996.

Vernier, Phillipe, and Dorothy Berkeley. *The Choice Is Always Ours*. San Francisco: HarperCollins, 1989.

"Voter's Self-Defense Manual." Project Vote Smart. 2002. www.vote-smart.org/program_publications.php.

Walther, J. B., and Lisa Tidwell. "When Is Mediated Communication Not Interpersonal?" In K. Galvin and P. Cooper, *Making Connections*. Los Angeles, Calif.: Roxbury Press, 1996.

Weil, Andrew, M. D. *8 Weeks to Optimum Health*. New York: Alfred A. Knopf, 1997.

Wheatley, Margaret. *Leadership and the New Science*. San Francisco: Berrett-Koehler 1994.

Wheatley, Margaret. *Turning to One Another*. San Francisco: Berrett-Koehler, 2002.

Williamson, Marianne. *A Return to Love: Reflections on the Principles of "A Course in Miracles"*. New York: HarperCollins, 1996.

Williamson, Marianne, ed. *IMAGINE: What America Could Be in the 21st Century*. Daybreak Books, 2000.

Williamson, Marianne. *The Healing of America*. New York: Simon & Schuster, 1997.

Wilson, Kristen. "Jill Ker Conway: In Her Own Words." *Here in Hanover*, Summer 1998, 7–8.

"Witnesses and Documents Unveil Deceptions in a Reporter's Work," *New York Times*, May 11, 2003 (conducted by a team of researchers and reporters), www.CBS.MarketWatch.com.

Ziglar, Zig. *Success and the Self-Image*. New York: Simon & Schuster, 1995.

Zinn, Howard. *People's History of the United States*. New York: Harperperennial Library, 2003.

Index

Accomplishment, recognizing
partial, 84
Accountability, 5
Accuracy, of Web sites, 33
Ackerman, Bruce, 182
Action (*see also* Advocacy;
Citizenship):
and change, 169–172
and thoughts, 23
call to, 163
critical thinking and, 28
frame of, 16–17
matching values to, 23
sample plan, 88–90
timeline of democratic,
169–170, 171
Action strategy (*see also* Advocacy;
Citizenship):
choosing partners and resources,
79–80, 89
considering obstacles, 82, 89
creating, 76–83
creating a timeline, 81–82, 89–90
fear of failure, 84
identifying goals, 79, 89
procrastination and, 85–86
project management and, 91–96
reviewing the project or issue, 76,
78, 89
staying on track, 83–88
targeting your audience, 78, 88
Actions, values and, 24
Activist, problem solving style, 21,
167 (*see also* Advocacy)
Activities:
choosing appropriate, 23
evaluating necessary, 81
Ad hominem, 36
Ad verecundiam, 36
Adams, John, 176
Advertising, campaign, 197

Advocacy, 187–198
clarifying objectives, 189–190
grassroots organizing, 196–198
working on a political campaign,
197–198
working with members of
Congress, 192–195
working with the media, 195–196
Agenda, meeting, 151
AIDS, 14, 46
Allen, David, 53
Alternatives, considering, 84
American democracy, *see*
Democracy
Analysis, Bloom's taxonomy and, 30
Appeals, to emotion, patriotism,
tradition, 36
Application, Bloom's taxonomy
and, 30
Arguments:
construction of, 99
straw, 36
Articles of Confederation, 176
Artist's Way, The, 59
Asynchronous communication, 135
Attitude:
change and, 168–169
values and, 2
Audience, targeting your, 78, 88
Authority, of Web sites, 33

Background knowledge, activating,
102–104
Balance, 68–69
Bandwagon, 36
Bates, Marilyn, 22
Beliefs, 2 (*see also* Values)
financial management and, 63
Beneficiaries, direct vs. indirect, 34
Bennis, Warren, 160
Berry, Wendell, 160

Bias, 36, 38
Bill:
how it becomes law, 186–187
timeline of, 190–191
Bill of Rights, 177, 183
Biological rhythms, 68–69
Blair, Jayson, 31
Blind self, 136
Bloom, Benjamin, 29
Bloom's taxonomy, 29, 30
Bohm, David, 158
Border security, 178–179
Boston Tea Party, 177
Boy Scouts, 62
Brainstorming, 41–42
about resources, 81
Briggs, Katharine, 22
Briggs-Myers, Isabel, 22
Brokovich, Erin, 83
Bronson, Po, 15
Budgeting, 63–67, 72–73
Bush, George W., 31, 178

Cabinet members, 178 (*see also*
Government, U.S.)
Cameron, Julia, 59
Campaign:
finance, 182–183
fund-raising and, 197
online, 198
public funding of, 183
working on a political, 197–198
Campfire Girls, 62
Card stacking, 36
Carson, Rachel, 87
Cathedral Within, The, 157
Cause and effect, 105, 106
false, 36
Change (*see also* Action strategy;
Advocacy):
allowing for, 82

characteristics of, 163–166
conviction and, 168
courage and, 168
creating environment for,
    168–172
defined, 163
effected by individuals, 158
effecting through
    communication, 137–142
leadership and, 157–160 (*see also*
    Leadership)
problem solving and, 166–167
systems thinking and, 158, 160
timeline of social, 169–170, 171
Chaos, change and, 164
Character traits, 5
Checks and balances, system of,
    178–180
Chief of staff, 185
Choice Theory, 144–146
Citizens Clearinghouse for
    Hazardous Waste, 87
Citizens, choosing where and how
    to engage as, 15–23 (*see also*
    Advocacy; Citizenship)
Citizenship (*see also* Advocacy;
    Democracy):
behavior patterns and, 22
choosing where and how to
    engage, 15–23
creating an action strategy, 76–83
creating sustainable, 198–199
critical thinking and, 27–38 (*see
    also* Critical thinking)
democracy and, 175–201 (*see also*
    Democracy)
effective engagement, 16
frame of action, 16–17
leadership and, *see* Leadership
personal resources and, 67–71
problem solving and, 38–47 (*see
    also* Problem solving)
resource management and,
    53–74 (*see also* Resource
    management)
self-awareness and, 1–26 (*see also*
    Self-awareness)
City Year, 161
Civic community, 172
Civic education:

reading skills and, 100–109
    skills for, 99–128
Civil Rights Act of 1964, 77, 189
Civil Rights movement, 56, 77–78
Classification, scientific, 29
Clean Money legislation, 183
Clinton, Bill, 31
Clinton, Hillary, 197
Collaboration, teams and, 148
Collective wisdom, 170
Columbus, Christopher, 37–38
Commitment, 5
Commitments, watching number
    of, 61
Committees:
congressional, 185–186
understanding the process,
    186–187
Communication, 131–142
accepting criticism and, 140–141
crucial conversations and, 138–140
defined, 131–132
effecting change through, 137–142
feedback, 133
listening with open mind, 138
method, 133
model, 132–133
negotiation and, 140–141
nonverbal, 135–136
nonviolent, 134, 142, 143
overcoming resistance and, 165
self-awareness and, 136
synchronous and asynchronous,
    135
types of, 135–136
verbal, 135
virtual, 135
Community:
civic, 172
connection to federal, 24
involvement, 62 (*see also*
    Advocacy; Citizenship)
Compare and contrast, 105, 106
Completeness of Web sites, 33
Comprehension, 100–109
Bloom's taxonomy and, 30
Compromise, 141
Compromiser, 146
Conceptualization, 17, 20
Confidence, 169

Congress, 178
acknowledging members, 194
committees of, 185–186
how a bill becomes law, 186–187,
    190–191
members of, 184–186
office staff, 185
working with, 192–195
writing to members of, 195
Congruence, 7–8
Constitution, U.S., 175, 176–177,
    180
Consumer Reports, 64
Content, of Web sites, 33
Context, evaluating, 35
Contribution limits, 183
Conversations, crucial, 138–140
Conviction, change and, 168
Convictions, 1
Conway, Jill Ker, 9
Cooper, Kenneth H., 69
Cooperation, 141
Cornell system of note-taking,
    112–113
Courage, change and, 168
Covey, Stephen, 8, 61, 62
Creativity:
problem solving and, 41–42
teams and, 148
Credit cards, managing your, 64–65
Crisis management, 62
Critical thinking, 27–38
Bloom's taxonomy and, 29, 30
creativity and, 41–42
defined, 27, 28
evaluating sources of information,
    29, 31–33
exercise in, 37–38
identifying false logic and bias, 36
identifying stakeholders and
    beneficiaries, 34
maintaining objectivity and,
    33–34
problem solving and, *see* Problem
    solving
separating facts and opinions,
    34–35
Criticism, accepting, 140
Critiquing, 103, 107–108
Crucial Conversations, 138–140

Dalai Lama, 138
Daley-Harris, Sam, 9, 80
Dance of Life, The, 54
Data, primary vs. secondary, 119
Davidson, Gordon, 169
Davis, Flora, 68
Debt, managing, 64–67
Declaration of Independence, 7, 176
Delegation, 57
Democracy, 175–201 (*see also*
    Citizenship)
  advocacy and lobbying, 187–189
  checks and balances, 178
  electoral college, 184
  founding documents of, 176–177
  how a bill becomes law, 186–187,
    190–191
  separation of powers, 177–180
  vision for, 1
  voting and electoral process,
    180–184
  working on a political campaign,
    197–198
Democracy Owner's Manual, The, 196
Democratic movements, timeline
    of, 169–170, 171
Department of Defense, 178
Departments, government,
    178–179
Descriptive words, 35
Details, supporting, 105
Development stages, of teams,
    146–147
Dialogue, 141
Dilemma, false, 36
Diplomat:
  problem solving style, 18
  style of problem solving, 166–167
Documents, founding, 176–177
Drucker, Peter, 55
During-reading process, 102

Editor, letters to, 122–123
Education, civic, *see* Civic education
Elected officials, letters to, 121
Elections:
  campaign finance, 182–183
  electoral college, 184
  primary, 184
  voting and, 180–184
Electoral college, 184

Electoral process, 180–184
E-mail, 61, 122, 135, 149
Emergency Preparedness and
    Response, 179
Emotions, 71
Empathy, 137–138
Empowerment, action and, 169
Encouragement, 170
Encourager, 146
Energizer, 146
Engage, EPIC and, 162
Engagement, effective, 16
Environmental issues, 87
EPIC format, 161–163
Esteem needs, 144, 145
Evaluation:
  Bloom's taxonomy and, 30
  leadership and, 163
Everything You Know Is Wrong, 32
Excellence, teams and, 148
Executive branch, 178, 179–180
Exercise, 68
Experimentation, 17, 20
Expert complex, 43
External motivation, 8 (*see also*
    Motivation)
Extroversion, 22
Eye contact, 135

Facial expressions, 135
Facilitation, of change, 165
Facts, vs. opinions, 34–35
Failure, fear of, 84
False:
  cause and effect, 36
  dilemma, 36
  logic, 36
Fear:
  change and, 165
  money and, 63
  of failure, 84
  of success, 85
Federal Communications
    Commission (FCC), 31
Feedback:
  communication and, 133
  teams and, 148–149
Feeling, 22
  NVC model and, 143
Feelings, responsibility for, 139
Fifth Discipline, The, 141, 158–159

Finance, campaign, 182–183
Financial management, 62–67
  budgeting and, 63–67, 72–73
  credit cards and, 64–65
First Amendment, 188
Fishkin, James, 182
Five-minute principle, 55–56
Flexibility, goals and, 12
Flowers, Betty Sue, 2
Forming stage, teams and, 147
Frame of action, 16
Franklin, Benjamin, 176
Functional literacy, 100
Fund-raising, 197

Generalities, glittering, 36
Generalization, hasty, 36
Getting Things Done, 53
Gibbs, Lois, 87
Givingness, 5
Glaser, Ronald, 131
Glasser, William, 144
Glittering generalities, 36
Goals, 2
  adaptable, 14
  attainable, 13, 23
  challenging, 13–14
  collective, 11
  conflicting, 12
  congruous, 14
  forming manageable, 83–84
  identifying desired, 79, 89
  individual, 10–11
  measurable and specific, 14
  meeting, 151
  positive, 14–15
  prioritizing, 11–12
  realistic, 13
  revisiting, 83–84
  setting, 12–15
  short-term and long-term, 11
  teams and, 147
  time management and, 57
  time-sensitive, 14
  translating values into, 10–15
  types of, 10–11
  written, 13
Goleman, Daniel, 143, 192
Gore, Al, 31
Government, U.S., 175–201
  branches of, 178–179

departments of, 178–179
how a bill becomes law, 186–187, 190–191
voting and electoral process, 180–184
Grant, James, 175
Grassroots organizing, 196–197
Gratification, delaying, 87–88
Green, Mark, 196
Greider, William, 29
Groups, 142–152 (*see also* Teams)
Groupthink, 144

Habit, change and, 164
Habits, developing good, 61–62
Hall, Edward T., 54
Harmonizer, 146
Haywood, Martha, 149
Healing of America, The, 1
Health, as personal resource, 68–71
Hidden self, 136
Hill, Julia "Butterfly," 159
Homeland Security, Department of, 178
Honesty, 5
Hopi Indians, 54
House of Representatives, 178 (*see also* Congress)
How, why, 108
Human Motivation Research Group, 9
Human traits, 86

I statement, 139
Illustrate, EPIC and, 162–163
Imaging, 105
Independent Sector, 189
Index cards, note-taking and, 114
Individual, change and, 158
Inferencing, 102–103
Influences, 70
Information:
　ability to research and integrate, 99
　accuracy of, 33
　applying, 109
　background, 102–104
　community sources of, 32
　evaluating on Web sites, 33
　evaluating sources of, 29, 31–33
　gathering for problem solving, 40–41, 45–46

identifying stakeholders and, 34
Internet sources and, 32–33
media sources, 29, 31–32
nonpartisan, 182
separating facts and opinions, 34–35
sources of for research, 118–120
Information seeker, 146
Initiator, 146
Integrity, 7
Intention, communication and, 133
Interests, landscape of, 16
Internal motivation, 8–9 (*see also* Motivation)
Internet, evaluating information on, 32–33
Interviews, 119–120
Introversion, 22
Intuition, 17, 20, 22, 42–43
Issues:
　environmental, 28
　social, 27–38

Jefferson, Thomas, 176
Jingshen, Wei, 87
Johari window, 136
Judging, 22
Judicial branch, 178, 180
Jung, Carl, 22

Keirsey, David, 22
Kennedy, John F., 161
Kennedy, Robert F., 168, 169
Key words, 35, 106–107
Kick, Russ, 32
Kiecolt-Glaser, Janice, 131
Kimball, Richard, 182
King, Jr., Martin Luther, 56, 87
Kiwanis, 62
Knowledge, Bloom's taxonomy and, 30

Land, E.H., 84
Landscape of interests, 16
Law, how a bill becomes, 186–187, 190–191
Leaders, 157 (*see also* Leadership)
Leadership, 157–174
　advocacy and, 194
　continual learning and, 160
　defined, 160–161

effective speaking and, 161–163
qualities, 160–163
sharing in teams, 148
systems thinking and, 158, 160
vision and, 161
League of Women Voters, 62
Learning as a Way of Being, 160
Learning, continual, 160
Learning style, 100
Lecture, note-taking during, 110–111
Lecturers, styles of, 112
Legislative:
　branch, 178, 179
　director, 185
　process, 186–187, 190–191
Lesser, Elizabeth, 70
Letters:
　to elected officials, 121, 195
　to the editor, 122–123
　writing, 120–122
Life areas, defining, 2–4
Life, wheel of, 4, 12
Lions Clubs, 62
Listening:
　note-taking during, 110–11
　with an open mind, 138
Literacies, multiple, 103
Literacy:
　computer, 103
　financial, 103
　functional, 100
　math, 103
Living Alive, 68
Living History, 197
Livingston, Robert B., 176
Lobbying, 187–189 (*see also* Advocacy)
Locke, John, 176
Loeb, Paul, 1, 9
Loehr, Jim, 61
Logic, false, 36
Long-term goals, 11 (*see also* Goals)
Loss, change and, 165
Love Canal, 87
Luna, 159

Macrosystem, 158
Madison, James, 180
Main ideas, identifying, 105

Malcolm X, 56
Mandela, Nelson, 87
Mapping, 114, 115
Maslow's hierarchy of needs, 144, 145
Mature readers, 100
McLaughlin, Corrine, 169
McQueen, Mary, 64
Means, living beneath your, 64
Media, 29, 31–32, 195–196
Media, The Second God, 195–195
Meditation, 70
Meetings:
    agenda for, 151
    effective, 150–152
    leader and participant roles, 151–152
    with members of Congress, 195
Members of Congress, 184–186
Messaging, 78–79
Method, of communication, 133
Mind, open, 138
Mission statement, 5–6
Mitchell, Peter, 31
Money, beliefs about, 63
Montgomery bus boycott, 77–78
Moral soundness, 7
Mosvick, Roger, 150
Motivation:
    internal and external, 8–9
    translating into goals, 10–15
Motivators, 145
MoveOn.org, 101
Moyers, Bill, 175
Multiple literacies, 103
Myers-Briggs Type Indicator® Instrument, 22

NAACP, 77
National Adult Literacy Survey (NALS), 100
Needs:
    Maslow's hierarchy of, 144, 145
    NVC model and, 143
Negotiation, 140–141
Nelson, Robert, 150
Network, support, 170, 196–197
New American Spirituality, The, 70
Nixon, Richard, 183
Nonpartisan information, 182
Nonverbal communication, 135–136

Nonviolent communication (NVC) model, 134, 142, 143
Norming stage, teams and, 147
Notes, reviewing, 117
Note-taking, 109–117
    Cornell system, 112–113
    formats of, 112–117
    mapping, 114, 115
    outline format, 115, 116
    reviewing notes and, 117
    tabular format, 114, 116
    T-format, 112–113
    while listening, 110–111
Nutrition, 68

Objectives, clarifying, 189–190
Objectivity, maintaining, 33–34
Observation, 17, 20
    NVC model and, 143
Obstacles:
    considering, 82
    identifying, 89
Open self, 136
Openness, 5
Opinions, vs. facts, 34–35
Opponents, 34
Optimism, learned, 168–169
Others, working with, 80, 170, 172, 196–197
OtterMedia.com, 159
Outcome, evaluating, 82–83
Outcome thinking, 55
Outlining, note-taking format, 115, 116
Overhead, personal, 65

Pareto's 80/20 principle, 57
Pariser, Eli, 101
Parks, Rosa, 77–78
Partners, choosing, 79–80, 89
Patience, 170
Patriotism, appeals to, 36
Patterson, Kerry, 138
People, as resources, 67–68
People's History of the United States, A, 37
Perceiving, 22
Performing stage, teams and, 147
Perseverance, 157
    change and, 170
Personal:
    overhead, 65

resource management, 67–71 (*see also* Personal resources)
Personal digital assistants (PDAs), 61
Personal resources:
    emotions, 70
    health and well-being, 68–71
    other people, 67–68
    sleep/exercise/nutrition, 69
    spirituality, 70
Personality, Myers-Briggs and, 22
Perspectives, identifying, 34
Pert chart, 93, 95
Pessimism, 168
Physiological needs, 144, 145
Poland's Solidarity movement, 87
Policy, public, 27
Post-reading, 102
Posture, 135
Power of Full Engagement, The, 61
Powers, separation of, 177–180
Predicting, 104
Pre-reading, 102
Press:
    conference, 196
    releases, writing, 122, 123
    secretary, 185
Pressure, 86
Previewing, 103, 104
Primary data, 119
Primary elections, 184
Primary target, 78
Principles, 2 (*see also* Values)
Prioritizing, 60–61
Problem, defining, 39–40, 44
Problem solving, 38–47, 166–167
    defining the problem, 39–40, 44
    defining the terms, 40, 44
    developing solutions, 41–42, 46
    exercise, 21, 44–47
    gathering and interpreting information, 40–41, 45–46
    identifying stakeholders, 40, 44
    inventory, 19–20
    obstacles to, 43
    preferences, 16–21
    skills, 17–18
    steps, 39
    styles of, 18–21
Procrastination, 85–86

Profiteers, 34
Programming, communication and, 132–133
Project:
  management, 91–96
  naming, 79
  reviewing, 76, 78, 88
Project Vote Smart, 180, 182
Propaganda, of Web sites, 33
Propose, EPIC and, 162
Psychological Types, 22
PTA, 62
Public disclosure, 183
Public policy, 27
Purpose, determining, 104
Putnam, Robert, 62

Quantum physics, 158, 160

Racial injustice, 56
Racism, 56
Readers, mature, 100
Reading, 100–109
  activating background knowledge, 102–104
  determining purpose, 104
  determining structure, 105–106
  exercise, 124–126
  literacies and, 103
  note-taking during, 111–112
  post-, 102
  pre-, 102–104
  previewing and predicting, 104
  summarizing and, 108
Reception, communication and, 133
Reflecting, 108
  leadership and, 163
  self-awareness and, 9
Rejuvenation, 59
Reports, writing, 122–123
Request, NVC model and, 143
Research, 117–120
  interviews and, 119–120
  note-taking during, 111–112
  political campaign and, 198
  primary vs. secondary data, 119
  sources of information, 118–120
Resistance:
  considering, 82
  identifying, 89

overcoming, 165
to change, 164
Resource management:
  active citizenship and, 53–74
  financial management, 62–67 (*see also* Financial management)
  personal, 67–71 (*see also* Personal resources)
  time management, 54–62 (*see also* Time management)
Resources:
  brainstorming, 81
  choosing, 79–80, 89
  people as, 79–80
  support groups, 84
Responsibility, 5, 139
Rest, 68
RESULTS, 47
Reviewing, 103, 109
Rogers, Chester, 184
Roles, team, 146, 148
Rosenberg, Marshall, 134, 142

Safety, communication and, 139
Safety needs, 144, 145
Schedule, time management and, 57–58
Scheduler, congressional, 185
Schoeffel, John, 31
Schultz, Jim, 183, 196
Schwartz, Tony, 61, 195
Scientific classification, 29
Second Continental Congress, 176
Secondary data, 119
Secondary target, 78
Segregation, 56
Self-actualization needs, 144, 145
Self-awareness:
  and citizenship, 1–26
  character traits and, 5
  communication and, 136
  congruence and, 7–8
  goals and, 10–15
  integrity and, 7
  mission statement and, 5–6
  motivation and, 8–9
  of values and convictions, 1–15
  problem-solving preferences and, 16–21
  reflection and, 9
  setting goals and, 12–15

Self-esteem, 169
Self-questioning, 105
Self-worth, 169
Seligman, Martin, 168
Senate, 178 (*see also* Congress)
Senge, Peter, 137, 141, 158
Sensing, 22
Separation of powers, 177–180
Service clubs, 62
Seven Habits of Highly Effective People, 8
Shared human traits, 86
Sherman, Roger, 176
Shore, Bill, 157
Short–term goals, 11 (*see also* Goals)
Sierra Club, 3
Sierra Student Coalition, 3
Silent Spring, 87
Skills:
  communication, *see* Communication
  for civic education, 99–128
  note-taking, *see* Note-taking
  problem solving, 17–18
  reading and comprehension, 100–109
  research, 117–120
  speaking, 161–163
  writing, 120–123
Sleep, 68
Social change, timeline of, 169–170, 171
Social issues, critical thinking and, 27–38 (*see also* Critical thinking)
Social needs, 144, 145 (*see also* Advocacy)
Socioemotional role, 146
Solutions:
  developing, 41–42, 46
  evaluating, 42–43, 46–47
Soul of a Citizen, 1
Speaking:
  effective, 161–163
  EPIC format, 161–163
Spiritual Politics, 169
Spiritual practice, 70
Stakeholders:
  identifying, 34
  problem solving and, 40, 44
Standard, reinventing, 86–87

Storming stage, teams and, 147
Strategist:
  problem solving style, 18, 20, 21
  style of problem solving, 167
Straw arguments, 36
Stress, 86
  change and, 164
Structure:
  determining, 105–106
  team, 146
Sub-subtasks, 93
Subtasks, identifying, 92–93
Success:
  evaluating, 43, 89–90
  fear of, 85
Summarizer, 146
Summarizing, 108
Support:
  enrolling others in advocacy, 197
  group, 84
  network, 170, 196–197
  of change, 165
Synchronicity: The Inner Path of Leadership, 2
Synchronous communication, 135, 149
Synergistic compromise, 141
Synthesis, Bloom's taxonomy and, 30
Systems thinking, 158, 160

Tabular format of note-taking, 114, 116
Target, primary and secondary, 78
Task specialist role, 146
Tasks:
  combining with goals, 12
  identifying important, 91–92
Teams, 142–152
  characteristics of effective, 147–149
  Choice Theory and, 144–146
  development stages, 146–147
  effective meetings and, 150–152
  forming stage, 147
  groupthink and, 144
  norming stage, 147
  performing stage, 147
  roles in, 146, 148
  shared leadership and, 148
  storming stage, 147

structure of, 146
  virtual, 149–150
Technician:
  problem solving style, 18
  style of problem solving, 166
Technology, paradox of, 53
Television, habit of, 62
Temperaments, 22
Ten-minute approach, 86
Terms, defining for problem solving, 40, 44
T-format of note-taking, 112–113
Thinking, 22 (*see also* Critical thinking)
  categorizing, 29
  defined, 28
  faulty, 36
  outcome, 55
Thoughts, and actions, 23
Tiananmen Square, 87
Tidwell, Lisa, 135
Time management, 54–62
  active citizenship and, 59–60
  procrastination and, 85–86
  scheduling and, 57–58
  steps in, 55, 57–59
  tools of, 60–61
Time order, 106
Timeline:
  creating, 81–82, 89–90
  of U.S. social change, 169–170, 171
Tradition, appeals to, 36
Traits:
  character, 5
  human, 86
Turning to One Another, 137
Types, personality, 22
Typical compromise, 141

U.S. Congressional Handbook, 184
U.S. Constitution, *see* Constitution, U.S.
U.S. Government, *see* Government, U.S.
Understanding, 137–138
UNICEF, 175
Unknown self, 136
Utne Reader, 137
Utne, Eric, 137
Vaill, Peter, 160

Values, 1
  action and, 23
  character traits and, 5
  defined, 2
  determining, 2–9
  how they affect your viewpoint, 38
  identifying, 4–5
  life areas and, 2, 4
  translating into goals, 10–15
  using your, 36–37
Verbal communication, 135 (*see also* Communication)
Vernier, Phillipe, 75
Virtual communication, 135
Virtual teams, 149–150
Vision:
  creating, 78–79, 88–89
  leadership and, 161
Vocabulary, 107
Voters, contacting, 198
Voting, 1, 180–184

Walesa, Lech, 87
Walker, Shaun, 159
Walther, Joseph, 135
Washington, George, 176–177
Watergate scandal, 183
We've Got to Start Meeting Like This!, 150
Web sites, evaluating, 32–33
Well-being, 68–71
Werbach, Adam, 3
What Should I do with My Life?, 15
Wheatley, Margaret, 137
Wheel of Life, 4, 12
Who Runs Congress?, 196
Who Will Tell the People, 29
Williams, Jody, 135
Williamson, Marianne, 1
Wisdom, collective, 170, 172
Words, descriptive, 35
Words, key, 35
Working with Emotional Intelligence, 143, 192
Writing, 120–123
  letters, 120–122 (*see also* Letters)

You statement, 139

Zinn, Howard, 37